ENCOUNTERS
with the
BRIDEGROOM

ENCOUNTERS

with the

BRIDEGROOM

A Journey Through the Song of Songs

GARY HOPKINS

FOREWORD BY DAVID CRONE

For more information, contact the author: Gary Hopkins,
 6391 Leisure Town Road; Vacaville, CA 95687
Email: ghopkins@imissionchurch.com
Cover design: Shelby Gibbs, shelbygibbsgraphicdesign.com
Editing, interior formatting and design: Creatively Inspired, LLC, Creativelyinspiredlife.com.

Printed in the United States of America

Endorsements

When one first meets Gary you become aware of his heart of love for God and compassion for others. In spending time with Gary and Karissa it becomes obvious why—they are sold-out to pursuing the greater depths of intimacy with God. In his book, *Encounters with the Bridegroom*, Gary unpacks much of his own personal journey with candid stories of his ups and downs in life, and invites us to join in this adventure of the heart towards intimacy with the Bridegroom. You will be encouraged and built up in your own walk with God into an activated life of experiencing His love. I highly recommend you invest in your true calling by prayerfully working through this book and allow Holy Spirit to lead you through the beautiful lyrics of the Song of all songs.

—John and Lisa Crumpton
Pastors of Breakthru Life Church, Johannesburg, SA

It is a rare and precious treasure to find a "manly man" utterly captivated by the divine romance. The author of this book, Gary Hopkins, is such a man. I know Gary to be one firmly held in the grip of the most transforming of all truths—that the ubiquitous, transcendent, Creator of the Universe passionately pursues us with His unquenchable love. To read *Encounters with the Bridegroom* is to rediscover love and to feel yourself being pulled ever closer to the holy flame of God's burning love for you.

—Dan McCollam
International Director of Sounds of the Nations, Vacaville, CA
Author of *Prophetic Company* and *The Good Fight*

Throughout history, the moves of God have been about God's love. Nowhere is His love more poetically stated that in the Song of Songs. Gary takes us on a vulnerable and personal walk through his own issues (and yes, we all have them!) while each day apprehending the unfathomable and intimate love of God afresh—for him . . . and for us. *Encounters with the Bridegroom* is a practical guide through the stages of intimacy with Jesus with its crafted prayers and space for personal reflection. I believe this book will lead you into a deeper revelation of His powerful and unstoppable love for you.

—Bill Dew
Founder and Director of DEWNAMIS, San Diego, CA
Author of *Living The Miraculous Life*

In this timely book, my friend, Gary Hopkins, writes from his own personal journey about the believer's invitation to encounter the Lover of their soul, Jesus. I have seen Gary walk out this heart-provoking message. This book explores more than bridal intimacy; it is a life-transforming *encounter* with your Bridegroom waiting to happen. Jump in with your heart wide open and you *will* encounter the King!

—Keith Ferrante
Founder and Director of Emerging Prophets, Vacaville, CA
Author of *Reforming the Church, Restoring the Father's Heart,* and
There Must Be More

Encounters with the Bridegroom is the essential map for becoming a radical receiver! As soon as I began to read this book, a spirit of nurturing calm came over me as if I had just arrived home—to the ultimate love and acceptance environment. To a fatherless generation, or a generation who had parents that were unable to adequately express love or build relationships, this book allows them to connect in love with an intimacy that supersedes all the ramifications of those issues. It opens up all the possibilities of the Kingdom of God through connection to the King—a surprisingly deep, personal connection. If you in any way 'must have more', this book is a *must-read*.

—Tim Dickerson
Businessman, Suisun City, CA

Encounters with the Bridegroom is an amazing journey of vulnerability and intimacy with Jesus, the Lover of our souls. In this book, Gary Hopkins does a great job of explaining the journey of the Shulamite woman in the Song of Songs, while sharing his own personal journey in becoming the beloved of God. If you desire an intimate relationship with Holy Spirit, Gary lays out a clear path to the secret place of God and gives practical tools and examples on how to build your own private history with God.

—Rick McCoy
Director of The Mission School of Deeper Life, Vacaville, CA

Encounters with the Bridegroom draws us deeper into the heart of God. Gary challenges us to truly understand and experience the fierce passion and romance of this love story with Jesus. The more I read, the more I wanted to worship!

—Heath Wise
Counselor, LPC, CST, CSTA, Asheville, NC

Some people *have* a message. My friend Gary *is* the message. Because he has experienced a powerful transformation, his message carries powerful transformation for those who have eyes to see and ears to hear.

—Magnus Sund
Prophetic Life Coach, Vacaville, CA

As Gary shares his personal journey of failure and success, you'll gain understanding on how to develop, upgrade, or renew a tangible and vibrant connection with God.

—Josh Cawley
Director, First Year School of Prophecy at The Mission, Vacaville, CA

For you reach into my heart.
With one flash of your eyes
I am undone by your love,
my beloved, my equal, my bride.
You leave me breathless—
I am overcome by merely a glance
from your worshipping eyes,
for you have stolen my heart.
I am held hostage by your love.

Song of Songs 4:9
The Passion Translation

Contents

Acknowledgments

When you experience God so powerfully, you just want to share it! But often describing a life-changing experience in a teaching series, and then, putting that message into a book can be especially challenging. That's why I'm so grateful for the wonderful people that came alongside to help in this process. I'd especially like to thank:

- My daughter, Amber Garza, author of 27 books, for sitting with me for hours and turning my notes into a first draft;
- My niece, Malarie Plaugher, for diligently and tirelessly going over the document and editing the content;
- Carol Cantrell, and her husband, Ron, for their encouragement, creative contributions, and commitment to excellence;
- My wife, Karissa, for her love and constant encouragement every step of this journey;
- All the ones who actively participated in this series from the Song of Songs at the Wednesday Encounter Nights at The Mission, and were rocked by His presence again and again. Observing His work in you gave language for this book, and fueled my own fire for more encounters.

Thank you.

Foreword

My wife, Deborah, was raised on the Monterey Bay in a quiet little fishing village in Northern California by the name of Moss Landing. I first met her when I was nine years old and we grew up together in the same church. We were friends long before we became lovers. On December 25, 1970, while traveling in my 1968 Mustang from Moss Landing to Santa Cruz, I nervously asked her to marry me, and she agreed. We were married nine months later on October 23, 1971. I have loved getting to know Deborah. She has always been a bit of a mystery to me, and learning about the things she likes or dislikes, coming to understand her thinking and her emotions, and trying to see life through her eyes has been an amazing journey. As much as it has been an adventure getting to know these things about her, I didn't marry Deb for that primary purpose. I married her because she captivated my heart and I wanted to experience—to participate personally—life with her. To simply know *about* her was not an option.

Experiencing the manifest presence of God and living in an intimate, life transforming relationship with the Bridegroom is as normal in the Kingdom of God as experiencing the presence of one's spouse. His presence is the essence of the Kingdom. Being possessed by His presence is our privilege as born-again people and is the absolute intention of God for us. He wants to be experienced, and He sealed this intention when He sent His Holy Spirit to be "God in us". If this were not so, He would have simply written a book and not bothered sending His Son or His Spirit.

In the Preface of A.W. Tozer's book written in 1948, *In Pursuit of God*, he stated the following:

> *Sound Bible exposition is an imperative must in the church of the Living God. Without it no church can be a New Testament church in any strict meaning of that term. But exposition may be carried on in such a way as to leave the hearers devoid of any true spiritual nourishment whatever. For it is not mere words that nourish the soul, but God Himself, and unless and until the hearers find God in personal experience they are not the better for having heard the truth. The Bible is not an end in itself, but a means to bring men to an intimate and satisfying knowledge of God, that they may enter into Him, that they may delight in His presence, may taste and know the inner sweetness of the very God Himself in the core and center of their hearts.*[1]

Gary Hopkins is an obvious lover of the Bible, but in reading his book, it becomes increasingly clear that he is captivated by something—no—*someone* greater. It is important to study, memorize, even categorize Scripture, and we can run our life according to the principles of Scripture. But until we experience the living Word—Jesus, God with us—we have not discovered the true purpose of Scripture—to point us to intimacy with the Bridegroom.

In *Encounters with the Bridegroom,* Gary passionately alerts us to the emptiness of a religious relationship with God. His heartfelt expressions reveal the futility of studying God, gaining a historic or intellectual knowledge of Him, without personally experiencing Him. The reader comes away from this book with the caution that it's possible to fight the good fight and overcome the struggles of our humanity, yet miss the whole point of warfare—the embrace of the Father.

When my oldest granddaughter, Samantha, was about three years old, her mother brought her by our house to see

---

[1]   Tozer, A. W. *The Pursuit of God.* Harrisburg PA: Christian Publications Inc., 1948, p. 9.

her "Papa". Deborah was home, but I was at the church office. When Samantha stepped into the house, she stopped in the entrance, stood silent for a moment, then finally declared with both confidence and disappointment, "There's no Papa in this house." Samantha, a child with a very sensitive spirit, had measured the atmosphere and knew that I was not there. She then wanted to know where I was, for it was her Papa that she had come to see. A house without Papa was not the house she wanted to be in.

The promise expressed throughout *Encounters with the Bridegroom* is that we need not serve God with all our strength and diligently study the Book He left for us, while tragically leaving on the table the delights of love offered to His bride. He has prepared a table for us, even in the presence of our enemies, and at His right hand of favor and blessing there are pleasures forevermore.

I have had the privilege of walking in relationship and ministry with Gary for many years, and have found that he is not only the messenger but the message. Through his personal, authentic self-revealing stories, Gary opens windows of opportunity for the reader to explore his or her own new levels of freedom and intimacy with the one whose longing for them is greater than theirs for Him.

Encounters with the Bridegroom is a journey book—a journey that doesn't end when the last word of the last chapter is read. It will stir a longing that will draw you into a lifelong adventure exploring the passionate, unreasonable, and dangerous love of the Father.

—David Crone
Sr. Leader of The Mission, Vacaville, CA
Author of *Decisions That Define Us; The Power of Your Life Message; Declarations That Empower Us;* and *Prisoner of Hope*
www.nisventures.com

Preface

In 1997, I began a journey into the Song of Songs, and this book is the result of that ongoing journey. I was at a place in my life, where Jesus took me so deep, I encountered His healing and transformational love plumbed to a level I had never before experienced. I carefully notated those very private and intimate times with Jesus, not realizing at the time how my notes would eventually be used.

Around the same time as my transformational encounters with the Holy Spirit, there were many others who greatly influenced my life with their friendship and extraordinary teaching gifts: Graham Cooke, David Crone, Dan McCollam, Bill Johnson, Iverna Tompkins, my wife Karissa, Tim Dickerson, and especially, Mike Bickle, and Brian Simmons. I am incredibly grateful for the deep insight and great anointing on, *The Passion Translation,* by Brian Simmons, directly related to the Son. The passages from his translation of the Song of Songs quoted in this book gave language and articulated well the message on my heart to Jesus' Bride.

Most of the content of this book came from the notes I recorded during this transformational-healing season of my life and emerged into a ten-week series I presented to our congregation at our Wednesday evening services at The Mission Church in Vacaville, California, in the fall of 2014. Sharing some of these revelations from the Song of Songs created stunning opportunities for others to encounter Him where many received healing, salvation, breakthrough, or victory in areas where they had struggled. These Wednesday evening gatherings became known as "Encounter Nights," and are still ongoing. Testimonials of the Holy Spirit capturing the hearts of His beloved ones from these encounters always leaves me undone when I hear about the lengths He will go to have us exclusively.

We only have to observe our culture today and realize that the world is crying out for genuine intimacy in relationships—the very purpose for which God created us. Unfortunately, we can get our cravings, needs, and passions entangled in some very unhealthy and destructive ways. We allow offense and life disappointments to derail us. But God's pure passion and His redemptive nature always draws us back to the one intimate relationship that fully satisfies and flows out into every human relationship we have.

I have found the Song of Songs to be an unfathomable well of revelation into the depths of God's infinite love, providing nourishment and refreshment for the soul, and breakthroughs into freedom. The longing of the Shulamite combined with the passion of the Bridegroom set in its poetic literary form, is the perfect backdrop for our exploration into this divine romance. We soon discover that His garden of delights is readily available to His Bride.

The Song opens with a desire and ends in fulfillment. This is my prayer for you, dear reader, as you journey through *Encounters with the Bridegroom.*

—Gary Hopkins
Vacaville, California
June 2017

Introduction

The Song of Solomon was written around 900 BCE by King David's son, Solomon. In 1 Kings 4:32, we learn that King Solomon wrote 1,005 songs, and this is the one that he calls the Song of all songs—his self-proclaimed best song. When Solomon describes this song as the "Song of all songs", the connotation in the Hebrew language is "the highest of the highest." In the heart and mind of Solomon, there is no song that is higher than the Song of Songs.

Interpreting the Song of Songs

We understand the Song of Songs to be a prophetic song, and the purpose of the prophetic is to reveal the current and future heart of the Father. That's why it is good to study it and consider its interpretation.

While there are many valid approaches to interpreting this Song, three main interpretations have been studied throughout biblical history: the natural, historical, and allegorical.

The natural interpretation adheres to the view that the Song chronicles a human love story between King Solomon and his bride, the Shulamite. In the natural, this story is also based on biblical principles to honor and inspire deeper love within marriage. But this interpretation has only been a popular teaching for about the past 100 years.

The Jewish historical interpretation presents the Song as a description of God as the Bridegroom, and Israel as the one chosen and loved.

The third and most popular view of the Song is an allegorical interpretation. As well as being the most popular, it is also the oldest elucidation of the Song. For the most part, the Song has been studied as an allegory—a story that is completely symbolic without any historical facts as its basis. An example of this would be, *The Chronicles of Narnia,* and *The Lord of the Rings.* These are stories with messages hidden within them. Allegorical interpretations are helpful, especially when utilized to illustrate truths established throughout the New Testament. The meanings extracted from the symbolism in an allegorical study must already be established as central New Testament understanding.

Our focus in this book is to interpret the Song of Songs as an allegorical love song between Jesus and the individual believer.

The Main Characters

There are three main characters in the Song: King Solomon, the Shulamite woman, and the Daughters of Jerusalem.

- **King Solomon** is depicted in the allegorical interpretation as a type of our Bridegroom, Jesus Christ. Therefore, I will use the "Bridegroom" and "Jesus" interchangeably throughout this book.
- **The Shulamite woman** is depicted as a type of the Bride of Christ. She's introduced as a young maiden, who eventually becomes the mature **Bride**. Throughout this book we will identify her as "the Shulamite", or "the maiden", until later in the Song when she has reached full bridal status and the Bridegroom identifies her as His "Bride".
- **The Daughters of Jerusalem** are never clearly identified or defined in the song. These represent ones who love Jesus, but they never really press in for intimacy with the Bridegroom the way

the young Shulamite maiden does, and are characterized by spiritual dullness or passivity.

The Journey of the Bride

Throughout the Song, the Shulamite maiden is making a journey, finally emerging as the mature Bride of the King— Jesus. I believe you will be able to personally identify with the Shulamite/Bride, and perhaps at times, find yourself in her exact place. You may even discover that your responses mirror hers.

Along the way, the Shulamite/Bride makes four declarative statements regarding her relationship with her Bridegroom, which we will explore in this book. Each statement gives us insight about the progression of her journey into full bridal partnership.

What is revealed in the Song of Songs is the intention of the Lord to reveal our inheritance in the Beloved, our identity in Him, and the glorious characteristics of His beautiful nature. Through intimate encounters with the Bridegroom, we progress into an intoxicating intimacy of relationship with Him so that our testimony and declaration ultimately becomes: "I am my Beloved's and He is mine." This is our goal! Along the journey, the aggressive pursuit of the Bridegroom overwhelms the Shulamite so that it awakens a passion within her to find Him—no matter the cost. She literally lays down everything else.

Meanwhile, the Daughters of Jerusalem are observing all of this and question the Shulamite about this Bridegroom with whom she has fallen head-over-heels in love. Though the maiden has seemingly lost everything—her ministry, possessions, relationships—the desire to have her Bridegroom is heightened. These Daughters, however, are not possessed with the same ardent desire for God and so their religious passivity is highlighted in the face of her pure and fervent devotion.

The description of the nature of the Bridegroom by the Shulamite becomes her testimony of Him. His beauty was an ongoing revelation on her journey to maturity and bridal partnership. Over time, and through many disappointing and arduous life experiences, she realizes that her Beloved has fulfilled all of her desires and deepest longings, and none compares to His love.

This is the Song of all songs. Exploring its themes and meditating on its truth will put to rest the unsettled within and will strengthen and empower a fragile, weakened interior.

Like the Shulamite maiden, each one of us is somewhere on this personal journey and process into our destiny and inheritance as a mature Bride. My prayer as you go through this book is for the Spirit of the Lord to encounter you with revelation that will both inspire and transform you more and more into a radical lover of your Bridegroom Jesus. Revelation is an invitation from the Holy Spirit to experience a specific facet of His captivating and glorious nature.

How to Use this Book

For the most part, this is not a verse-by-verse study of the Song of Songs. Rather, I have chosen specific verses and sections of the Song where God has given me revelation that I feel would be encouraging and strengthening. As you read through this book chapter by chapter, along with the Song of Songs, look for those invitations to encounter your Bridegroom.

In each chapter of this book, I have highlighted key Scriptures for a particular focus. Where I've quoted from a verse or section(s), in some cases I quoted the same Scripture(s) twice using two different translations. Unless other otherwise indicated, the first translation will be from the *New King James Version* ("NKJV"), while the second translation will be from *The Passion Translation* ("TPT"). At the end of each chapter I have included a Prayer, a word from the Lord, and/or a Declaration in response to the chapter theme, as well as an Activation. This is an opportunity for you to absorb and process what God may be saying to your own heart and record His personal word to you in some way. Pay close attention to where you are in your own journey with Jesus, your Bridegroom, and the changes emerging in your heart and life as you encounter His passion for you afresh. At the end of this study, you should have a journal of your progress and will have created a momentum for ongoing encounters with Him.

The Shulamite makes four progressive statements through the Song of her process in the prioritization of Jesus in her life.

1. The Shulamite: My life with Jesus is all about me.
2. The Shulamite: My life with Jesus is about me, but Jesus has a big part.
3. The Bride: Jesus is first in my life, but I am still a high priority.
4. The Bride: It's all about Jesus. I am solely His.

We, too, are in a journey of process. Spend some time with the Holy Spirit and track where you are in relation to the Shulamite as she moves through each of these four stages. Notice that in statements one and two, she is "the Shulamite"; in statements three and four, she progressed to an elevated matured position as "the Bride".

Expect Encounters with your Bridegroom!

As you study the most amazing Song of all songs, let me once again encourage you to allow what you read to take you into fresh encounters with the One whose heart is ravished over you—the Lord Jesus. Just respond to Him! What I have written here are truths that struck a chord in my own heart and energized me to dig deeper to find even more treasure. I hope you will do the same. I've organized this book so that it provides an opportunity to deeply ponder these truths with the Holy Spirit as He makes them real to your own heart.

So, *expect* encounters with Jesus! What He's about to show you will be so profound, you will never, never forget it.

A Word from the Bridegroom to You

As you begin your journey, hear the heart of the Lord as He speaks this to you.

> My beloved son/daughter, I have given you a Helper; listen to Him. Do not allow any other voice to overshadow His.
>
> I love what I am doing in your life—making you like Us—Father, Son, and Holy Spirit. We love partnering with you. We love listening to you; we love being with you; We love encouraging you; We love anointing you, and We love lifting you up.
>
> Beloved, We are in a passionate pursuit of you. We are romancing you . . . drawing you to Us. We are in pursuit of **you**; so simply continue turning your heart of affections towards Us.

A Bridal Response

Now, my friend, pray this back to Jesus:

> Thank You for pursuing me . . . thank You for coming after me, Lord. From here on, I will make it easier for You to catch me. I invite You to touch me today.
>
> Thank You for all Your kind intentions towards me. Thank You that it is going to be better in this next season of my life than it has ever been. Thank You that I am walking away from my history of failure; I am walking away from depression and fear. With You by my side I am walking **into** a new territory, right into a land of blessing and a land of laughter and fruitfulness.
>
> I'm ready for this next season, Lord. I am ready for the best time of my life. I say to You, "Yes, Lord . . . yes."

ONE

The Awakening Kiss

*Let him kiss me with the
kisses of his mouth—
for your love is better than wine.*[2]

An author of more than a thousand songs, King Solomon wants his readers to know that out of all of them, this song tops them all. Right from the first words of his song, he attributes it with the utmost importance:

The song of songs, which is Solomon's (1:1).

Then the Song starts off with a stunning encounter right out of the gate—

Let him kiss me with the kisses of his mouth—

This is a metaphor of intimacy with Jesus. Right away I think it's important to add a little context to the mindset of the Shulamite when she experiences this life-changing encounter with the Holy Spirit. From various places in the Song, we are able to discern the mental, emotional, physical, and spiritual condition of the maiden when we first meet her. She is not in an intimate relationship with her Bridegroom. In fact, she seems to

---

[2] Song 1:2.

have withdrawn from Him and from others in the Body because of offense. She experienced some wounding and rejection in the past along with some disappointments, and has allowed those to painfully lodge in her heart. She has aimed that pain at God, at people, and to some degree, at herself. This is the state in which we meet the Shulamite here in the opening verses of the first chapter of the Song.

A Desire for Passion

And yet, the Shulamite expresses a true desire of her heart for intimacy with her Bridegroom here. This one verse contains two key points to the entire book:

> *Let him kiss me with the kisses of his mouth—for your love is better than wine (1:2).*

> *Smother me with kisses—your Spirit-kiss divine (1:2, TPT)*

It is important we do not miss those first two words of verse two, "Let him". We are the beloved of our Bridegroom Jesus, yet so often the most difficult thing about being the beloved is just allowing ourselves to be loved. Let Him love you! Let Him kiss you with all the passion He has in His heart. There is no striving or working for this; it is simply yielding to Him, which positions us in perfect alignment to receive all the passion He has for us. Why not start your journey by waking up every day and saying to Him, "Jesus, today I am letting You kiss me with all the passion You have in Your heart for me"? I can think of no better way to start the day.

The life-transforming process of the Shulamite becoming the Bride begins right here as she responds to the Holy Spirit and yields herself to Him: "Let Him kiss me . . ." That's the way this process towards intimacy with Jesus always begins. Yielding is a resignation of our will to His desires for us.

Awakened out of Dullness

This young maiden is in a place of self-imposed distance

from Jesus. She's angry at God, she's upset with leadership, and she's bitterly resentful against the Body of Christ. She feels she's been deceived, abandoned, and misused. She has withdrawn from God and from people, and she's actually really bored with her life. She is in great need of having her heart awakened out of a dull spiritual condition. Acts 28:27 describes this condition of "dullness":

> *For the hearts of this people have grown dull. Their ears are hard of hearing, and their eyes they have closed, lest they should see with their eyes and hear with their ears, lest they should understand with their hearts and turn, so that I should heal them.*

This word "dull" describes those believers who have lost the excitement of Jesus and the joy of faith. They are living drab, colorless, dreary, stale, and unimaginative lives in Christ—clearly not the abundant life of which Jesus declared[3] He came to bring us. Instead, the Shulamite is in a place where she is no longer astonished or amazed by Jesus and His ways, and in the eyes of the Holy Spirit, that is never an acceptable place. He will never leave us in that condition.

Romanced by the Holy Spirit

The Holy Spirit is continually romancing and wooing us back into the heartbeat of Father God who adores us. Part of why we were even created was because the Father wanted someone in whom He could pour His love. He wanted someone with whom He could have an intimate relationship—someone He could hang out with and share life with at a deep level. The Holy Spirit romances us by drawing us into encounters with the passionate Lover of our soul, Jesus, our Bridegroom. We have a choice, of course: to respond to Him, or not respond; to yield to Him, or not to yield.

The Passionate Kiss of His Presence

Back in 1996, I was thriving in my ministry as a pastor, but I felt so distant from the Lord. At that time, the Holy Spirit was

---

[3] See John 10:10.

being poured out all over the world and people were encountering the love of Jesus in ways they had never before experienced. One weekend, our family attended a service at Bethel Church in Redding, California, where I had a "kiss"-experience with Jesus. The Presence of the Lord was so powerful and I felt His romancing—a drawing of the Holy Spirit. I cannot articulate really well what I was feeling, but I can say all my physical and spiritual senses were awakened at a whole new level. I was literally stunned and overwhelmed with this warmth of love. I felt such safety, value, self-worth, peace, and acceptance like never before in my life.

This is what the kiss is all about. It's encountering a love that is powerfully addicting that you find yourself crying out to your Bridegroom for more and more kisses.

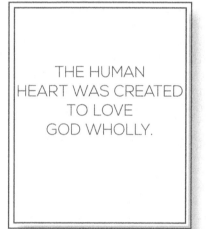

THE HUMAN HEART WAS CREATED TO LOVE GOD WHOLLY.

The Holy Spirit is always romancing us into "kisses,"— a deeper and much more intimate relationship. While you may be satisfied with being forgiven, having the guarantee of Heaven and experiencing the occasional blessing, the Holy Spirit has a greater level of passion for you. He wants to upgrade your vision to mirror the vision of the Shulamite. This is the journey and process He has you in right now.

I personally desire the deepest encounters with Jesus that the human spirit can experience. This is my vision, this is my passion, and there is no price too great for me to pay to go after it. Obviously, there are many blessings and passions in my spiritual life, but what I crave and pursue above all else are the kisses of intimacy and passion from Jesus that ignite my heart with a greater, captivating, and consuming love affair with my Beloved.

That is the vision of the Shulamite we see here.

Seven Longings of the Heart

We read in the Gospels that we are to seek God with all our hearts, and as we do, everything we need will be provided for us. Everything. I agree with the writers who declare that humans have seven longings in their heart, and here's how I identify them:

- The longing to be **enjoyed by God.**
- The longing to be **accepted.**
- The longing for **significance.**
- The longing **to be great.**
- The longing for **intimacy.**
- The longing for **passion.**
- The longing to be **wholehearted.**

All those longings find their fulfillment in that place of intimacy and abiding in Jesus.

The Holy Spirit has come and stirred the heart of His Bride and begins to draw her out from that place of dullness, and we find her responding to the drawing of God as she cries out for an increase of passion for her Bridegroom. That's how the process works. He is always the initiator and we are always the ones who respond to His initiation. Then He responds to our response, and we respond to His response, and that's how this process unfolds. God loves making the first move. He sends out His love to us and we respond to it, and it changes something inside of us. Out of that place of experiencing His love and passion, we release our ignited passion back to Him in worship, in adoration, in praise, and in lifestyle transformation. We give back to God the very thing He gave to us. We never give back to God anything that originates in us. Rather, we always give back to God what originated in Him and we became the recipient of His generosity.

A Clash of Passions

Passion and intimacy for Jesus works the same way as

His redemption. When you couldn't have cared less about the Lord, He couldn't have cared more about you. The Holy Spirit kept drawing . . . wooing . . . and just wowing your heart with the love of Jesus until you responded by opening your heart . . . and whoooosh! In He came. When the Shulamite prays, *Let me know the kisses of your Word,* she is asking for help to give her whole heart to Jesus. She longs to have a heart inflamed with passion for her Beloved. She knows that she cannot muster up that kind of love; she can't "work it up." She knows it is birthed out of supernatural encounters—that which is birthed in Heaven—and so she is crying out for that encounter.

The human heart was created to love God wholly. We were made to cry out for the kisses of Jesus. God has made each one of us with this great capacity for deep cravings—deep thirsts. Now His goal, of course, is for us to fulfill those cravings and thirsts in Him and in His Kingdom. We, however, are a very self-absorbed, self-centered people, and we often turn away and find fulfillment for those cravings in some worldly offering.

That's why we see such an incredible clash of passions in our culture today—a global warfare between the kingdom of Satan and the Kingdom of God. The book of Revelation speaks about this "clash." I believe Revelation has several levels of applications, and one of those levels deals with the end of the age. When we study Revelation, especially chapters 17 and 18, we discover that the power of immorality is very pervasive across the world, especially at the end of the age. Immorality and fornication occupy a major scheme in the strategy of Satan in these chapters of Revelation, where it says that the "spirit" of pornography is going to be so incredibly strong, even the "kings of the earth"[4] will become drunk under the power of this darkness.

It is clear that we are presently living in a clash of passions as we witness an epidemic onslaught of sexual perversion sweeping the world to degrees we've never witnessed before. It is an all-time explosion of sensuality and pornography that is intoxicating the nations of the earth, including our own. We

---

[4] See Rev 18:9.

have easy access to globally connect with every type of sensual content simply by using almost any mobile device. We are witnessing children at very early ages being introduced to sexual images. This kind of assault against our God-given sexuality with its unbridled immorality is unparalleled in history.

Who are the "kings of the earth" mentioned in Revelation 18:9? I interpret it to be Christians. Jesus is the King of kings and we are the "kids" of the King. As King's kids, we have dual citizenship. The Apostle Paul tells us in Ephesians 2:6 that we are seated with Christ in heavenly realms while living on earth. I have a theory regarding our inheritance position in the heavenlies. I envision a conversation in Heaven where the Father is speaking with the Holy Spirit regarding the Bride for whom His Son will one day return to earth. That Bride would be one who is passionately and demonstrably in love with Him. As the Father viewed the Bride in this moment, however, He could see she was not even close to the radical, fiery heart of love for Jesus that will precede His return. But she must be . . . she will be! So the Father dispatched the Holy Spirit with a directive: "Reveal My Son in such a way that all the distorted images carried in the hearts of His Bride would be crushed, and they would encounter His love and passion in ways never before experienced." The Bride would then know true satisfaction of all hunger and thirst the soul craves. This was Heaven's directive. The Holy Spirit rolled out that strategy and the Bride began to experience Jesus in such phenomenal ways, so that we saw an explosion of love, an energized passion, and joyousness breaking out all over the world. Churches in Argentina, Florida, Toronto, and so many other places throughout the world found satisfying refreshment and blazed with the manifested love of Jesus. Hearts were set on fire once again from the wonder and awe of His glorious presence.

My theory continues. I believe the devil saw what was happening and he immediately released a counterfeit to the authentic love that was being released—an explosion of a powerful demonic spirit of lust and sexual perversion like we have never before seen. I believe the unparalleled outbreak of pornography and incomprehensible sexual perversion is a direct counterfeit of Heaven's outpouring of holy passion for His

Son that the Father is releasing to the Church—a demonically-charged assault against the holy-intimacy directive.

Created for Deep Cravings

As I previously mentioned, God has made every one of us with the capacity for deep cravings, deep thirsts and passions. His desire is to see them all fulfilled *in Him*. But so many of us fall prey to our carnal passions, and then we spend hours, days, weeks, months, year after year battling them, working to be free. But we will never get free from addictive carnal passions until we displace them with new and holy passions— until we take those desires, cravings, thirsts, and passions and turn them toward the One who put them into our hearts in the first place. We will never see immoral souls healed by rebuking them or teaching them about drawing back or gritting their teeth and doing their best. Carnal passions will only be healed as they are replaced by a stronger and more abiding passion. And the passion that the Holy Spirit puts into our hearts is way more than sufficient to heal all manner of perversion.

The Apostle Paul wrote about this in Galatians 5.

> *As you yield freely and fully to the dynamic life and power of the Holy Spirit, you will abandon the cravings of your self-life. For your self-life craves the things that offend the Holy Spirit and hinder Him from living free within you. And the Holy Spirit's intense cravings hinder your old self-life from dominating you. The Holy Spirit is the only **one** who defeats the cravings of your natural life.[5]*

This verse is such a significant truth. The word "craves" is so powerful, and it is important to know why God made each one of us with this great capacity for deep cravings in our life. The dictionary defines craving in this way: "a very strong desire for something; an intense, urgent abnormal desire or longing

---

[5] Gal 5:16-17 (TPT), emphasis added.

for something." I'm pretty sure all of us have experienced this at some point in our life. When my wife, Karissa, was pregnant, I got a pretty good understanding of the word "craving" when it came to hot dogs and dill pickles!

The human heart craves and has deep thirsts and was created to be fulfilled in Jesus and His Kingdom. But we sometimes find ourselves addicted to cravings that entrap our physical appetites in enslaving ways that actually oppose God and the priority of His Kingdom in our life.

The Entrapment of Destructive Emotions

Before I became a Christian, I was utterly locked in to my cravings for drugs and alcohol. It took me a long time to realize that I was allergic to alcohol: Every time I drank, I seemed to break out in handcuffs. Anger and rage was another thing I have dealt with much of my life. It often would get the best of me no matter how hard I tried, and resulted in dropping me into a dark place of shame and guilt.

When Karissa and I were dating, she came over to the house one hot summer afternoon to make us dinner. This was the first meal she would be preparing for us. For some reason I decided that while she was making dinner, I would do her a favor and repair a little rattle in her car under the dashboard that had been disturbing her. Just to clarify, I have no skills to repair anything, least of all something in a vehicle. I allowed my passion for Karissa, and my desire to do something nice for her, overrule wisdom.

Armed with a long, heavy screwdriver and a flashlight, I headed out into the 100-degree day to tighten the screw. Utilizing the flashlight I had no problem in locating the loose screw. I affixed the flashlight to the car and began to tighten the screw. The heat inside the car was stifling, and I was sweating profusely, but my determination to help Karissa kept me focused.

Working steadily, I felt the screwdriver beginning to secure the screw, but way too slowly for the discomfort I was enduring. Suddenly, the sweat from my hands caused the heavy screwdriver to slip out of my hand and fall to the floor of the car.

Now I should mention that in a Nissan Sentra, getting my hands to reach up into the cramped area of the dashboard with a screwdriver was very costly to the skin. My goal was to only force them up under the dashboard *one time*. However, over the course of the next fifteen to twenty minutes, that scene of the screwdriver getting sweat-soaked and falling to the floor of the car was on a repeat cycle. Each time the screwdriver hit the floor, my infamous temper began to escalate, until rage finally won the battle. The final straw was when the screwdriver slipped off the screw and hit me directly in the face on its familiar path toward the floor. As it did, I lost total control and snapped my head up, smashing it into the steering wheel. Grabbing the screwdriver, I flew out of the car in a rage. At that exact moment, Karissa was coming out of the door cheerily calling out, "Dinner is ready!"

As she spoke those words, I launched the screwdriver, throwing it up the long walkway towards my neighbor's house. He had a large plate glass window and I watched the screwdriver airborne and spiraling directly towards it. Both Karissa and I were glued to the screwdriver as it neared the window. Fortunately for me, it lost its momentum before slamming into the window, so that instead of shattering it, it simply shook violently. By this time, I had lost steam, as is usually the case when I released my temper in a fit of anger. I looked over sheepishly at Karissa, who, by now was wide-eyed, turned on her heels and quickly headed back into the house.

As I started towards the front door, I could already feel the guilt and shame beginning to wash over me. While Karissa forgave me, I found it impossible to forgive myself, and I allowed that incident to push me into a dark place.

A New and Holy Passion

Here's the thing—the enemy would beat me up for days after an event like that, and I convinced myself I would never get free. I would promise the Lord I would never lose my temper again, and I would grit my teeth and set my determination. But it never worked. Then one day, the Holy Spirit revealed this truth to me: **I would never experience freedom from addictive, destructive passions until I replaced them with a new and holy passion.** I learned I could never be completely set free by determination of my will or attempting to do my best to not engage in that destructive activity. I found that I could only experience a consistent freedom when I replaced destructive passions with the passion the Holy Spirit put into my heart for God and for the things of His Kingdom.

Here's the key: love the Lord your God with **all** your heart. Be intentional in your pursuit of intimacy with Him. Actively and passionately seek the Lord with all your heart, mind, and strength, and you will discover that at the very least, you are distracted from the evil passions of this day. When you are consumed with a passion for Jesus, carnal passions seem to dissipate.

In this clash of passions in the Song, the Shulamite responds to the wooing and the romancing of the Holy Spirit. She yields her heart and her emotions to the heart, emotions, and passions of her Bridegroom Jesus, and she is flooded with a sense of His overwhelming love. She feels His passionate love physically, mentally, emotionally, and spiritually, and in the moment she cries out, "Come and kiss me again, for your love is better than wine."[6] The Shulamite cries out for the Lord to "smother me with your kisses," and, of course, the Lord will always respond to every prayer that He initiates. Wave after wave of the passionate love of Jesus floods the heart, mind, soul, and life of this young maiden. She is absolutely stunned as she encounters the love and the passion that is in His heart for her. Her heart is ignited with a passion that she has never experienced before, and she longs for more, so she cries out, "Please come and kiss me again, and again, and again."

A Heart Aflame Renews Hunger

The Shulamite is saying, "I have never felt love like this before. Are you kidding me? Where has this been? Please come

---

6   Song 1:2, NLT.

and kiss me again." She has tasted of the passion of Jesus, and it ignites a renewed hunger in her heart for more and more and more.

That's the way the Kingdom works. In the world we get hungry and we eat, and are satisfied. In the Kingdom we eat, and we get hungrier for more. That's what the kiss is all about. She longs to have a heart inflamed with passion for her Beloved, and she knows that she cannot muster up that kind of love. She has tried to muster it up or work it up in the past, but she discovered it simply doesn't work. The way passion will come and increase in our lives is to receive the passion the Lord has for us. As that passion hits our hearts, it ignites our passion, and we release it back to the Lord in worship, in praise, in joy, and in a transformed lifestyle.

As I said, we were created to love God with our whole heart. We were made to cry out for the kisses of His mouth. And right here at the beginning of the Song, the journey begins for this Shulamite as she cries out: "Jesus, come and kiss me again . . . come and ignite a passion in my heart for You. God, I serve You from a distance. I don't really know You very well anymore, but I just encountered Your heart again and *I have* caught another glimpse of You. Now the cry of my heart is that I need You, I long for You. I have to know You more. I know there is more, and I want more! Nothing else matters to me but You and Your Presence."

Intoxicating Love

The maiden then declares to her Bridegroom:

Your love for me is better than wine.

She uses the wine metaphor because wine exhilarates the heart. It's a picture of a heart intoxicated by the love of the Father. She's setting forth the idea of a stunned heart, a heart that is just intoxicated by Him. "Your love is more intoxicating than anything in this world You allow me to enjoy and experience." She's not only saying, "Your love is better than sin;" that's a given. She's saying, "The unfolding of Your love to my heart is even better than all those things that I love to experience in this world but that doesn't bring me into a deeper experience of Your love.

My wife, Karissa, and my daughter, Amber, have talked with me about another aspect of this wine metaphor. Both of them mentioned how they enjoy a glass of wine in the evening because it has a way of calming, soothing, and quieting the stress that attacks the mind. That's definitely a picture of the Holy Spirit.

I love to read. I love to exercise. I love going to the movies, and I even love the popcorn with the imitation butter. I love watching my boys play baseball. I love traveling and spending time with my wife. I love spending time with my children and my grandkids. But all of those things, as wonderful as they are—and I would die for any member of my family—all pales in comparison to my love for Jesus. His love is intoxicating, and He always initiates it.

God always responds to prayers for intimacy, because, again, He is the One who initiates it. We see this with the Shulamite as God responds to her heart-cry and He begins to flood her with an incredible sense of His Presence. He begins to touch her, and in that touch, she experiences all the love, the joy, the pleasure, the adoration the Father has for her. And what naturally begins to rise up out of her is a spirit of adoration. When God comes and touches you and whispers in your ear, a smile comes to your face, and something so much deeper than you've ever experienced begins to flow out of you.

We serve a God who loves to touch us, because we are His kids. Think about how much you loved being touched by a loved one, or touching a loved one. You hug your child, and everything within you is released in that touch to your child. All your hopes, all your dreams, all your non-negotiable love, all your desires, all your unyielding support and commitment—everything you feel for that person is translated into that hug. So it is with our Father. There is absolutely nothing like the intoxicating presence of God's love. He has come to give us His presence—to touch us in a tangible and healing way.

That's His passion. He has a fire in His heart that burns for you.

The Fragrance of His Presence

Because of the fragrance of your good ointments,
your name is fragrance poured forth; therefore
the virgins love you (1:3).

The idea of fragrance speaks of the emotional make-up of our Bridegroom Jesus. Think for a moment of the fragrance of a rose. That fragrance arises from the internal properties or the internal qualities of that rose or that flower. In that light, this perfume refers to the way Jesus thinks and the way that He feels. It is His interior life, His emotional make-up, and His thought life. The good perfume of Jesus that moves us the most and moves us at the deepest level is His affection and emotion for His people.

In the presence of the Lord, you smell His wonderful fragrance, and you know He is near. There is such a sweetness to the fragrance of the presence of God. The Shulamite is consumed in the sweetness of His wonderful fragrance being poured out all over her.

The young maiden starts out by saying, "Because of the fragrance of your good perfumes . . ." Think about perfume for a moment. Perfume is not an activity; it's not even a visible substance. When perfume is in the air, we can't grab a handful of it, but we can still sense its impact. I've heard someone use a "rose" to describe this beautiful fragrance of His presence. The rose is really beautiful in its external appearance, but its fragrance comes from within. The beautiful fragrance that comes from the rose is hidden within the rose itself. In the same way, the Shulamite is speaking of her Bridegroom's internal qualities. She declares that it is because of the nature of who He is that overwhelms her. She declares how He stuns her heart and she is overwhelmed by the sweet perfume of the goodness that emanates from within Him.

The unique thing about perfume is that although we cannot see it or touch it is very real, and has the ability to genuinely impact us—even our emotions. It stirs our olfactory senses and creates a response within us. "Perfume" speaks of Jesus' wonderful personality, which especially includes His passion and pleasure for His people. All of Heaven is filled with the perfumes of Christ Jesus—but that perfume is not limited to Heaven only. We are the fragrance of Christ[7] to every person we encounter.

I once heard a story about a man walking through an airport with his wife to catch a plane when they passed by a group of men. The pastor stopped, dropped his luggage and said to his wife, "I'll be right back."

He approached one of the men in the group they had just walked by and after a short exchange, the wife watched her husband hug one of them. The husband then returned to his wife, picked up his luggage, and continued walking toward their gate.

"Who was that?" she inquired.

"Well," her husband answered, "I do not know him, but when we passed that group of men, I smelled the exact same fragrance I smell in the throne room of Heaven! I simply had to meet him."

Paul spoke about the fragrance of Jesus each one of us carries.

> *Now thanks be to God who always leads us in triumph in Christ, and through us diffuses the **fragrance** of His knowledge in every place.*
>
> 2 Corinthians 2:14, emphasis added

God has a literal fragrance and I'm certain it is a supernatural fragrance that surrounds His throne—a fragrance unlike anything of earth. Something beautifully powerful is released throughout all of the universe because of this fragrance. I believe it is a reflection of the state of God's heart and is the result and expression of His internal beauty. The fragrance of Jesus is His cologne that lingers, but you have to get really close and intimate with Him to smell it.

---

[7]   See 2 Cor 2:15.

Again the Holy Spirit plays such a huge part in the type of fragrance that emanates from us. When we yield our heart to the Holy Spirit, we will know the peace of God because we will be filled with it. We will know the joy of the Lord because we will be filled with it. We will know the presence of God because we will be full of God, and when you are full of God, you will overflow. We are meant to be people who are overflowing and dispensing the fragrance of Jesus. Everywhere we go we leave evidence that the Lord was there. Every arid and stale place we enter will be infused with a heavenly deposit of the Lord Jesus.

"Therefore the virgins love you"

The "virgins" here are the Daughters of Jerusalem—those who love the Bridegroom with sincere hearts. They have yet to experience encounters that have filled them with a greater passion for Jesus than they have for all the other passions in their life. In the coming chapters, we will follow these Daughters in this journey as well, and discover that it is the passion of the Shulamite, and her testimony and life that cause these Christians to begin to pursue and love the Bridegroom with all their heart, soul, mind, and strength.

I believe it is God's desire to ignite this same passion into your heart.

"The Awakening Kiss" Prayer

If you are sensing in your heart a stirring for more intimacy with Jesus as you read these words, then I would like to pray for you as you agree in your own heart.

Holy Spirit, I pray You would release Your passion for Jesus into the heart and soul of the reader. We know we cannot work up or muster up a passion for You. We know our passion for You comes as You release the passion You have in Your heart for us, and it touches our heart. So Holy Spirit, please encounter our hearts with the heart Jesus has for us.

We are sensing a hunger for more intimacy with You, Lord, and You always feed hungry people. We have tasted of Your goodness, Lord. We have tasted of Your love, Your joy, Your power, Your favor, Your immense pleasure over us, and we are hungry for more.

So, we turn and yield our hearts toward You, Holy Spirit, and I ask that You would increase the awareness of the love and passion Jesus has on His heart for the one reading right now.

I pray as well, Lord, if the reader is in need of a touch from You, whether it be physically, mentally, emotionally, or spiritually, I ask You to please touch them now, in Jesus' name.

Lord, You are everything we need, and I pray You would drop the things we need into our spirit. We want Your presence, God. My prayer is if the one reading these words does not feel loved, let their heart feel the flood of Your love wash over them right now. For that one who does not feel accepted, overwhelm them with the feeling of acceptance. For that one who has never felt Your arms surrounding them with comfort, let them feel Your embrace right now and allow them an opportunity to feel Your unceasing, unending, unlimited love.

I pray for a tenacious love to overwhelm the reader. Let him/her experience a love that never quits, a love that never gives up, a love that persists through all opposition to it, and a love that keeps our eyes fixed on You, Jesus.

Ignite their heart to another place of passion as they are being overwhelmed with the passion You have for them.

We ask all of this for the sake of our Lord and Savior, Jesus Christ.

Amen.

ACTIVATION #1
The Awakening Kiss

All of God's dealings with you are geared towards creating maximum dependency upon Him, and drawing you into a closer place of intimacy with Him. As you read through this book, make it a goal to allow the Holy Spirit to carry you into encounters with Jesus right into His most secret, intimate place. Determine to live as close to God's heartbeat as you possibly can. If you dwell deeply embedded in the heart of a God who adores you, there is not a circumstance on earth that will distress you out of the safety of His presence, because it is a place of perpetual peace.

ACTIVATION

When difficult circumstances come into our life, instead of concentrating on the event and getting overwhelmed, determine to praise and thank the Lord, and the Holy Spirit will use that to carry you right into the Presence of Jesus. You will discover the reality of Jesus with you in this situation and His presence and peace will carry you right on through.

With that in mind, consider the external situation(s) you are presently facing. Ask yourself these questions:

- Is this situation causing me anxiety, worry, fear, or stress in my life?
- Am I inadvertently taking these external assaults onboard in my soul, my mind, and emotions?
- Or am I, rather, using these circumstances as vehicles to drive Him deeper into my spirit and right into the heart of God with His abundance of peace?

Think of that specific situation, and then consciously use them as springboards into expressing praise and gratitude to the Lord. Begin to thank Him *in* that circumstance. Notice, I am not saying, thank Him *for* the circumstance, but thank Him that He is *in* the circumstance, and that this specific situation is increasing your intimacy and trust levels with Him.

45

"The Awakening" Prayer

I would encourage you to read aloud the words of this crafted declarative prayer, and take them personally to heart.

Father, thank You for Your Presence. I thank You that You are pursuing me, that You are after me. Lord I plan to make it really easy for You to catch me. I invite You to touch me again today. I invite You to bless me. I invite You to speak to my heart and to give me wonderful thoughts about who I really, really am in Your eyes. I invite You to teach me how to pray like Jesus and the Holy Spirit, because I want to pray *with* You, not towards You. I want to pray with the answer, not try to find one.

I thank You for all that is happening around and about me right now, and I declare that I am in the best time of my life, and I am going to make the most of what You are doing. I am not going to hang back this time. I am not going to be late to this party. I am going to move quickly; I have my running shoes on and I am coming after You. Thank You for all that You intend towards me and my house, towards my family, and my loved ones. Thank You for the prodigals in my family that are coming home. Thank You that You are restoring all the enemy has stolen. Thank You that You are going to teach me how to rob my enemy blind. I am not just getting back what he stole from me, but I am going to get back what he has stolen from my neighbor as well, because I am also praying for them.

Thank You, that it is going to be better for me in this next season than it has ever been in my life. I am trusting You today for that. Amen.

TWO

A Two-Fold Call

*Draw me away! We will run after
you. The king has brought me into
His chambers (1:4).*

With her heart inflamed with passion for Jesus, the Shulamite cries out for God to draw her into an even greater place of intimacy.

Draw me into your heart and lead me out. We will run away together into your cloud-filled chamber.

We will remember your love as we laugh and rejoice in you, celebrating your every kiss as better than wine . . . (1:4, TPT)

The Shulamite has experienced a beautiful intimacy of the "kiss" with her Bridegroom. Now she knows she must go deeper—right into His heart. She doesn't realize, however, that she is asking to be taken away from what has become comfortable, but her passion is speaking. "Lead me out" is an urgent plea for Jesus to take her from her present place of comfort into the place where He dwells.

I love *The Passion Translation* wording, "into your cloud-filled chamber". This is the holy place where He resides. In answer to her heart's cry, the Holy Spirit takes her into the very throne room of the Lord. This is a huge thing that the Shulamite is asking of the Bridegroom, but she really has no clue, at this point in her walk with Him, what she is asking for.

Going to the Next Level

Sometimes when we ask God for something, especially something really big, we, too, don't realize that we are actually asking the Lord to transform us. It would be impossible to go from our present state into the next advanced level without His transforming work. What we are really asking is to leave our present comfort zone and relocate into a season of processing where our character can develop the weight with which to carry it.

In Mark 10:35, the mother of James and John came to Jesus to make a request of Him. Kneeling down before Him with her two sons, she started off by announcing, "Teacher, we want You to do for us whatever we ask!" That may seem funny, but in reality, the disciples had heard Jesus say numerous times, "If you want something, just ask for it." He told them:

> *Ask, and it will be given to you . . . For everyone who asks receives . . .* [8]

So, here they are asking. But they don't realize that what they are really asking for is a promotion. They have seen the power and authority of Jesus. They have heard Him talking about setting up His Kingdom, and they believe it will happen soon, and they want to be placed into prominent positions in His earthly Kingdom.

I think Jesus probably had a half-smirk, half-smile on His face when He answers them by saying, "What is it You want Me to do?"

She responds by asking on behalf of her sons—

[8] See Matt 7:7-8.

> *Grant that these two sons of mine may sit, one on*
> *Your right hand and the other on the left, in Your*
> *glory (Matthew 20:21).*

I guess they figured, *Hey, if you are going to ask, ask big!*
Jesus responded to their request by asking them yet another
question:

> *You do not know what you ask. Are you able to*
> *drink the cup that I am about to drink, and be*
> *baptized with the baptism that I am baptized*
> *with? (v 22)*

The disciples are clueless as to what He meant by that so
they responded with one of the top ten really dumb responses
in the Bible: "Yes. We are able. For sure. No worries. We got
this."

But the "cup" Jesus is referring to here is suffering. In
Luke 12:50 He talks about this cup of suffering when He says:

> *I have a baptism [of great suffering] with which*
> *to be baptized, and how [greatly] I am distressed*
> *until it is accomplished! (AMP)*

Obviously Jesus is not talking here about water baptism;
He is talking about the extreme distress of the crucifixion—
His baptism into death. This distress is weighing so heavily on
Him, that we see in three of the Gospels where He prays and
asks the Father if it might even be possible to remove the cup
of suffering from Him. But He ends the prayer by saying, "Not
My will, but Yours be done."[9] When He asks these two disciples
of His if they are able to drink of "the cup", this is to what He
is referring . The disciples are asking for a significant personal
promotion in the Kingdom, and Jesus is about to show them
one of the keys to achieve that promotion. It comes through the
way you handle the cup of suffering.

Jesus then answered these inquiring disciples:

---

[9]   Luke 22:42.

> *But to sit on My right hand and on My left is not Mine to give, but it is for those for whom it is prepared (Mark 10:40).*

In other words, such positions of honor come with a significant price. This brings me back to an earlier statement. I do not think we always understand that when we ask for such big things in the Kingdom, we are actually asking the Lord to *transform* us—to prepare us for an experience where God's greater grace will be appropriated.

That is what is happening here with the Bride in her request.

Two-fold: Intimacy and Co-laboring

The bride's heart is stirred for her Bridegroom, Jesus, and out of that place of deep intimacy she cries out:

> *Draw me away with you and let us run together!*
> *(v 4, AMP)*

This is a two-fold call: The Shulamite wants to be drawn into deeper places of His heart, and into a more intimate partnership with Him. She's asking to be drawn into deeper encounters and experiences of His affection and intimacy toward her, and then out of that place of intimacy, partner with Him to touch the lives of other people. She has a desire to co-labor with Him and others within the Body of Christ with whom the Lord joins her. She wants to "run" in ministry with Him and desires partnership with the purposes on His heart.

The word, "run," is always phrased in the plural, whereas "draw" near to God in intimacy is singular. The divine order is always to be **drawn into intimacy**, and then **run together in ministry**—to co-labor with Jesus. Out of the deep intimacy we develop with Jesus, our ministry to others is birthed.

Jesus taught His disciples that the priority in the Spirit is in the first and greatest commandment, "love the Lord your God with all your heart, with all your soul, and with all your mind,"[10] which then empowers us to live out the second commandment: "love your neighbor as yourself."[11] As you saturate yourself in His love, it enables you to love others. There's just no other way to have a sustaining effective ministry.

Throughout my years of vocational ministry, I have seen how people often **"run"** without having first experienced the **drawing** into intimacy, and this reverse order of priorities leads to a whole lot of issues and problems. Of course, there is also the flipside where we only want to be drawn in, but we don't want to run.

Rediscover First Love

Sometimes people come to a point in vocational ministry where the joy all but disappears; it is no longer fun. In fact, ministry becomes laborious. A loss of joy is often a signpost indicating we may have lost the drawing aspect of our ministry. When you sense that loss of joy, if you will turn your heart toward the Spirit of God, you will discover that He is romancing you back into encounters of your first love. The Spirit's agenda in your life is for you to rediscover intimacy with Jesus. It is great to love ministry, but it is greater still to love intimacy and that nearness with Jesus.

In Revelation 2:4, the Scripture talks about the Church at Ephesus who lost their first love. This verse describes them as a good, hard-working church, but who were operating out of a diminished first-love passion for Jesus. The Holy Spirit is saying to us: *It is time for your heart to be captured and captivated by Jesus once again!*

It is not healthy, nor sustainable to have a functional, working relationship with the Lord that isn't coming from a place of extreme intimacy. Always be aware that if your ministry is growing, flourishing, and blossoming but your intimacy with Him is not, you may be heading for trouble. Perhaps today, even as you are reading this, you are feeling a tug on your

---

[10]   Matt 22:37.
[11]   22:39.

heart to be drawn into deeper places of nearness and intimacy with Jesus. Like the Shulamite maiden, when you pray, "Lord, draw me," I promise He will respond to that prayer, and just like the song we sing declares, He will "break every chain" that is holding you back. "Draw me" is a continual, lifelong journey and fervent prayer of our hearts to the Lord. Every time you ask Him, the Holy Spirit will draw you into that first love passion again and again, right into the heartbeat of a Bridegroom who is absolutely enraptured by you.

Into His Private Chambers

The king has brought me into his chambers (v 4).

The Shulamite prays for her Beloved to draw her away, and in response, the Holy Spirit picks her up and carries her into His "cloud-filled chamber",[12] His most private place, His innermost chambers. In the Song of Solomon, the King's "chambers" is the Holy of Holies. This is the place of no distractions where the two of them will share their most private thoughts. In this place, they begin to build a private history together. The private "chambers" is a magnificent picture of intimacy. The Bridegroom is romancing His lover . . . just the two of them alone. This is where a genuine life exchange really takes place.

This holy place of His chambers refers to the times in her life where she develops her secret life in God. Everyone in the Kingdom of God has a private life in God—a life that is carefully recorded by Him. Maybe we do not give much thought to it, but we do have a life in God others do not see that is actually the most important part of our lives.

The secret place—the Most Holy Place—secluded away from everything is where Jesus begins to reveal all of who He is to us and where we have an opportunity to open up our innermost life to Him as well. You see, He already knows everything about us, but He can only really *know* us by our transparent exchanges through conversation, and giving Him permission to view every hidden thing.

---

[12]   TPT.

On a Wednesday evening back in 1998, I received a prophetic word that rocked my world and set my course for the next 19 years. The prophet declared that the Lord was going to give me some powerful keys on the inward life and living out of that internal castle of God where the Presence dwells within me.

"You will be a man that can usher in the manifested Presence of God because you will live in it," she said to me. "There are going to be many times—just in the gentle, tender kindness of the way you speak—that people will know the touch of God and the sense of the heart of God. And it's all because you will be living in that secret place."

As she was speaking these words to me, the Presence of the Lord so filled the room, we were physically affected by it, and stunned.

The prophet then said to me, "Do you feel that?"

Both Karissa and I responded together, "Oh yes!"

She then went on to say, "That is what I'm talking about! What you experience in the secret place will be felt externally by every person you encounter."

Even today, I am still unfolding that word I received about the secret of living in that intimate place of His chambers.

Identity Upgrade

This is an important time for the Shulamite. She's had an incorrect image of her Bridegroom, and she desperately needed to upgrade her identity of Him. This is based around the question Jesus asked the disciples: "Who do men say that I am?"[13] They came back with four distorted images.

Following that Jesus asked them the most important question of all: "But who do *you* say that I am?"[14] At some point each one of us must all answer this question, because the

---

[13]   See Matt 16:13.
[14]   See v 15.

image and identity of Jesus that we carry in our heart will be the motivation for how we respond to everything in our life. Just like the Shulamite, we need to develop a personal testimony of who Jesus is to us. Our testimony is not just what we were like before we were saved; that is our history. Our testimony about Jesus should say something like this:

> *This is who I know Jesus is to me: He has proven Himself trustworthy. He is faithful and good all the time. He is the kindest person I have ever met. He is always for me and never against me. He has the best listening skills of anyone I know, and He always speaks the truth wrapped in love preceded by grace. He always points out the treasure in me, and His workings in my life never cause me a single moment of guilt, shame, or confusion.*

As we develop our own private history with God in the secret place of His presence, that hidden life in His chambers will result in our transformation and be publicly revealed through the activities of our daily life.

Jesus is drawing His beloved Shulamite into His most secret place. He is captivating her heart as He begins the process of reconciliation and reconnects at deeper and deeper levels. This is the time and place where He reveals Himself as our Healer, and begins to anoint our wounds with His healing balm. This is the place where we discover our truest identity—His beloved one. This is the place where we come to know how accepted and loved we really are, and our hearts are becoming softer, sweeter, and more easily accessed as our trust in Him begins to grow. As we take to heart that we are truly His beloved, we begin to experience how lovingly He responds to us, even in our failures.

In this secret place, we are finally allowing ourselves to be loved by Him, and in response, our affections are aroused.

The Secret Fort

Have you ever had a secret place? I mean, an actual

hideaway where you could escape and retreat from the pressures of life? I had such a place when I was in the fourth, fifth, and sixth grade. There were these huge pine trees behind the elementary school I attended. I loved climbing up 15 feet and sitting on those large branches as the cool breeze blew through them.

One summer, I begin to haul up various sizes of lumber scraps over a period of weeks and built a very flimsy, but somewhat safe, fort. It became my "secret place." It was in this place where I would go to get away from my brother and sisters and escape any of the pressures that a 10-12-year-old may face. It was in that secret place I would contemplate life.

I remember escaping to this place in a panic one afternoon, following a harrowing experience at my friend's house, about a half-mile from my secret hideaway. His house was located in a residential area, but because it was zoned as an agricultural lot, his family had turned part of the land into a farm where they raised sheep, goats, chickens, a couple of pigs, and grew vegetables. But our classmate never invited us over to his house, and so we determined amongst ourselves that it was because of his very stern, grumpy old grandfather who lived with them and worked their farm.

> THE MORE WE CONSISTENTLY BEAT A PATHWAY TO OUR SECRET PLACE, THE MORE IT BECOMES OUR DEFAULT.

On that particular Saturday, my buddies and I decided to visit our classmate at his house anyway. We parked our bikes up near the front door and began walking towards the house just as the old grandfather rounded the corner. He was sweating something fierce and looked really agitated. Terror filled us immediately. The big-bearded old man was carrying a huge shovel and growled at us, "What d'you want?"

"Is Craig home? . . . Can he come out . . . and . . . and, uh . . . play ball?" we asked hesitantly, eyes riveted on that big 'ol shovel in his hand.

"No! He cannot play today . . . or ever! You'll never see him again. He disobeyed me . . . and I . . . I disciplined him *good!*" By now our eyes were huge as saucers.

The old man menacingly pointed his shovel in our direction. "Like I said, you'll never see him again . . ." I was so scared . . . the palms of my hands were sweating so bad and my legs felt like jelly.

"Now get outta here," he bellowed.

We looked at the shovel, then at each other, and sprinted for our bikes. Flying down the path as fast as we could peddle, we were out the gate, racing down the road as if our life depended on it. Finally arriving at one of our other friend's house, we caught our breath and debriefed.

Later on, I rode my bike to the pine trees and climbed up to my secret place. Immediately I felt such safety . . . such peace and comfort. I had been terrified to my core earlier that day, but here in my little hideaway, it all changed.

After that, I found that every time I would go to my secret fort, I discovered it to be a refuge, a quiet, safe place where I could retreat and find amazing restful peace. In the same way, Jesus is a secret hideaway for each one of us—a true safe place. He is that strong tower we can run into and feel absolute safety. Psalm 91 calls the Presence of God a "secret place". It is called a secret place, because when we abide there, no external circumstance or demonic influence can find us there. The secret place is the Presence of Jesus within us. It is that internal stronghold where God's holy Presence dwells. It is where our spirit, our soul, and all of our emotions and feelings are safely guarded by His Spirit.

Building a Private History with God

In John 5:19, we read that Jesus did what He saw the Father doing, and He only spoke what He heard the Father saying. He lived in absolute response to His Father. Now, that does not mean Jesus spent time with His Father just to get the latest revelation, teaching, assignment, or strategy. Jesus was motivated solely by **intimacy** with His Father. He walked in such deep communion, fellowship, and intimacy with Him, and He heard the sounds of Heaven being heralded because He *lived* in that realm. He lived *from* that realm *toward* this world. In the same way, we, too, can live in response to the Father in Heaven as we enjoy continual intimate fellowship and friendship with Him. We can live from that realm, hearing the sounds of Heaven, and communicate the message of the Father to this realm. In this way, we can do as we see our Father in Heaven is doing, just as Jesus did.

My prayer for me, and for us all, is that we will not get too busy with life to "come away" and spend quality time with Him. A prayer I always pray—and I encourage you to join me—is this:

> Holy Spirit, set boundaries in my life to protect
> my private time with You, just as Jesus did.

This private history is developed in those quiet times alone with Him and becomes our lifeline to trust Him, even when our faith is challenged. It is in this place where you find your joy again, especially if the world around you is crashing. Psalm 46 opens with an earthquake and ends with an admonishment:

> *Be still, and **know** that **I am God** (v 10, emphasis added).*

Even with your life reeling, rolling, and rocking, you have a secret place inside where you know the Great I AM God and instead experience His peace, stillness, and joy. *Joy?* Yes, joy. Because as Christians, joy is not circumstantial, nor is it tied to an event or a circumstance. Joy is tied to a Person, and that Person is Jesus.

The more we consistently beat a pathway to our secret place, the more it becomes our default. When we start to feel depressed, discouraged, or unhappy, that should alert us immediately to set aside some time to be alone with Jesus.

ENCOUNTERS WITH THE BRIDEGROOM

It is in this secret place where you start to fall in love with the people that God loves, and you love them with authenticity because you are seeing people through God's lens. We often do not esteem people the way He does because we just don't see them quite the way He does. Spend time with Him in the secret place and watch your eyesight change; watch your heart fill up with love for people. This love for people doesn't come because the Scripture commands you to love others the way you love yourself; it comes because the place of intimacy with Jesus has moved you from hearing it as a command to believing it to be **a privilege and a joy.**

In the secret place—

- You love mean people;
- You love people who don't like you;
- You love people that don't look like you;
- You love people you would never choose to hang out with;
- You even love your enemies.

The love of Jesus has so permeated your heart and transformed you that you just love people as He does. You are simply possessed by His love.

Consider the following transformational results of your time well spent in that hidden place of His presence:

- Your history is shaped and developed in the secret place.
- Your intimacy is developed in this place.
- Your truest identity is discovered in this secret place.
- The upgrade of your Father comes in this place.
- The upgrade of the true identity of Jesus is discovered and activated in this place.
- Exchanges with God are made here.

Dying also takes place in this place—private, gut-wrenching death to things about which God is saying, "This will not travel well where I'm taking you."

"But Lord," you may say, "I have a strong attachment to [whatever it is]. I've lived with it all my life and have come to love it. I can't just let it go."

"Yeah, I know," He says. "But it is actually not that great for you, and it will be a huge hindrance to the better thing I've prepared for you. So give Me that, and take this. I promise, you will love this *so* much more."

Private victories are often gut-wrenching and very, very hard. Nobody knows what's happening in you, but everyone notices that *something* has happened, because you're totally different! Remember, whatever we do in secret will be made obvious publicly.

One last thing about this private place: it was not often that I would leave this secret time having my circumstances changed. In fact, I would often have to face the very same circumstances. The guy that was facing those circumstances going in, though, was not the same guy facing those same circumstances coming out. Something of the Spirit of God altered my heart and changed the way I perceive, changed the way I see, changed my perspective, and changed the way I act toward the opposition before me. It could be people who are causing opposition; it could be pressures from finances, pressures from work, pressures brought on by relational issues, ministry or work-related pressures—these are the things that drive us into the secret place.

But here's the reality: if you are not setting aside consistent times to hang out with God and going to Him when things are great, when life comes crashing in with its difficulties, traumas, and challenges, you will discover your default is **not** to go to Him. Rather, we will pull into our mind, emotions, and intellect and just try to figure things out. We often go to others to ask them for advice. Eventually we do consider prayer, but only after our own attempts fail, because it has *not become* our habit to build that pathway in the good times. But we can make the secret place our priority and default by taking a new direction beginning today.

Determine your heart will go after this two-fold calling: "Draw me away" and "Let us run together." And make a commitment to build a life with God in the secret place of His private chambers.

"A Two-Fold Call" Prayer

Father, I thank You that You walk with me through the good and the bad. You walk with me on the mountaintops and through the valley. Your commitment to me is never less than 100% because that is who You are. Father, right now, let Your Presence touch me. I pray that I can sense Your Presence tangibly.

I give You this moment, Lord, to draw me deeper into Your heart. Holy Spirit, would You come as Comforter? Would You come and touch my heart, touch my emotions, touch my mind, and replace the mindsets I have about You with a better one? Replace the mindsets I have about myself with the mindset You have about me, so that the eyes of my heart will be opened to really see how You see me and just how much You really love me.

Holy Spirit, I long for You to pick me up and carry me into that most secret place—into the private chambers of my Beloved. I pray for fresh encounters with Your love. I pray for a desire to open my heart wide and allow my Beloved into every part of my life. I trust You, Jesus. I long to develop an intimate friendship with You, and I commit to a lifestyle of communion with you. I love You, Lord.

Amen.

ACTIVATION #2
A Two-Fold Call

The Shulamite requests intimacy with her Beloved so they will "run together" in ministry. She knows it is the drawing into His passionate, compassionate heart of love where she will experience upgrades in her love for others.

Activation

I want to recommend that you review the main themes of this chapter and come up with your own questions to evaluate your progress, but here are a few questions to consider.

1. How am I demonstrating in the natural the spiritual reality I have of living deep in the heart of the love of God?

_____

_____

2. Whom am I serving? How could I improve?

_____

_____

3. How am I handling suffering?

_____

_____

4. In what ways has the Holy Spirit been drawing me to rediscover first love?

_____

_____

5. How could I improve on creating those secluded times in His private chambers to make it my default?

_____

_____

_____

_____

6. What is the theme/focus of the Holy Spirit in recent weeks/months in the secret place?

_____

_____

_____

_____

7. From these recent encounters with your Bridegroom, write out an answer to Jesus' question to His disciples: "But who do YOU say that I am?" (This will be a result of your private history with God as you have been discovering a specific facet of His character revealed to you applied in a particular area of your life, i.e., healing, faithfulness, etc.)

_____

_____

_____

_____

_____

_____

_____

Prayer

> Father, thank You for loving me so well and for filling me with a true agape love for others. Holy Spirit, create in my heart an even greater passion to choose to serve and love You, and to serve and love others as You do. Draw me, and let us run together in a co-laboring partnership to demonstrate to people just how much You love them, and how good You truly are. Amen.

THREE

Guilt, Shame, and Failure

> *I am dark, but lovely, O daughters of*
> *Jerusalem, like the tents of Kedar,*
> *like the curtains of Solomon (1:5).*

The Shulamite is moving into another significant life-transforming encounter with the Lord as she faces her first spiritual crisis.

> *Do not look upon me, because I am dark, because*
> *the sun has tanned me (1:6a).*
>
> *Jerusalem maidens, in this twilight darkness I*
> *know that I am so unworthy—so in need. Yet you*
> *are so lovely! (1:5, TPT)*

As she is carried into the bedchamber of her Beloved, the maiden discovers the darkness buried in her heart. Here in the atmosphere of the Presence of God, all those things within her that she does not like—all her poor choices, her failures, her sin—begins to rise up, and she feels unworthy. The deeper we move into the heart of Jesus, the more our weaknesses and failures manifest.

"I am dark, but lovely"

The Shulamite says, "I am dark in heart, but I am lovely to God." This is the first crisis she will face on her journey—the revelation of her own sinfulness. In this place of His Presence she makes an incredibly revealing statement known as the paradox of grace. At the beginning of every believer's journey, we run into this conflict where we discover the magnitude of the darkness of our heart. This crisis is an essential part of our spiritual growth. When we see the darkness of our heart, and yet we know we are loved even in our weakness, there is the spirit of thanksgiving and praise that simply erupts from deep within us. This truth has a way of humbling us, and releases a significant level of praise and gratitude erupting from the core of our being.

When she declares, "I am dark, but lovely . . ." the maiden is beginning to have confidence before God in spite of her weakness. She sees within herself all those things that frustrate her—those habits she struggles with, the poor choices that led to failure, and those thoughts she knows are not right. She has the incredible revelation that, in spite of all this, her Bridegroom still sees her as lovely. This is foundational for her as the Bride-to-be and for us as well. If we don't get this, we won't progress into maturity, because we will find ourselves engulfed in a vicious cycle of a performance-based life in God.

Dealing with Guilt, Shame, and Failure

This statement, "I am dark, but lovely," is similar to the instance when Jesus told Peter he had a willing spirit, but he also had weak flesh. Peter had a very difficult time navigating failure and reconciling this issue of "dark, but lovely." He was unable to get past the "I am dark"-phase of his mistakes, and Jesus had to break the power of guilt, shame, and failure in his life (as He does with the Shulamite) in order to move forward in an intimate relationship. Peter was shocked by his failure, and he was convinced that God was shocked by it as well. Peter had talked himself into believing that because of his failure, God was renegotiating His relationship with him. (We will take a more in-depth look at the process Jesus took Peter through later in this book.)

We see that the Bridegroom succeeded in breaking through the Shulamite's guilt and shame because she admits, "I am dark, but I am lovely." She is finely discovering her truest identity—who Jesus and Heaven says she is—even as she is confronting her own weaknesses and life failures. Though she acknowledges those frustrating things within herself, she does not allow the spirit of guilt and shame to lock her in a prison of self-deception. In the private chambers alone with her Bridegroom, she is overwhelmed by the stunning revelation that He still considers her beautiful and it causes her to feel loved and accepted. This is foundational for the Bride, and for every Christian. We, too, must get this revelation, so that when we fail, we will not be stuck in a cycle that demands a better religious performance. Those twin towers of guilt and shame are two insidious tools the enemy uses to keep Christians living with a poor self-image, and thus focused on how to please God by what they *do for* Him instead of *intimacy with* Him. Guilt and shame keep us locked up in the "I am dark"-aspect of life. Shame keeps us under the influence of two convincing lies: "I am not good enough", and "I do not measure up in God's eyes or in the expectations of people."

Guilt and shame work together, but they are not the same emotion. Shame has a self-focus, while guilt focuses on behavior. Guilt says, "I did something bad," while shame says, "I *am* bad."

I remember when I was nine or ten years old and I was hanging out at my best friend's house, who lived just across the street from me. It was a typical summer afternoon where we would go in his backyard and look for something to do. Suddenly, we heard some music playing in the next-door neighbor's yard. The people who recently purchased this house were a young married couple with no children. For our neighborhood, this was unique, because most of the homes on our block were made up of families with children. All of us boys had a huge crush on the wife because she was so pretty.

Hearing the music next door, my friend and I decided to climb up on a couple of big bricks next to the fence to look

67

over and see what was happening. To our shock, the wife was sunbathing topless! Now this was definitely a marquee moment for my friend and I. We stared at her, mesmerized, and just couldn't stop staring . . . We never even heard my friend's dad walk up behind us.

His deep voice suddenly interrupted our dream-state. "What are you boys doin' there?"

We immediately jumped down off the bricks, nearly tumbling backwards as we watched his dad step up to survey the other side of the fence. Quickly scanning his neighbor's yard, he, too, saw why we were so mesmerized. Stepping off the bricks, my friend's dad grabbed us both and hurried us into the house. We knew we were in big trouble. There my friend's dad lectured us about what we had done and how wrong it was . . . and in that moment, I felt such incredible guilt and shame wash over me. I just felt dirty. I understand that my friend's dad was handling the situation in the way he thought best; we all operate from our current place of revelation. Certainly it could have been handled in a manner where my friend and I would not have taken on such a depth of guilt and shame. But the result of this particular event was that I continued to experience guilt and incredible shame for a very long time.

This story actually has quite a humorous ending. A couple of days after that event, I was again hanging out with my friend at his house when we decided to shoot his BB gun in the backyard. As we came around the side of the house and entered the backyard, we saw my friend's dad standing in the same place, on the same bricks where we stood just a few days earlier peering over the fence. Needless to say, we shared a funny moment "catching" my friend's dad in a very compromising situation—the very one he had lectured us about long and hard. I cannot say it helped me in dealing with the guilt and shame that was heaped upon me, but it was definitely a moment of comic relief for us both that we have recalled again and again down through the years.

Guilt, that feeling of doing something bad, was made real

to me that day. I think we can all relate to such moments in our life. Being so young, I did not know how to be relieved of it. Shame, however, was the bigger threat to my peace of mind. Shame tells me I am a "bad" person *because* I did this thing. I did not think I was a bad person, but I remember struggling with this particular event for a long time as a young boy.

In the same way that guilt and shame differ significantly, conviction and guilt are not the same. There are times when we make choices that hurt or injure someone, but then we are moved with compassion to apologize. That apology can come out of guilt, or out of conviction from the Holy Spirit. Both guilt and conviction cause us to feel bad that we hurt someone. But the difference is that with the conviction of the Holy Spirit, after you address the situation with the one you hurt, you are able to forgive yourself.

With guilt, even after you have asked for forgiveness, you are unable to forgive yourself. Guilt loves to take you down the pathway to shame where you determine in your heart, *I am bad.*

Shame is such an epidemic in our culture, and it has been proven to tie directly into peoples' struggles with depression, suicide, eating disorders, and addictive behaviors.

As the Lord shows the Shulamite who she really is, who He is for her, and how He sees her and feels about her, He breaks off her shame. This is key to deliverance from shame in our own lives.

Identifying with Guilt, Shame, and Failures

Failure, guilt, shame, and rejection are significant weapons in the hands of the enemy. These will cripple intimacy with Jesus and with people in your life. They will cause you to hide from God, because you have an extremely hard time believing He loves you when *you* are having a difficult time loving you.

One of the things we absolutely cannot ever do is let a failure progress from an action into an identity fueled by guilt and shame. That is exactly what the Apostle Peter did, and it caused him to run and hide from God and everyone else as he came under the power of guilt and shame. Peter had built his relationship on his commitment to God, and when he failed, he was devastated.

It's really important for us to understand that we are to build our life in God on *His* commitment to us. No matter what, He is endlessly and outrageously committed to you! God desires that you walk with Him in your brokenness, your pain, your suffering, and yes, even in your weaknesses. He longs for you to keep walking closely with Him, because the closer you walk with Him, the more you walk *out* of those things and *into* the territory He has prepared especially for you.

If you want to be strong and do great things, you have to learn the art of bouncing back quickly. In other words, learn to practice getting healed right away as you go on your journey into maturity in God. Get healed as you go. If you get wounded, get healed right away. That pleases God and annoys the enemy immensely.

The Holy Spirit desires that you know you are of great worth and value to Him. Your failures never disqualify you from His love—from your destiny. Does He want us to change our negative behaviors? Yes, of course. He loves us too much to leave us where we are, but He will love us into transformation. He is never going to stop transforming you. At this very minute He loves you, and your failures—that will never change due to your poor choices and decisions. He is also transitioning you through His transforming work.

In my role as a pastor, I have had to spend countless hours counseling and encouraging people who believe that failure has crushed their relationship with God and destroyed their opportunity to be used by Him for the Kingdom. That's such a lie from the demonic realm. You are the beloved of God. He's not obsessed by your sin; He's already dealt with it. Instead, He's consumed by giving you life. He has an abundance of grace that He provides every day of your life; it is like a continual fountain that washes you clean. There is never going to be a moment when He will not be merciful to you, or when He is not full of kindness and generosity toward you. He is not embarrassed by any of your failures. When you've failed, He does not pick you up and set you aside and say, "Well, give Me a call when you do better." The truth is, when you fail, He never moves away from you; rather, because of who He is, He steps in closer and holds you tighter.

Yes, we still have the ability to sin, because we have weak flesh. But we also have a willing spirit, and the Lord sees our heart to please Him way more than even we do. I love what Bill Johnson of Bethel Church in Redding, California, says:

> *When we were saved, we didn't lose the ability to sin; we just lost the ability to enjoy it.*

We know the Shulamite understands and is embracing who God says she is when she states, "I am dark, but I am lovely." She is embracing the reality of who God says she is. She knows she's not there yet, and this new experience—that God loves her with a radical love all the time whether she is in the best place she's ever been or in the worst failure she's ever experienced—is shocking to her. But she's connecting her mind with her spirit, and her spirit is letting her mind know the truth.

So many of us struggle with our negative self-views, with our own self-made identities. We see ourself in the poorest light viewed through the lens of our failures. Yet if we will listen to the voice of the Spirit of God, we will hear His words, "You are so lovely." God never lies. He never distorts the truth. He never flatters. He never exaggerates the truth. When He says you are lovely, even if your mind is telling you that you're not, listen to the highest form of truth—what God says. Facts are true, but they are the lowest level of truth. A higher level of truth is God's truth—what He has said.

The Disconnect in Failures

God always defines us by our willing spirit. Your failures do not disqualify you from intimacy with God. Peter had to work through this because his failure caused him to believe he simply could not be a safe leader in the Body of Christ. Peter prided himself on his own personal commitment and his *lack* of failure. So if someone failed, he wouldn't have any patience for them; he would consider them to be a weak person because *he* would never fail. That's why we hear him say again and again, "These guys will fail You, Lord, but not me! I will *never* let You down." Peter had never failed, he did not have compassion on those who did fail, which greatly affected his role as a good leader. Because Peter had built his relationship with the Lord upon his own full commitment to Him, when he failed, that failure crushed him.

Jesus needed to replace Peter's incorrect mindset with the mind of Christ so he would view failure through a different lens. At the Last Supper, He prepares His disciples by forewarning them all of their upcoming failures.

> *Then Jesus told them, "This very night you will all fall away on account of me. . . . But, after I have risen, I will go ahead of you into Galilee (Matthew 26:31-32, NIV).*

Here they are in the Upper Room breaking bread for the final time, and they are all sitting around enjoying themselves. It's just hours before the Crucifixion and Jesus makes an announcement: "Each one of you will fail Me this night." These disciples are unaware of what is about to take place that evening, even though a couple of days earlier, Mary of Bethany had anointed Jesus for His death. Jesus Himself has been telling these guys for months that He was going to Jerusalem to die. Even with those clues, the disciples don't seem to have grasped the fact that Jesus really is going to die in Jerusalem.

So Jesus speaks to each of the disciples and prophesies that all of them will stumble that very night. Peter hears the words, but he does not receive them. Instead, he responds in typical Peter fashion by announcing:

> *Even if all fall away on account of you, I never will (v 33, NIV).*

There it is. "No way . . . not a chance. I will never fail You. These other guys . . . well, yeah, I'm sure they will, but *I* will never fail You!"

Jesus looks directly at Peter and says, "Well, Pete, actually, before the rooster crows, you will deny Me three times."

But Peter would have none of it. The Gospel records His response:

> *Even if I have to die with you, I will not deny you*
> *(v 35).*

Then Jesus pushes it a little bit as He gives Peter a two-fold description of His heart.

> *Watch and pray so that you will not fall into temptation. The spirit is willing, but the flesh is weak (v 41, NIV).*

In essence, Jesus says, "Let me tell you something, Peter, that you just aren't getting. You have a willing spirit . . . oh my goodness! Do you ever! But you also have such weak flesh. You have a heart that is so for Me, and I see that, and I love that in you, Peter. It moves My heart to see how passionate your heart is to love Me, to please Me, to be with Me."

That's a truth about the Lord that most of us really don't understand; but our lack of understanding does not alter truth. Jesus sees our heart of passion, our heart of obedience, our heart of desire to please Him, to serve Him, and to love Him, way more than we even see it. He sees our failures, of course, but He also sees that "yes" in our heart to please Him, to love Him, to obey Him, and serve Him. Jesus says to Peter, "You have a heart for Me, but you also are a human being, which means you will fail on occasion."

Luke gives us another piece of the story.

> *Simon, Simon, Satan has asked to sift all of you as wheat. But I have prayed for you, Simon, that your faith may not fail. And when you have turned back, strengthen your brothers.*

But he replied, "Lord, I am ready to go with you to prison and to death."

Jesus answered, "I tell you, Peter, before the rooster crows today, you will deny three times that you know me."[15]

There are a lot of interesting and intriguing exchanges going on here. Jesus tells Peter that Satan has asked to sift him like wheat. Now I don't know about you, but that statement right there would really get my attention. That would put such fear into my heart. But Jesus immediately goes after that fear when He tells Peter, "I have prayed for you, so you will be all right." Then Jesus told Peter what He prayed. "I am praying that when you fail, you will get up. Peter, do not let Satan take this failure and lead you into failing faith." In other words, "Peter, don't leave Me when you fail because You think I'm upset and have quit on you. Don't believe the lie of the enemy." Listen, the enemy is really good at distorting reality in failure. When you do something you aren't proud of, the enemy is quick to accuse you. That is his job and his identity: he is a liar, and he is called the "accuser of the brethren." So Jesus is warning Peter here. He is saying, "When you fail, do not believe the lie of the enemy, because he wants to sift you like wheat. So when you fail, get right back up, and then strengthen your brothers who have failed as well—all those who need your leadership, courage, and strength."

However, Peter doesn't take this prophetic word from Jesus to heart. He again declares that what Jesus is prophesying is *not* going to happen: "I am not going to fail. Period." Or so he thinks.

Jesus responds and tells Peter, "Since you are pushing the point, here is a two-fold description of your heart. You have a willing spirit, but you have weak flesh." Peter just had to get this truth. Weak flesh and failure are not the same thing as outright rebellion. So, just as Jesus prophesied, Peter does deny the Lord three times before the rooster crows, and then

---

[15]   22:31-34, NIV.

he completely falls apart. He not only denies knowing Jesus, he reacts by declaring a curse where he vehemently denied ever knowing Jesus. That may explain why Peter is so devastated and paralyzed with guilt and shame that caused him to disconnect from life. He is absolutely crushed by his choice that led to failing Jesus. In the movie, "The Passion of Christ," the portrayal of Peter after his failure is so accurate. He was devastated and felt his life was over. When he told the others that he was going fishing, he was not talking about fishing for fun or recreation. He is basically saying, "I am a hopeless hypocrite, and I am going back to my old lifestyle. I failed my Lord, and I can never face Him again."

Jesus will not let Him go, however. He is going to have a face-to-face encounter with Peter and tell Him He is wildly, passionately in love with Him. We must understand that our failure will never affect His passion for us. Jesus saw the love in Peter's heart. He sees the love in your heart.

What happened to Peter was exactly what Jesus prophesied and prayed would *not* happen. Peter was indeed allowing his failure to lead him to failing faith. He allowed it to lead to an identity, and he was going to hide from God. This is also what Eve did in the Garden when she failed God. The serpent approached Adam and Eve and declared, "If you eat this you will know the difference between good and evil, and you will be like God."[16] Eve listened to the voice of the enemy, and by doing so, she gave him a platform to speak into her life, and the cost of that exchange was her losing the awareness of her truest identity. By entertaining and giving authority, credence, and value to what the enemy said, she put herself into the position of being deceived. When the enemy told her, "If you eat this, you will be like God," that spirit of deception caused her to forget she had been created in His image—that she was already like God.

So Eve disobeyed God and ate of the forbidden fruit. The result was guilt and shame came upon her in such a powerful way that she immediately felt a disconnection in her heart

---

[16] See Gen 3:5.

against God and ran away from Him and hid. That's one of the enemy's objectives of guilt and shame: to cause us to disconnect and to hide. But God will never allow us to do that. We see that God pursued Eve, and when He reconnected with her, He asked her, "Why did you eat the fruit?"

The Scriptures usually translate Eve's response as, "I was deceived . . . and I ate." However, if you look at the same passage in the Young's Literal Translation, the verse is translated like this:

> *And Jehovah God saith to the woman, "What [is]*
> *this thou hast done?" and the woman saith, "The*
> *serpent hath caused me to forget, and I did eat."*[17]

What did she forget? She forgot who she was. She forgot her identity. She forgot that she already was like God. I am convinced that we really do not have a sin issue; we have an identity issue. We either forget who we are, or we do not believe who God says we are. The enemy never wants us to discover our truest identity. He does not want us to know how beloved we are as a child of God. He doesn't want us to know that God's heart is ravished over us, that we are the Father's beloved children, and the Bride of His Beloved Son.

Even if you discover that you are a son or daughter of God, the enemy does not want you to know how deeply and passionately you are loved, and that there is nothing you could ever do to increase His love for you, or nothing you could ever do to decrease or negatively affect His love for you.

We see a perfect example of this at Jesus' baptism when the voice of the Father made a declaration from Heaven.

> *When all the people were baptized, it came to*
> *pass that Jesus also was baptized; and while He*
> *prayed, the heaven was opened.*
>
> *And the Holy Spirit descended in bodily form like*
> *a dove upon Him, and a voice came from heaven*

---

[17] See Gen. 3:13, YLT.

which said, "You are My Beloved Son; in You I am well pleased."[18]

Then the Spirit led Jesus into the wilderness where He was tested by Satan.

And the devil said to Him, "If you are the Son of God, command this stone to become bread."[19]

In this first temptation, the enemy revealed one of the most successful strategies that he uses against us today: He does not want you to ever discover you are a son or daughter of your Father in Heaven; but if you do discover that truth, he does not want you to know the amazing extent to which you are loved!

In this first temptation of Jesus, Satan said to Him, *"If you are the Son of God."* But he left off a critical word, "beloved". The enemy may have to concede your knowledge and belief that you are a son or daughter, but he definitely doesn't want you to know how deeply loved you are as a son or a daughter—that you are the "beloved" of the Father.

Like I've said, the favorite tool of the devil is to use failure to keep people disconnected from God and living under the influence of guilt and shame. When we discover how God the Father, Jesus, and the Holy Spirit respond in our failures, we will take that tool away from the enemy by exposing it and thereby render it useless in our life.

We seem to have a tendency to magnify our failures, while the Lord always seems to magnify our heart to please Him. God has a passion for restoration, and there is no way failure can ever release a power greater than that passion of God for reconciliation and restoration.

The reason I have a personal vendetta against failure is because it was one of the tools the enemy used to take me out significantly for long stretches at a time. Like Eve or Peter, I would follow that same pattern. I would fail, I would take on

---

[18] Luke 3:21-22.
[19] Luke 4:3.

the spirits of guilt and shame, and then I would hide. I would allow my failure to progress from an action into an identity, and guilt and shame would make sure that I stayed locked into that place of low self-esteem.

Shame causes us to have a real strong dislike and value for ourselves. We cannot value others, because we really do not value ourselves. Shame is anything that keeps you from loving yourself and seeing yourself the way God sees you.

I met Jesus and got saved in 1977, but it was not until 1997 that I really had a breakthrough in revelation of how He loves me even in my failure—the exact same way He loves me when I am in the greatest place in my life. The enemy had me convinced that every time I failed, God was angry, disgusted, and on the verge of giving up on me.

Grace For An Adulterer

It was at this point the Holy Spirit took me to a very familiar setting in the Bible, the story of the woman caught in the act of adultery, where the Gospel of John reveals how Jesus deals with a person in their failure.

> *Now early in the morning He came again into the temple, and all the people came to Him; and He sat down and taught them.*
>
> *Then the scribes and Pharisees brought to Him a woman caught in adultery. And when they had set her in the midst, they said to Him, "Teacher, this woman was caught in adultery, in the very act. Now Moses, in the law, commanded us that such should be stoned. But what do You say?"*
>
> *This they said, testing Him, that they might have something of which to accuse Him. But Jesus stooped down and wrote on the ground with His finger, as though He did not hear.*
>
> *So when they continued asking Him, He raised Himself up and said to them, "He who is without*

sin among you, let him throw a stone at her first."
And again He stooped down and wrote on the
ground. Then those who heard it, being convicted
by their conscience, went out one by one,
beginning with the oldest even to the last. And
Jesus was left alone, and the woman standing
in the midst.

When Jesus had raised Himself up and saw no
one but the woman, He said to her, "Woman,
where are those accusers of yours? Has no one
condemned you?"

She said, "No one, Lord."

And Jesus said to her, "Neither do I condemn
you; go and sin no more."[20]

This woman is devastated by her own actions. She has
been dragged through the streets of her hometown, and her
failure has been broadcast for all her friends and neighbors
to hear. She is brought into this public place, placed before
someone she does not know to be judged for her sin. She knows
that the penalty for what she has done is to be stoned to death,
and being in this place where her failure has led her, and with
the way she is feeling about herself, she's probably okay with
that penalty. She is so humiliated, there is no way she can face
anyone in that city again, and so, being put to death would
seem more like a blessing. I'm certain these types of thoughts
were raging in her mind: "I deserve to die. I don't want to face
anybody else in this town. I'm too embarrassed and humiliated.
I just hate myself. I really am ready to die."

Jesus is standing there, probably not saying anything for
the longest time. Then He stoops down and the two of them
make eye contact. As you can imagine, this is a profound
moment, because you simply cannot look into the face and the
eyes of Jesus and not be overwhelmed with His love. As she
stares into the eyes of the Lord, she is completely overcome as

---

[20]   John 8:2-11.

His peace, love, compassion, care, and tenderness floods her heart. I would imagine at this point that the woman was no longer aware of anyone else in that area, because when Jesus shows up, He consumes you. He makes you feel like you are the only one alive; it is just the two of you.

Then Jesus begins to write something on the ground. And as he does, I'm sure this lady becomes conscious of all the movement of people around her as one by one they begin to leave, until it is just her and Jesus standing alone together.

Then Jesus speaks to her and inquires: "Where are all those people who were condemning you?" You see, Jesus spoke to the ones who wanted to stone her, even giving them permission to do it, but with one caveat: only the one without sin could cast the first stone. All those holding stones, ready to throw them at her fled away. The fact that the one who legitimately could actually cast the first stone, is the very one who stepped in and extended mercy with authentic love.

All the others who stood in judgment of her were gone. Looking around her, the shamed woman answered Him, "No one, my Lord."

Then Jesus fixed His gaze upon her and said: "Neither do I condemn you." That was not what she was expecting. Jesus came and stood in the very place of her failure and He forgave her and accepted her. That's what Jesus does with us in failure. He doesn't move away; He draws near.

That is a lesson we must learn. Your failures have not caused the Lord to change how He feels about you. The enemy's desire is for us to define our lives by our failure and our struggles. Jesus wants us to be defined by our truest identity as a son/daughter of a loving Father in Heaven whose heart is ever for us. He is consistently focused on our heart to please Him, so far beyond how we see our own heart.

Peter's Upgrade

Peter was struggling to believe this truth, as Jesus knew He would. He knew He would have to have a face-to-face encounter with Peter. Eight days after His death, Jesus appeared to Peter.[21] He would have to rescue Peter from Himself. He had prayed for Him, and now He was going to be the answer to His own prayer.

Peter is out fishing one day when he hears a voice calling out to Him from the shore. He recognized that voice . . . it was the voice of Jesus. He was so impacted by His voice that he dove into the water, swam to shore, and discovered Jesus making him breakfast.

Now put yourself in Peter's sandals. You know he's so excited to see Jesus, but he's also embarrassed and humiliated—filled with guilt and shame. The memory of what he's done is vividly replaying in his mind. He must be thinking, "How disappointed Jesus must be in me. In His hour of greatest need, I quit on Him and left Him all alone." I'm sure Peter felt there was no way he could even look Jesus in the eye ever again.

Peter is broken, depressed, discouraged, and he feels defeated. Jesus knows this, and so He begins to speak tenderly to him by inviting him to eat with Him, setting him at ease, and then asking key questions that would draw him in.

> So when they had eaten breakfast, Jesus said to Simon Peter, "Simon, son of Jonah, do you love Me more than these?"
>
> He said to Him, "Yes, Lord; You know that I love You."
>
> He said to him, "Feed My lambs."
>
> He said to him again a second time, "Simon, son of Jonah, do you love Me?"
>
> He said to Him, "Yes, Lord; You know that I love You."
>
> He said to him, "Tend My sheep."
>
> He said to him the third time, "Simon, son of Jonah, do you love Me?"

---

[21] See John 20:26.

Peter was grieved because He said to him the third time, "Do you love Me?"

And he said to Him, "Lord, You know all things; You know that I love You."

Jesus said to him, "Feed My sheep. Most assuredly, I say to you, when you were younger, you girded yourself and walked where you wished; but when you are old, you will stretch out your hands, and another will gird you and carry you where you do not wish." This He spoke, signifying by what death he would glorify God.

And when He had spoken this, He said to him, "Follow Me."[22]

These are questions geared and aimed to draw Peter out of his depression. He was giving him hope for his future. When Jesus asks us questions, they are always for us. They are questions that give us insight and revelation to our own identity and into the particular circumstance or situations of life we are currently in. Jesus asks Peter three questions, because Peter needed an upgrade in his understanding of commitment and love. He needed to understand that it's really not all about his commitment to Jesus, but it is also about Jesus' commitment to him.

So He asks him, "Peter, are you a lover of God?"

Peter responds, "Well, I denied You before a lot of people when You really needed me. I failed You miserably. I let You down."

"Peter, do you remember what I told you a week ago, that you have a willing spirit, but weak flesh? You didn't believe Me. In fact, you argued with me!"

"Yes, I remember. I didn't understand You or believe You, but I do now. I was shocked at how easily I failed."

---

[22] 21:15-19.

It is as though the Lord was saying, "Peter, I was not surprised or shocked by your failure. But you need to understand that I am not looking at the failure; I am looking at your heart. Of course, I see your failure. I am not denying that or covering it up; but it is not that failure that defines you. What defines you is your heart, and what I see in your heart is a passion to love, to serve, and to please Me."

"I see your heart—way beyond how you see your own heart," says the Lord. "Yes, I want you to continue to grow and mature in Me. And Peter, you will, and failure will happen less and less in your life. But you have to understand, I look at failure and success differently than you do."

"How beautiful you are, my darling!"

The lesson Peter learned was a lesson the Shulamite needed to learn as well. Near the end of the first chapter of the Song, the Bridegroom says this to the Shulamite:

> *How beautiful you are, my darling, how beautiful (1:15, NLT).*

The Passion Translation renders that verse like this:

> *Look at you, my dearest darling, you are so lovely! You are beauty itself to me . . . (1:15a)*

Those words, from the Lord Jesus to you and I, are so stunning and should ignite our hearts. He is telling us how He feels about us! He is saying, "You look good to me, and I like you." He is drawing your heart to a place where you will recognize the truth that you are His favorite, even in the midst of failure. He is desperately trying to get us to upgrade our image of who He really is and how He really feels about us. That truth will result in breaking off the lies of the enemy that keep so many Christians locked up in the "I am dark"-phase of life and away from the "but I am lovely"-place we should be living. Christians seem to have a natural religious resistance to the truth that we are beautiful in Jesus' sight. We love the idea of it, we applaud it, but it is still difficult because it is not easily grasped in our hearts and minds. The reason for this is that we always feel such guilt over the things that we do, or don't do. When we hear God say that we are beautiful to Him, it is a huge struggle to believe. Our minds can talk us out of what God honestly feels about us.

We always seem to want to measure ourselves by our successes or failures. If we are walking in what we define as success, then we feel right before the Lord and we can almost grasp the truth that we are beautiful to God. However, if we are experiencing the result of some type of failure and we feel "unsuccessful" in His sight, we will never receive that truth. We get this idea that God likes us more when we do "good stuff," or when we think we are having a "good" day.

Let's consider what you might describe as a good day. You start out your morning by waking up—so already, it is a good day. You get up, and with your coffee you have a conversation with God, you read some Scripture, and pray for some people.

At work, you are nice to everyone all day, even to those people you know do not really like you. You pray over your lunch before you eat it, and you don't extend your ten-minute break to twenty-five minutes like you might sometimes do. It has been a good day.

On this good day, God likes you. In fact, God loves you. He is very proud of you.

A Tangled Mess

But what about a day that you would describe as not good? In fact, it would be considered the opposite of good. Maybe you went outside to put up the outdoor Christmas lights so your house would match all the other houses in the neighborhood you live in, and a "not so good"-day ensued. Let me tell you about such an incident.

When my son, Kagen, was about five, I decided to put up our outdoor Christmas lights. You probably should be aware that I would never be considered a handyman. Hammers, screwdrivers, wrenches, plus Gary are not a good mix.

The process started out poorly as I tried to untangle all the strands of lights we had stored in a box last Christmas season. I should have recognized a familiar trigger, and I should have been aware of my rising frustration. It took me quite awhile to get those lights all laid out in some semblance of order on the lawn. Internally, I could feel my patience being tested, and I could also sense anger looking for a landing spot, but I took a deep breath and moved on with the next phase of the project. I tested all the strings and threw out the ones that no longer worked, and then I put all the strings of lights across the front of the house. We had a fairly long, ranch style house so it took quite a few strands. Trying to be careful as I stepped around and over the various strands of lights, I started hearing popping sounds—lights exploding—as I clumsily stepped on them. This did not help my increasing frustration level . . . not at all.

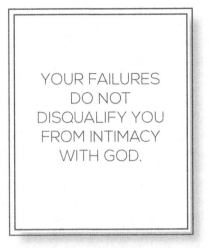

YOUR FAILURES
DO NOT
DISQUALIFY YOU
FROM INTIMACY
WITH GOD.

Next, I began stringing up the strands of lights along the house using a staple gun. The idea, of course, is to staple the cords along the gutter, not your hand, which I did on a few occasions. Frustration. Rising. I dropped the gun a couple times too . . . just for good measure. More frustration.

Finally, after getting all the lights properly affixed, I plugged them in, and what a beautiful sight! . . . for about five seconds. I watched an entire carefully-stapled string of lights fizzle out completely. *Never mind* (keeping myself in check). *I'll just go check each bulb*, I thought, and after my careful inspection came to the conclusion that this string was, indeed, defective. As I was taking the defective string down, the working string of lights next to it came down also, and then the one further down the line came loose. I could feel myself starting to get *very* agitated, but again, I took a deep breath, and continued with the project.

To this day, I still cannot comprehend why the project went the way it did, because I had tested each string of lights before I put them up. But each time I would put a new string in to replace the defective one, another string of lights would go out—I'm talking about a whole complete strand!

Again, fighting the rage building within me, I continued to replace bulbs and strands, until, about the fifth time I put a staple from the staple gun through my finger, I snapped. I completely gave in to my rage and anger, and jumped off the ladder. I grabbed the string of lights from the end strand, and pulled it from the house. Each succeeding strand followed suit, and as I was flowering the air with words of discouragement, drawing neighbors from their homes, I stomped to the middle of the court where we lived and swirling the lights around and around, I launched them down the street.

Standing there admiring my work, looking like the Big Green Hulk, I could hear a neighbor kid asking, "Mommy, is that Pastor Gary?"

"Yes, honey . . . go back in the house."

Definitely not my finest moment. I soon calmed down, walked around the court picking up the strands, cleaned up the broken lights, and walked back toward my house thinking to myself, *That went well.*

Later as I contemplated it all I realized, even though I did not like me very much on this day, and I'm not sure Karissa really cared for me much either, the reality is, *God liked me.* On this not-so-good-of-a-day, God loved me the same way He did on a really good day.

Pre-Approved and Accepted

You have to know that no matter what, you are accepted

in the Beloved. Now, notice I did not say He *approved* of my actions. He did not. But He still accepted me. In the same way that I did not always approve of my children's choices as they were growing up, their choices never had any negative affect on my accepting and loving them 100-percent of the time. We may not always approve of what our kids say and do, but we always accept and love them.

In the same way, God is committed to you—with all the good and the ugly. He loves to embrace us in our weakness and He loves us right into transformation. But His love for is unconditional and 100-percent *all* the time.

If you are one who is inclined to highlight all your shortcoming and failures, you need a different lens through which to view yourself. Right where you are, right this moment as you are reading these words, take this time to speak these truthful words over your life:

> God loves everything about me. He loves me
> when I'm doing great. He loves me in my worst
> failures. God loves me . . . all the time.

I would love to be in your head as you are reading this right now listening to the argument you are having with yourself. This may be a stretch for you, but I will tell you that your spirit knows it's true. This truth is nourishing food for your soul. You need to take it in and let it nurture you by allowing your spirit to tell your mind this truth. Our minds deal in facts, but our spirit deals in truth. As we see in 1 Corinthians 2:14, our natural mind cannot receive the things of God. God speaks to our spirit man, who in turn speaks truth to our mind.

God speaks to the Treasure within us

God is in passionate pursuit of you because He longs to hang out with you, and your failures have not caused Him to change His mind on how He feels about you. The reality is, God never measures success, but He does measure faithfulness.

Think about Ezekiel for a moment. God tells him that He

is raising him up as a prophet to the nations, sending him out with words of warning to a nation of people who will not listen to one thing he is saying. The people rejected everything that Ezekiel had to say. How then do you measure Ezekiel's success? In reality, it appears he did not have any success. You have to measure his success by his faithfulness to the Lord. God doesn't measure success by results. He measures success by the faithfulness we display—day in, day out, week after week, month after month, year after year.

So few of us really understand the incredible power of faithfulness. It is not about what you are doing or not doing that draws God's attention. It is what is in your heart. What is the value that is driving the behavior? Like Peter, the Shulamite had to get that. Like Peter, we have to get that. God sees, and He believes in, the sincerity of your heart even more than you do.

So there on the shore, Jesus asks Peter a second question: "Do you love me?"

"Well, I blew it. I cannot be a leader because I can't stand the pain of my failure."

The Lord replies: "Peter, do not define yourself by what you do or do not do; rather define yourself by who you are in Me."

So a third time Jesus asks Peter, "Do you love Me?" It's like the Lord is saying, "I have to push you on this, Peter. I know it's really hard, but I have to cleanse this wound. I have to remove this accusing spirit that is lodged in your heart. You are almost there, Peter. Do you love me?"

Three failures. Three denials. Three times Jesus brings Peter to the place of pronouncing the truth of who he is; Jesus is breaking the power of shame, guilt, and accusation in the heart of Peter. He is reinstating Peter and giving him back his true identity in God. And Peter responds with, "Yes, I am a lover of God."

Though Satan wants us to define our lives by our failures and weaknesses, the Father looks at you today and is not the least bit concerned with what you are not, because He sees within you what He most loves about you. You are of great worth and value to Him. He only sees the treasure within you.

Does God want us to change our negative behavior? Of course. But He points to the treasure within us and He always speaks to that . . . all while He encourages us toward maturity. However, like Peter, you are going to have to work with the Holy Spirit. As we see in the Song with the Shulamite, the Holy Spirit will pick us up and carry us into that most private place of the Lord to build a history with us. He wants us to know Him—the one who is available for all we need Him to be.

Part of the history-building is that the Holy Spirit will begin to touch areas in your life that will not do well where He is taking you. Now the Holy Spirit will never point out anything in your life unless you are ready to deal with it, and He is ready. He never points out anything to make us feel bad. If He's touching something, He is ready, and you are ready to move all the way through it.

The Ketchup Story

As I've already recounted, one of the areas that I personally struggled with for many years is anger and a rapid-rising violent temper. You already read about one of my episodes with the Christmas lights, but the one that probably tops them all is what has become known around our home and church as, "The Ketchup Story."

But just to give a backdrop to this story, I'll share a stunning encounter with God just a few nights before the Ketchup incident. Karissa and I were associate pastors at a church in Northern California in 1996, and we decided to visit a church a few miles from ours that was having a "revival" or "renewal" service. The visiting speaker, a very powerful prophetic speaker, picked me out of the audience and spoke a prophetic word over me. When we typed out the word single-spaced, it was four pages long and contained information that spoke to my gifts, my ministry, my present, my future, and my destiny. As she was speaking these powerful prophetic words over my life, she made this statement: "Gary, you will be a man who always responds to crisis events, to pressure, and to opposition with rest, stillness, and peace."

Now to be honest with you, I was a little disappointed, because when I heard those words I started looking around to see if she was actually speaking to someone else, because those words were so far from who I was that I could not even wrap my mind around them. In fact, my mind was talking me out of the words I was hearing, while my spirit-man inside of me was leaping for joy. My spirit-man knew that was my truest identity—that I was a man who lived in incredible places of rest and peace all the time. So, I decided right then that I wanted to become the man God said I already was. But I knew, I would be moving into a time of process, because all prophetic words put you into a process of **declaration, development, and demonstration**.

The **declaration phase** is exactly what it sounds like: declaring the prophetic word that releases truth about you that God wants you to know. Then comes the development, or process part of the word, where all those things that oppose that word get dealt with in a loving, kind way. When there is something in our lives that stands opposed to our truest identities, such as an extreme temper, those things get dealt with in the development phase of the process.

The way God deals with those things is wonderful. The Holy Spirit will never point out anything in your life without a purpose. He does not touch things in your life, or make you aware of them, simply to make you feel badly about yourself. If He is speaking to you about an area of your life, and putting His finger on something, it is because you are at a place in your life where you are ready to deal with it, and so is He. Then the Spirit institutes a process called, "divine exchange." This is when He lets you know that where you are going in your destiny and inheritance, this particular habit or action will not travel well on the journey. He then reveals something to you that *will* travel well, and He asks you to make the exchange with Him. Then to make it even easier, He releases waves of His love and passion from His heart for you, and you put that old habit on the waves going out and receive this new thing on the waves coming into your heart.

Then comes the **development stage**, where you begin to see more and more of that prophetic word of destiny, identity, and purpose coming to fruition in your life. The Lord will also allow tests to come into your life, and these tests will reveal to you where you are in this process of development.

Deuteronomy 8:2 tells us that these tests are for us, because they will reveal where we are on this pathway or journey into our destiny. God already knows where we are; but the way we respond or react to the test is revelatory to us as to where we are on our personal journey.

My development process started immediately. I received the word on a Wednesday night, and on Sunday morning, a number of tests came my way revealing where I was on this journey of responding to every crisis and opposition with rest and peace.

On that particular Sunday, I was the only pastor on site for the two services. It was a cold November day and I arrived early at the church to open up and prepare for the morning. I was not feeling well: I had a headache, which aspirin did not alter, and I was, for some reason, extremely tired. I know the triggers that set off my anger, and being tired and having a headache contribute significantly to cocking the trigger of my temper.

Nevertheless, I preached both services, and by the end of the second service I was ready for everyone to leave so I could put things away, lock up the church building, and head home to rest. My head was throbbing, my strength had dissipated, and I was extremely irritated. Karissa left after the second service to attend a function, while our boys, Matt and Kagen, were to come home with me.

On the way out of the facility, Matt, who was thirteen at the time, and Kagen, who was four, wanted me to stop at McDonald's for hamburgers and fries for lunch. I succumbed, and headed for the drive-through so we could quickly order and take our food home. This was back in 1996 when the technological drive-through experience was not so easy, and I had a lot of trouble communicating my food order effectively through the little box.

I drove up and, as expected, the employee on the other end was having difficulty understanding what we ordered. I tried to communicate that my son, Matt, wanted his hamburger a specific way, and Kagen wanted his plain with nothing on it—no sauce, no ketchup. Nothing. Seemed simple enough. My head was throbbing . . . I just wanted those burgers so I could get home and rest.

After I placed my order, I waited for what seemed like five minutes before a voice came through the box. Then I heard the words, "Order whenever you're ready."

A bit exasperated, I went through the extensive, very specific, specialized order once again, and waited. Realistically, it was probably less than a couple of minutes, but because I was tired and didn't feel well, it felt like ten.

A voice finally came back on and repeated, "Please order whenever you're ready." *Are you kidding me? I just left a five-minute order!* I could feel myself starting to slip over the edge, but I kept hearing in my mind, *You are a man who always responds to everything with rest and peace.*

Okay, I thought, *let's try this again.* As calmly as I could, I leaned into the little box and ordered Matt's specialty burger. The employee finally acknowledged that he received that order.

Then I ordered for Kagen: "And we would like one plain burger, please." That's when we encountered yet another problem. My order was pretty clear . . . *one plain burger.* Simple.

But the response from the box was, "Would you like our special sauce?"

"No, thank you . . . just plain."

"Would you like any ketchup?" I was starting to teeter over the edge.

"No. Thank you. Just a *plain* burger."

"Did you want any lettuce . . . tomato?" That was it. Over the edge I tumbled.

92

Leaning out my car window, I yelled directly into the box, "We do not want any special sauce, or ketchup, or any lettuce or tomato. But what you could do is take one side of the hamburger bun, put a cooked patty on top of it, then take another hamburger bun, and put it on top. You know . . . like a sandwich. Then wrap it up in some of that special paper wrapping you have in there, put it inside of a paper bag, and hand it to us!!"

The woman on the other side of the voice box responded in perfect calmness with, "Sir, you don't have to be angry or rude."

I'm not being angry or rude! I thought. *Because, you see, I am a man who always responds to everything with rest and peace.*

We *finally* got our food, and as we were about to drive away, Matt yelled, "Dad! Stop!"

I slammed on the brake and asked, "What's the problem, son?"

"Mom always has us check the bag to make sure we got everything we ordered."

"Do you see mom in the car?" I countered. "Because I don't see mom in the car!" and roared off. The drive home was about ten minutes and most of the way, the boys argued about what they were going to watch on television as they ate their burgers. Since I had already gone over the edge, I slowly, mentally came back to teetering on the edge, but their argument about watching football versus cartoons was keeping me in the dangerous teetering zone.

We arrived home and the boys rushed to the living room. Matt, being the oldest and strongest won the TV battle, so football filled the screen. I pulled the food out of the bag, and realized immediately that we *should* have checked the contents, because the one hamburger that did not make it into the bag was, of course, the one I'd ordered for myself.

I distributed the burgers and fries to the boys with their drinks, the game was on, and I was ready to move off the brink of disaster . . . when it hit. As I moved into the kitchen, Matt yelled out, "The bag doesn't have any ketchup!"

Great. They needed ketchup for their fries. That was it for me. Even though I am a man who always responds to all crises and opposition with rest and peace, I snapped.

"No worries . . . no need to get up and trouble yourself by walking ten feet into the kitchen to get the ketchup out of the refrigerator . . . I'll bring it . . ."

I grabbed the Costco-sized, full-to-the-brim ketchup container, walked into the living room, stood in front of the boys as they were seated on the couch watching TV, and brought the ketchup bottle down full-force onto the coffee table in front of them. The force with which I slammed that bottle down caused it to explode. Ketchup shot everywhere throughout the family room: all over the head, face, and body of my boys, all over the TV, all over the walls, and even up to the ceiling.

Kagen began howling, but Matt was all business. He simply grabbed a fry, reached up to his face, dipped it in ketchup, and carried on eating and enjoying the game.

Retaking the Test . . . Again

In that moment I realized I had a long process ahead of me, but I had a passion and a desire to see that anger broken in me. I am very happy to report that twenty years later, I am seeing fruit of that prophetic word. I am not 100-percent there yet, but I am closer than I have ever been, and I seem to pass more of those tests than not.

A friend of mine, Graham Cooke, used to say that you can never fail a test of God. You simply get to take the test over again, and again, and again, and again . . . until you pass it.

What helped me so significantly with this area of my temper was when I did what Peter did: spend time with Jesus and answer the probing questions the Holy Spirit asks that allowed me to see truth. Three times Jesus asked Peter probing questions. The questions were not for Jesus; they were for Peter so he could have revelation of truth. So it was with me. My outbursts of temper were not the problem; they were the evidence of something deeper within me. All my behaviors of anger were tied to some value that drove that behavior and I needed to spend time with the Holy Spirit to discover the value that was driving the anger.

That really is such an important step to getting set free. Prior to my rooting down on this issue, I had the same cycle: I would explode, manifest my anger with a violent temper, feel bad, then hide from God and from people. After a long period of time, when I felt better about myself, I would come back to God and quasi-apologize about the event. I was almost casual as I talked with God about my problem.

I would have these one-way talks with Him: "I know you saw me go crazy again. I mean, did you see me swinging those lights? Whoa, that was some kind of event, wasn't it! Did you see me throw that ottoman through the wall? I mean, I didn't even know ottomans could *go* through walls. That was crazy. Anyway . . . sorry 'bout that. I promise I'll do better next time."

I thought that was enough . . . and for asking His forgiveness it was, because I was truly sorry and repentant. But deep in my heart, I knew it was not enough. I am not saying that I had to jump through any religious hoops to be forgiven. I *was* forgiven, because forgiveness is an act of faith. But I knew there was another step, because all behavior is tied to a value. I have a value to live at peace and to respond to everything with the fruit of self-control. That's a core value of mine, and the behavior I was evidencing was not the behavior that comes from that value. So I needed to take a journey with the Holy Spirit to discover what value was driving that behavior.

For so many years, I was doing a "weed-whacker" job on this area of struggle, instead of taking time and seriously getting to the root of my issues. When Karissa and I would do yard work together, and she would ask me to help her weed the garden, we had polar opposite ideas on what she meant. When I would weed that garden, I would take our trusty weed-whacker power tool, fire it up and whack the tops off of the weeds. I took them all the way down to the dirt, and it sure looked great. But within a few days, or weeks, they were all back, because I only took off the tops, but obviously, I did not get the roots. Karissa finally stopped asking me to do any weeding, and I would see her get out her little knee pad and gardening tools, get down in the garden beds, and spend a long, sweaty session of pulling out the weeds from their roots.

I realized that's what I had to do with my temper . . . my anger issues. I was dealing with the behavior—the tops of the weeds—but not getting to the roots. When I did get to the roots, I discovered that it turned out to be a Lordship issue, and the Holy Spirit showed me some events and situations from my past where I needed to be healed and made whole. It was obvious I had something going on deep down within me, something deeply rooted in my personality, and simply saying, "Sorry, God . . ." was not going to set me free.

That's what we see with Peter, and that's what is happening with the Shulamite in the Song as the Bridegroom, Jesus, takes her into His most private place for times of intimate exchange and transformation. We know that this process was happening with the Shulamite by her comment, "I am dark, but I am also lovely to my Bridegroom." Unfortunately, not a high percentage of Christians have the ability to make that same statement. I know, because it was something I struggled with for so long.

"Like the dark tents of Kedar, like the curtains of Solomon"

These dark tents of Kedar that the Shulamite is referring to are grayish-black tents woven out of the dark hairs of goats that is still very common all over the Middle East. Symbolically and spiritually they speak of spiritual darkness. The Shulamite is using the common imagery of the day when she says, "I am like the dark tents of Kedar; however, I am also like the bright white curtains of Solomon." The curtains of Solomon were in the Holy Place in the Temple. These bright white curtains of the Holy of Holies speak of the inward grace of God and His glory in her life, because the beauty of these curtains was hidden from the public's view. They were only visible to the priests who were assigned to serve in the Holy Place.

There is a beauty in you that others cannot see, like the hidden curtains in the sacred place of Solomon's temple, which no one was able to see except for those special anointed ones. The Shulamite says, "I know I am dark like the tents of Kedar on the outside, but I have an inward work of beauty like the curtains of Solomon. I am beautiful in the holy place before God, even in my struggles." We truly are beautiful to God in that holy place, even in our failures and struggles, because of His outrageous grace toward us.

You are beautiful to your Bridegroom, Jesus, *all* the time. You are in a process of becoming more Christ-like in your nature and in your character, and you are accepted by Him all the time. You are the beloved of God, and He loves you right now just the way you are. Yes, He has plans to transform you, but even in this place where you are at this very moment, He is pleased with you and He loves you with all His heart.

Failure Does Not Disqualify Us

Often we allow our failures to disqualify us in our relationship with God. When we fail, we tend to pull away from God if we have not upgraded our image of His divine nature. He truly responds with unconditional love in all our moments of failure. Our inaccurate picture of the Father's heart allows guilt and shame to disqualify us from loving God and serving others. This is the greatest tool of the enemy, and therefore, it is vital that we expose it for what it is and recognize how much destruction it creates in our lives.

I find it interesting in reading the story of the Mount of Transfiguration that God chose two men from the Old Testament, Moses and Elijah, who both ended their lives in failure, to minister encouragement to His Son, Jesus, in His most difficult hour—just before He endured the cross.[23] Moses' failure came when he was instructed by God to *speak* to the rock, but in his anger at the people's constant whining and

---

[23]   See Matt 17:1-13.

complaining, he snapped and *struck* the rock instead.[24] That failure cost Moses the opportunity to enter the Promised Land. There are consequences to our choices. But God never withdraws His love as a consequence of our wrongdoing. Never. Why? Because God radically loves us, and He radically loved Moses.

Elijah was given three assignments to complete before turning everything over to Elisha:

> Then the LORD said to him: "Go, return on your way to the Wilderness of Damascus; and when you arrive, anoint Hazael as king over Syria. Also you shall anoint Jehu the son of Nimshi as king over Israel. And Elisha the son of Shaphat of Abel Meholah you shall anoint as prophet in your place. It shall be that whoever escapes the sword of Hazael, Jehu, Elisha will kill; and whoever escapes the sword of Jehu, Elisha will kill. Yet I have reserved seven thousand in Israel, all whose knees have not bowed to Baal, and every mouth that has not kissed him."[25]

Though the Angel of the Lord gave Elijah three assignments, we see that he only completed one of the following:

1. Anoint Hazael as King over Syria.
2. Anoint Jehu as King of Israel.
3. Anoint Elisha as prophet in your place.

He only anointed Elisha as prophet to take his place. He leaves the other two for Elisha to finish after God sent a chariot to bring Elijah home. Yet neither one of those failures cost Moses or Elijah their place in God's heart, or their place of service opportunities for God.

Take this to heart my friend: Our failures do not disqualify us on any level.

---

[24]   See Num 20:9-12.
[25]   1 Kings 19:15-18.

God's Book of Remembrance

Do you remember the story from Genesis 18:9-15, when the Lord told Abraham that Sarah would conceive and bear a son? The Bible says Sarah was listening at the tent and she laughed out loud. Her laugh was derisive; it was mocking . . . kind of like: "Yeah, right! In what universe is this actually going to happen? I'm 90 years old . . ."

The word used for "laughter" in this Scripture actually means, "a mockery." Sarah was mocking God, and He called her on it. God asked her, "Sarah . . . why did you laugh?"

She was so stunned that she got caught, she lied to God in response: "I didn't laugh!"

But God replied, "Oh yes . . . you *did* laugh, Sarah."

It's bad enough to fail, and then when you get called on it, even worse. But then we sometimes compound it by lying. We actually deny our very own actions!

Later, in Hebrews 11 when the Lord is listing the heroes of the faith, it says about that incident:

> *By faith Sarah herself also received strength to conceive seed, and she bore a child when she was past the age, because **she judged Him [God] faithful who had promised** (11:11, emphasis added)*

Wait . . . what?!? Sarah had **great faith**?? That's not how I remember it. Exactly. But that's how *God* remembers it . . . for all eternity. What is written in Genesis 18 about Sarah laughing at God's prophetic word to her was written for our benefit. He wanted us to be able to identify with her weakness and humanity. What was written in Hebrews 11 was what God put in His Book of Remembrance. He recorded that story after it was touched by the **blood** of Jesus.

We seem to always want to magnify our personal failures. God always magnifies our heart to please Him—those moments of faith where we choose to trust Him.

As you read this, perhaps the Holy Spirit is revealing to you that there is an area—or areas—where guilt and shame are finding an entry point. Perhaps you are still living connected to some ties to your past failures, or you have some habit that is not necessarily sinful, but it is certainly not beneficial to you in this season of your life. If you are feeling some prompting by the Spirit, it is because He wants to walk you through the displacement process, where you give Him that failure or sin, and He will give you the Kingdom of Heaven's replacement.

Remember the key we mentioned earlier? The Holy Spirit has an intentionality in these moments to make a divine exchange with you. Then at the moment of exchange, He will release wave after wave of the passionate love Jesus has in His heart for you. His love will overwhelm you and His Presence will overshadow you with such peace and joy that you will readily engage in the exchange. But here is the catch: He is very serious in these moments, and you need to be as well. They are opportunities of a lifetime, and as a friend of mine likes to say, "When the opportunity of a lifetime comes, make sure you act in the lifetime of the opportunity."

"Guilt, Shame, and Failure" Prayer

I have crafted a prayer for you as you and the Holy Spirit engage in this displacement assignment. Hear what the Lord has to say to you.

> In this season, I am increasing within you a courage to trust Me at new levels, where you find yourself relying on your testimony of Me, and you hear yourself saying: "I know My God, and He is with me and He is for me!" I am drawing you to this place where you fix your eyes upon Me and walk in this place that I have prepared for you.
>
> I am here to sustain you. I am here to bring you through. I am here to lift you up to the next place—to the next level—for I AM for you and if He who is I AM is for you, who can be against you?

I have crafted a prayer for you as you and the Holy Spirit engage in this displacement assignment.

> Father, for the person reading these words and activating this process, I ask You to draw up next to them so powerfully that there is an increase in Your manifested Presence.
>
> If the reader is still holding on to some failure from their past, I ask You, Holy Spirit, to sever that stronghold.

I ask you, reader, to get an image in your mind of a wire. Now see that thin wire connected to that failure, that event, that circumstance, from your past. Now, see the Lord with supernatural wirecutters coming towards that wire. Once you are there, watch as Jesus takes those wirecutters and severs that wire that is connecting you to any past failure. Feel yourself becoming free.

Holy Spirit, I now ask that You break off any words that were placed on the person reading these words. (Allow the Lord to break off any words that tell you that you are lazy, you are not smart, you have no artistic ability, no athletic ability, you will never amount to anything.)

Holy Spirit, break the power of those hurtful words, in Jesus' name.

Holy Spirit, I ask You to exchange those words with truth.

Declare the following exchanges out loud and listen for the Holy Spirit as He speaks exchanges that may not be listed here. When you make these exchanges as a declaration, you are engaging the enemy in warfare, and you are taking ground from the dark world and setting new benchmarks in the realm of the Spirit. See these as gifts from the Lord direct to you.

I give you joy instead of depression.

I give you supernatural courage instead of fear.

I give you hope instead of hopelessness.

I give you a release to pursue your creative, artistic passions instead of hanging on to the lie that says you don't have any of those talents.

I give you beauty for ashes.

I give you the oil of joy for mourning.

I give you the garment of praise and worship instead of the spirit of heaviness.

I give you the spirit of abundance instead of poverty.

I give you laughter instead of sadness.

I give you confidence in God and confidence in who you are in God instead of low self-esteem.

Repeat these following words of affirmation out loud five times, because it takes five times for it to really begin to be sealed within you at a conscious level.

I AM LOVED. I AM VALUED. I AM ACCEPTED.
I AM LOVED. I AM VALUED. I AM ACCEPTED.
I AM LOVED. I AM VALUED. I AM ACCEPTED.
I AM LOVED. I AM VALUED. I AM ACCEPTED.
I AM LOVED. I AM VALUED. I AM ACCEPTED.

One more time—from your heart—like you really mean it:

I AM LOVED. I AM VALUED. I AM ACCEPTED.

ACTIVATION #3
Guilt, Shame, and Failure

God has a passion for restoration, and there is *no way* failure can ever release a power greater than God's passion for reconciliation and restoration.

As you read this chapter, perhaps the Holy Spirit is revealing to you that there is an area(s) where guilt and shame are finding an entry point. Perhaps you are still living connected to some ties to your past failures, or you have some habit that is not necessarily sinful, but it is not beneficial to you in this season of your life. If you are feeling some prompting by the Spirit, it is because He wants to walk you through the displacement process, where you give Him that failure or sin, and He will give you the Kingdom of Heaven's replacement.

Ask yourself the following questions:

- Is there any place in your life today where you have failed and not forgiven yourself?
- Are you disqualifying yourself from serving God in some capacity because you are holding yourself hostage to some failure?
- Is today the day to ask the Holy Spirit to sever that cord that is attached to that past failure that keeps you from thriving in your walk with God?

The Holy Spirit is ready to make an exchange with you, and so are you. Expect that at the moment of exchange, He will release wave after wave of the passionate love Jesus has in His heart for you. You will sense His love will overwhelm you and His Presence overshadow you with such peace and joy that you will readily engage in the exchange.

Make the Exchange

> I exchange *[name the past failure, that instance where you cannot forgive yourself. For example, "I exchange lying to my wife . . ."]* for God's best—*[name the opposite—God's provisional displacement. For example: ". . . full disclosure and bearing the consequences of my actions."]*.

(Note: the exchange will be redemptive and restorative. Ask the Holy Spirit what that is and make this transaction with Him.) Repeat this exchange exercise for each and every instance that comes to mind.

Pray this over yourself:

> I receive the forgiveness and cleansing of the Lord provided in the blood of Jesus Christ. Thank You, Father, for Your full provision to set me free and bring breakthrough in my life because of Your redemption.

> Amen.

FOUR

The Shulamite's Offense

Do not look upon me, because I am
dark, because the sun has tanned
me. My mother's sons were angry
with me; they made me the keeper of
the vineyards, but my own vineyard
I have not kept (1:6).

As we saw in the last chapter, the Shulamite had the power of guilt, shame, and failure broken off her, and now we get some insight on why she became so offended. In this verse, we see her addressing her issue of loneliness by asking the Lord where He feeds His flock.

Why is the Shulamite Offended?

The Shulamite is being very vulnerable as she opens up about why she has offense in her heart toward people. She felt they overworked her and kept her so busy working in everyone else's gardens, that her own garden was ignored and neglected. And because of that she lost her own personal connection with God. Her negative experience begins with rejection. Members of the Body of Christ were angry at her because of her zeal for her Bridegroom; they rejected her and took advantage of her by overworking her in their fields.

Have you ever noticed people who are living dull, passionless lives can get very offended and irritable when others around them are manifesting a tremendous zeal for God? Fervency and passion scare people who don't have it, and for that they will judge you.

We have a very sad illustration of this in 2 Samuel. King David's wife, Michal, saw David dancing in his linen undergarments before the Ark of the Covenant with such unbridled passion.

> *Then David danced before the LORD with all his might; and David was wearing a linen ephod. So David and all the house of Israel brought up the ark of the LORD with shouting and with the sound of the trumpet. Now as the ark of the LORD came into the City of David, Michal, Saul's daughter, looked through a window and saw King David leaping and whirling before the LORD; and she despised him in her heart. . . .*
>
> *Then David returned to bless his household. And Michal the daughter of Saul came out to meet David, and said, "How glorious was the king of Israel today, uncovering himself today in the eyes of the maids of his servants, as one of the base fellows shamelessly uncovers himself!"*
>
> *So David said to Michal, "It was before the LORD, who chose me instead of your father and all his house, to appoint me ruler over the people of the LORD, over Israel. Therefore I will play music before the LORD. And I will be even more undignified than this, and will be humble in my own sight. . . . Therefore Michal the daughter of Saul had no children to the day of her death (6:14-16, 20-23).*

People without passion are often offended at those displaying such raw passion for God. For context, David and his men were slowly moving the ark of God's presence up the mountains, carrying it home on their shoulders exactly as directed. They would take six small steps, and on the seventh step, they stopped and gave a burnt offering to the Lord. When they finally arrived to the city, David took off his kingly robes, and stripped down to only a linen ephod, basically his underwear. Linen is what the priests were instructed to wear in the presence of the Lord. They were not allowed to wear wool or anything that would make them sweat. God wanted His people to realize that our ministry before Him is not by our own works. Life in God and ministry is not by sweating and striving; it comes out of rest and trust in Him. Faith comes out of rest, and that's what David's linen ephod symbolizes.

The Religious Spirit Hates Passion

When King David took off his kingly garments and danced wildly before God and all the people, that's what he was demonstrating—a resolve of faith and trust in God alone. Meanwhile, his wife, Michal, stood observing all of this from her palace window, clearly embarrassed by the king's undignified display, and so attempted to humiliate him. But his response to her came as a big surprise. "If you think that was bad, you haven't seen anything yet! I can certainly be way more undignified than that." David was expressing raw passion, and the religious spirit hates it. Religious spirits prefer to align with those who have lost their heart passion for God and rely instead upon their intellectual and analytical processes.

The Fear of Man

Every person has a desire to be loved and accepted and made to feel they belong to something "special". The enemy knows that and he uses religion to instill the fear of man. The fear of man is obsessed with what people think about you; you need people to like you so they will accept and love you. When that spirit is prevalent in your life, you become overly concerned with how your actions are seen by people and consumed with what they are thinking and saying about you.

Religion was birthed out of fear, and so one of the things the fear of man will do is talk people out of displaying a lifestyle of passion by being more concerned about what others think of them. In this story, Michal is under a spirit of religion and she is very concerned about what people are thinking about her, and her husband, the king.

My real question is: what was Michal doing in the palace, anyway? All the people—just about the whole nation, in fact—were lining the streets in joy and great exuberance to celebrate the Ark of the Lord returning home. It's amazing how awkward extravagant worship and passion looks when others are doing it but you are far removed. Michal's heart is not joined with them, and so it was easy for the spirit of criticism to begin to overwhelm and influence her mind and perspective. The end result was a critical spirit tormented her.

This incident concludes with a very frightening outcome . . . and warning.

> *Therefore Michal the daughter of Saul had no children to the day of her death (v 23).*

From that moment on, Michal was barren, because passion is the key to fruitfulness in life.

The Spirit of Offense

The Shulamite was feeling the rejection of those under a spirit of religion. It was one of five pressures that she was experiencing that are directly related to this spiritual crisis. She feels—

- rejected,
- shamed,
- overworked,
- distracted from her first love, and
- she is serving Jesus from a distance.

The Spirit of offense is so destructive in our lives, and often we do not even realize that we are deeply offended, but our actions produce the **fruit of offense**. We see it in the life of John the Baptist. When John was in prison, he instructed his disciples, "Go and ask Jesus if He really is the coming Messiah." What initiated this request came out of a heart that was filling up with offense. John already knew Jesus was the Messiah, because he saw the heavens opened during Jesus' baptism and heard the voice say: "This is My beloved Son in whom I am well-pleased."[26]

Here is what I believe was John's struggle. In His inaugural address, Jesus declared that He had come to set captives free and to bring freedom to those in captivity. He also declared, "When you have visited someone in prison, it is like I am visiting them."[27] Well, Jesus had never visited John in prison nor did he set him free. I believe that John was building an offense in his heart towards Jesus, so he began to doubt his heavenly commission and sent His disciples to question if He *really* was the awaited Messiah. John's disciples communicated this burning question of John. To this, Jesus replies:

> *Go and tell John the things which you hear and see: The blind see and the lame walk; the lepers are cleansed and the deaf hear, the dead are raised up and the poor have the gospel preached to them. And blessed is he who is not offended because of Me.*[28]

That word "offense" means "stumbling block." However, the definition of offense that I think is really most descriptive is, "messed up in your head." Jesus is advising the disciples of John to tell him, "Blessed is the one who is not messed up in his head over something I am or am not doing in his life."

I think the best illustration in the entire Bible on how to deal with offense and see it lead to your greatest breakthrough is found with the Syrophoenician woman. She approached Jesus and asked Him to heal her severely demon-possessed daughter. We pick up the response of Jesus and His disciples in Matthew 15:23-26:

> *But He answered her not a word. And His disciples came and urged Him, saying, "Send her away, for she cries out after us."*

---

26   See Matt 3:17.
27   See Matt 25:36.
28   See Matt 11:4-6.

> *But He answered and said, "I was not sent except to the lost sheep of the house of Israel."*
>
> *Then she came and worshiped Him, saying, "Lord, help me!"*

Now there are some responses that could, for sure, cause offense to lodge in your heart. The following is one of those.

> *But He answered and said, "It is not good to take the children's bread and throw it to the little dogs."*
>
> *And she said, "Yes, Lord, yet even the little dogs eat the crumbs which fall from their masters' table."*
>
> *Then Jesus answered and said to her, "O woman, great is your faith! Let it be to you as you desire." And her daughter was healed from that very hour (vs 27-28).*

Here she is, a non-Jew coming to Jesus with a request. But He responds by telling her, "I can't give the children's bread [healing] to Gentiles (who are 'little dogs') . . . . " Yet even this seeming insult does not cause offense in her heart. There is a lot more to this story than what we read. You see, Jesus is dealing with cultural issues and attempting to change the mindset of His disciples in this exchange, as well. Amazingly, the woman does not take offense or get "messed up in her head" over what Jesus said to her. She refused to be derailed in her desperation to see her daughter healed by the words or actions of someone, and stepped right on past the offense that could easily have lodged in her heart, and received her miracle! That's the key. Actually, this faith-filled woman got even more than her miracle. She told Jesus, "Even the dogs get to eat the crumbs." But Jesus did not give her crumbs. Her desperate prayer for her daughter's freedom was exactly what He gave her.

There is "stuff" that happens to us in relationships nearly every day that has the potential to offend us and trip us up and cause us to stumble. This woman certainly had the opportunity to get disappointed and discouraged. She could have become so offended and could have countered with, "You have no right to talk to me like that! I deserve better treatment than this." However, instead of playing the victim, she used that moment to step into a breakthrough, and her daughter was completely healed as a result.

Perhaps the place of your greatest disappointment is an invitation into your desperately needed personal breakthrough.

Rejection

Let's take a look at rejection. Rejection is a lot like judgment: Whether perceived or pronounced, we often let it take us out, when in reality, it could be used to accelerate us deeper into embracing our truest identity. When we process rejection incorrectly, it can be devastating. But on the other hand, if you choose to respond correctly, rejection can be a very important opportunity to becoming a powerful person in Jesus. That's why it is important when you feel rejection that you don't fight back, but instead, embrace it, and hold it close. Then talk to the Lord about it: "Lord, I sure don't know what brought this on, but I'm asking You, Father, to use this incident to deepen my life in You . . . deepen my anointing, because I want more."

Embrace rejection—the rumor, or whatever form in which it might come. Do not fight it; treat it like a friend. Have a mindset that declares: "I am going to get as much out of this as I possibly can," realizing that in rejection, the part that hurts the most in me is the part that should have been dead anyway.

Rejection will come as a familiar pain, so recognize it, and celebrate the good result that is about to emerge. In such times of feeling the familiar results of rejection, here is a good prayer:

> Oh Lord, thank You for allowing me to experience this rejection with all these feelings of anger and resentment, feeling I need to defend myself, feelings of jealousy—which I thought were dead, but obviously are not. I pray You use this to

deepen in me my hatred for pride, my hatred for recognition, and those aggrandizing responses and behaviors. Lord, let's kill it for good this time. For the glory of Your name. Amen.

I went through a period of time where the Lord used me in unique ways in my pastoral giftings and opportunities. I found myself on three different occasions mentoring younger pastors who were all in Senior Pastor positions and I was the Associate Pastor. In all three of these seasons, I had specific pastoral duties and functions, which included preaching on Sunday morning. And in all three seasons, the spirit of jealousy invaded hearts of team members and created tensions and problems. This, then, resulted in a reduction of my teaching and preaching time, which, in turn, limited my pastoral outreach to the churches.

> PERSONAL BOUNDARIES ALLOW US TO STAY IN CONTROL OF OUR TIME, OUR ENERGY, OUR RESOURCES, AND OUR RELATIONSHIPS.

With each incident, I felt extreme rejection and I began to wonder why I kept finding myself in such a position. Looking back, I realize how much I learned from each of those experiences, and I also knew God was the one who directed me right into these seasons. Even still, there were great friendships built during those years, and I was able to be involved with many important breakthroughs and victories in the lives of those precious people.

My reaction to rejection from the first circumstance to the third reflected a measure of growth in me as well as more processing I still needed to go through. I remember the third rejection incident where I was sidelined from teaching and preaching, my initial reaction was very similar to the first experience. I felt all the emotions of hurt, pain, wounding, discouragement, and disappointment. I allowed the pain of that disappointment to settle unresolved in my heart and ended up offended at God and at people. It took the Holy Spirit quite a long time for me to process through that rejection where He revealed some wrong motivations I held for teaching and preaching. Then I read the words of the Apostle Paul:

> *God has given me grace to speak a warning about pride. I would ask each of you to be emptied of self-promotion, and not create a false image of your importance. Instead, honestly assess your worth by using your God-given faith as the standard of measurement, and then you will see your true value with an appropriate self-esteem (Romans 12:3, TPT).*

I realized that self-promotion was at the root of my ambition to preach and teach and found my identity and my self-esteem out of these ministerial activities. The response from people became more important than living out of my truest identity and in a healthy self-esteem from God's vantage point. It was then the Holy Spirit took me through a season where I allowed my pride to be broken, and the result was a true, authentic humility became a very high value in my life.

So, when the third rejection came, and I reacted again with anger, it lasted just a matter of minutes before I felt that spirit of humility rise up within me. I realized pride and a very unhealthy desire for recognition was still very much alive within me. It took this incident of rejection for me to see that pride had been hiding there all along. For that reason, I rejoiced in that particular instance of rejection because it exposed the very thing I thought was completely gone and dead inside of me. I knew instantly I had to deal with it, and with the Holy Spirit's wonderful assistance, we went through more processing.

When a situation of rejection comes again, and in partnership with the Holy Spirit, I believe the fruit of humility will be the prevailing response instead of pride and anger with its demands for self-recognition.

Protect Your Priorities and Establish Healthy Boundaries

The Shulamite in this chapter is facing five pressures: rejection, shame, being overworked, being distracted from her first love, and serving her Bridegroom from a distance. She has a heart to serve, but she has no idea how to say "no" to the demands of others, and because of that, they overwork her. She works every Sunday morning in the kids' church, Wednesday nights with the youth, she works in the nursery, she ushers, helps with clean-up after service, and she works as a greeter. Obviously I am overstating this, but there is validity in being overworked in the church. I know there is the other side—not serving on any level—which has become a disappointing epidemic. There needs to be a good balance.

It is clear that the Shulamite has lost her intimacy with God because she is being overworked. She has been hurt and wounded by the church leadership. She is no longer serving out of an overflow of intimacy with her Bridegroom Jesus, so her ministry service is not sustainable.

Because we are all very compassionate people, it is extremely important that we make decisions based on our Holy Spirit-birthed assignments, and that we establish appropriate boundaries in our life. Because we are loving and caring people, we automatically want to respond when we see a need. But that may not be the heart of the Lord for us. I am not saying to turn off your compassion, nor am I suggesting that you cannot respond to a need. But I am saying that a need that arises may not be yours to carry; it may be a burden that is assigned to someone else whom God has prepared for that season. The need cannot be the call. We must only take on needs and burdens that are part of our assignment.

Personal boundaries allow us to stay in control of our time, our energy, our resources, and our relationships. Without proper boundaries, it is nearly impossible to successfully manage the most important priorities in your life. Without boundaries, it is very easy to become over-involved in a variety of other activities, when, in reality, we're just not able to properly follow through. These potentially steal away our valuable time, resources, and energy, and then we end up neglecting that which we should be managing: our own families and household, and ourselves. If you cannot take care of yourself because you are so busy in everyone else's gardens, then you make it somebody else's job to take care of you. Boundaries are miracle workers that allow you to control your own environment. As much as you love other people, and as much as you want them to be blessed and happy, they are not always your assignment.

Jesus understood and lived with that principle. He was the freest person I've ever seen because He lived with boundaries. When Jesus walked the earth, He released healing everywhere He went. In the Gospels, He is batting a thousand: Every person who needed a healing and had the faith for that healing got healed; they got the miracle they needed. Jesus is famous for this. So you can imagine that everywhere He went, huge throngs of people were waiting for Him, especially those who needed healing. This was the case in Luke 8 when Jesus came to the edge of a city, and a throng of people were awaiting His arrival. In this large gathering of people from all over the region, there were those who desperately needed something from Jesus. There were those who brought their sick friends and loved ones in need of a healing, and they made sure to position them right where this Healer would pass by and could touch and heal them.

That's what happened with a man named, Jairus, who suddenly found himself face-to-face with Jesus as He stopped and fixed His gaze upon him. Jairus begged Jesus to go with him to his house and heal his dying daughter.

"Yes, I'll come . . ." Jesus responded, and off they went to Jairus' house. On this journey, Jesus walked right past thousands of hurting, broken, wounded, and desperate people crying out in need of healing. But Jesus had a specific assignment and so He set up boundaries to protect His time, energy, and resources. He continued walking right past a whole bunch of people who had real needs, real hurts, and yet He does not respond to those needs. He just seemed to pick up his pace as He passed by. We know that Jesus is full of compassion and loves people, and that He came to this earth to heal the sick and brokenhearted. But on this particular trip, He had an individual, clear-cut assignment, and He could not let Himself be diverted by losing sight of this one goal.

That is exactly what healthy people do. That is what makes you powerful in the presence of great needs. Your boundaries do not allow you to get diverted by the needs of the environment that often pull you in multiple directions. Jesus' number one priority is to get to Jairus' house. He's focused, determined, and disciplined to this one objective. By the time He arrived, however, Jairus' little daughter had already died. But, Jesus was undeterred, and raised his daughter from the dead, because He was *present*. He had not allowed Himself to get sidetracked with someone else's need on the edge of town, because He had strictly set His priorities based on this one specific assignment of the Holy Spirit, and the environment all around Him with its legitimate demands of desperate needs did *not* divert Him. In this particular instance, His focus was one little girl that would need to be raised from the dead.

To be most effective in our calling, it is vital that we establish healthy boundaries to safeguard the priorities God has given us in relationships, time, energy, and resources.

"The Shulamite's Offense" Prayer

Father, thank You for showing me the priorities in my life. I want to establish proper boundaries to protect all You have given me and I'm asking You for the wisdom to do just that.

Father, I am choosing not to put my head down under pressure. Instead, I am committing to You to not live in self-pity as an attempt to manipulate You into soothing my injured pride or soul. In this moment, I am choosing to lift up my head, to building gates out of pearls so the King of Glory can come in!

I will not ask You, "Why?" I choose to not hold my peace hostage by demanding to know why this is or is not happening. Instead, I choose to trust You.

Holy Spirit, release a supernatural courage and strength as I choose to worship you in this moment. I ask You to release upon me an enduring faith that says: "I put my hope and my trust in my testimony of who God is!"

Increase in me Your refreshment, hope, strength, joy, and courage that can say:

I don't know why this happened . . .

I don't know why that didn't happen . . .

It really looks like God failed me here . . .

It looks like I totally failed Him here . . .

But, in this moment, I choose to trust You, Lord!

Making this declaration positions me for revelation and understanding, because I know Lord, You actually measure my heart through my response to things that I do not understand.

As You said in the Gospel of John:

I have some things I would love to tell you but you are not at the place right now where you could handle it.[29]

So here I am, lifting up my head, Lord, and inviting You to come in and go places only You can go, and do things only You can do.

Thank You, Lord.

I put all my trust in You.

Amen.

---

[29]   John 16:12.

ACTIVATION #4
The Shulamite's Offense

When it comes to relationships we all have varying levels of friendship boundaries. This activation will help to define those boundaries. The hope is that by establishing them, we can protect the very place we need to be in order to maintain our own "garden"—our intimacy with the Lord.

Make Boundary Circles

Below are circles that will represent a boundary. In the first inner circle, place God. In boundary circle #2 put a name in there, and continue to do so until you have labeled all the circles. Be careful not to be too hasty in placing people in your inner circle boundaries. These should be reserved only for those who hold a special place of honor and influence in your life. I've discovered that some people who do not operate with boundaries will often attempt to penetrate yours, so be on your guard. It is important that you learn language to communicate your needs, such as, "We are still developing a relationship and I do not feel we are at a place in our friendship where we should be dialoguing about this . . ." or something like that. Respect and guard your boundaries well! It will guarantee peace in all areas of your life and create the healthiest environment for you and all your relationships to thrive. The result will be a productive and fruitful life and ministry.

1. God: The first boundary circle is reserved for God alone. He is the center of everything in our life. No one else should be in that center circle, which represents the central place of our life.

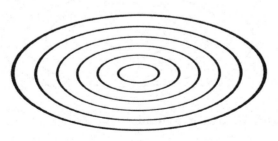

2. Most Intimate Friend: The next boundary circle is your most intimate friend. If you are married, it would obviously be your spouse—not your mom, not your dad, children, or a close friend. If you have *anyone* else in this circle besides your spouse, you are going to have conflict. If you are married and you have not removed your mother or father, family member, or close friend from this circle, you can *expect* marital conflict between you and your spouse.

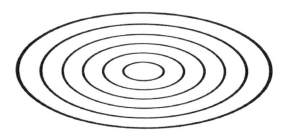

3. Family and Loved ones (immediate and extended family): The next circle would be your family, children, and loved ones (extended family members)—those who have deep access into your life. Each boundary circle determines the level of weight and input that person has in your life, and likewise, you hold that place in their life, as well. You do not want someone in an outer boundary to have the same access and input into your life as you would someone in your inner boundary circles. People move into boundaries based on your level of friendship, intimacy and trust levels. Those in your inner boundaries are people you have invested a lot of time in, and they have reciprocated.

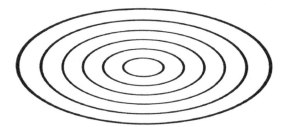

4. Close, Intimate Friends: The fourth boundary circle

would contain those you consider your really close intimate friends. These individuals do not have access to you that circles one, two, and three have, but they hold a great level of importance to you.

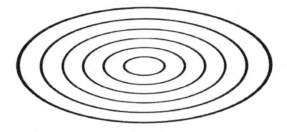

5. Business/Ministry Associates: This circle might be your business associates and others that you have contact with on a fairly regular basis.

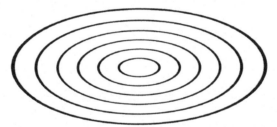

6. Church Community Associates: This circle would be those you have contact with at church whom you are just getting to know; the boundary clarifications continue depending on your level of friendship.

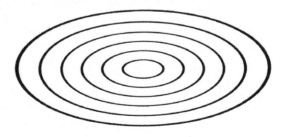

FIVE

The Strength of Community

Tell me, O you whom I love, where
you feed your flock, where you make
it rest at noon. For why should I be
as the one who veils herself by the
flocks of your companions? (1:7)

As we come into this chapter in the Song, the Bride is remembering the days she spent in the private chamber with Him, and she's going over in her mind all the amazing things that have happened so far. She's been awakened again to a place of passion for Jesus. She's had guilt, shame, and the power of failure broken in her life. She has had her first crisis in which she discovered that she is "dark", but she is also "lovely", and she's working through her offense.

Longing for More

Now she wants more. She wants to deal with the loneliness in her life, so she asks the Lord, "Where do you feed your flock?" The Shulamite has come to the understanding that it is not the church, ministries, or others that have her heart, but it is Him—the one she loves with all her heart. She wants to get back to that place where her sole desire was the kisses of His mouth. She remembers the touch of Jesus and the romance of His heart, and she says, "Tell me, where will You make me lie down and rest like the old days? I want to get back to where I was." This is a cry for another level of intimacy. This is a desperate cry for experiencing Jesus, not merely seeing Him from afar, or doing things for Him, but knowing Him at another level of experience.

> *Tell me, O* **you** *whom I love, where* **you** *feed your flock, where* **you** *make it rest at noon. For why should I be as the one who veils herself by the flocks of your companions? (1:7, emphasis added)*

> *Won't you tell me, Lover of my soul, where do you feed your flock? Where do you lead your beloved ones to rest in the heat of the day? For I wish to be wrapped all around you, as I go among the flocks of your under-shepherds. It is you I long for, with no veil between us! (TPT)*

The Shulamite sees her Beloved as a shepherd. This is a metaphor of the role He takes in her sight. She is basically saying, "Tell me, You whom I love, where can I find You? I do not care about ministry, about church responsibilities and obligations, about all I am *supposed* to do; I simply want to be with You. So, where can I find You?"

In the phrase, "Where do **you** feed your flock?" the key word is "you." The Shulamite uses the word "you" three times in the verse. It's my understanding that sheep will only lie down at noon if their stomach is filled. The Shulamite is not completely fulfilled being fed by others. She is still left with an emptiness inside because she has this ravishing hunger for Him alone. Jesus responds in the imagery of the day.

> *If you do not know, O fairest among women, follow in the footsteps of the flock, and feed your little goats beside the shepherds' tents. I have compared you, my love, to my filly among Pharaoh's chariots. Your cheeks are lovely with ornaments, your neck with chains of gold.*

We will make you ornaments of gold with studs of silver (vs 8-11).

Listen, my radiant one—if you ever lose sight of me just follow in my footsteps where I lead my lovers. Come with your burdens and cares. Come to the place near the sanctuary of my shepherds— there you will find me (1:8, TPT).

All of this is in the imagery of a shepherd, and it's all about her finding her path again. He hears her prayer of despair inquiring, "Where can I find You?", and as He always does, every single time, He addresses her, He affirms her. He renews the romance with her again. He calls her "most beautiful of women."

Commit to Fellowship

Then He gives her a general answer, three specific answers, and three affirmations to back up the three answers. He calls her to the commitment of Body-life. He calls her to follow in the footsteps of the flock. He calls her to get involved. When He says "the footsteps of the flock," He is talking about the place where all the sheep reside. He is telling her to get back into fellowship. He is encouraging her to get over her offense, reopen her heart, and get back into community again.

Jesus did *not* establish His church for us to work in isolation. It is not just "me and Jesus" and all is well. It is "me and Jesus", but it is also me and Jesus plus you. It is a deceptive ploy of the enemy to keep us isolated from one another. When we separate ourselves and disengage from our spiritual community, we can easily get picked off by the kingdom of darkness. It is always the sheep that lags behind the herd or wanders off that becomes easy prey. Protection and safety is found within the herd.

The Power of Community

The Lord will *always* lead us into a protective, secure

environment. The enemy tries to lure us away into a solitary place. We were never meant to struggle alone with our personal battles. In the following verse, He instructs His Bride:

Follow in the footsteps of the flock (1:8).

The Bridegroom tells her to get back into her community—get reconnected again. Why? A distracted sheep wandering the fields alone can easily be attacked. Connecting with those in your community—with people who are *for* you—is the second part of the key to breaking the power of sin and shame in your life.

All healing is completed in relationship—in community. I had a friend tell me one time that God heals you 90 percent of the way, and then He gives you friends to complete the healing. As you look through the gospels, you see that Jesus did exactly that. He would heal someone, and then turn them over to a community of people who knew how to love that person well to complete the healing process.

I was speaking to one of the young married men in our congregation who was struggling a bit in his marriage. I asked him how their community was helping them, and he told me they had not talked about it with anyone in their community. He felt he could not burden them with their struggle, and he declared to me they were doing the best they could to work it out. I have to be honest: that's not going to be enough. God has not set up this life in Him to work that way. This is a relationship we have entered into; it is about family.

Certainly God is asking us to do the best we can, but He is also asking us to get the best we can from our community. I need the best that my friends can give me of themselves, and they need my best. Two of the most powerful words that I hear in my community when I am sharing a struggle are, "Me too!"

One of the ways the enemy focuses his attack on relationships is with the spirit of offense, unforgiveness, misunderstanding, rejection, and divisiveness, because his intent is to rob, destroy, and ultimately kill relationships on every level. That's why it is so important for us to build community and develop strong relationships, because these become a defensible stronghold the enemy cannot penetrate.

The Bible says that you and I are "living stones;"[30] we are "buildings" joined together. Relationships are the stronghold—a hiding place—where you and I are the safest.

Let me ask you some questions about community: Who are you doing life with? Who are your friends? Who are those people with whom you celebrate life: birthdays, holidays, amusement park trips, ball games? Who is such an intimate friend in your life that if you were struggling with something, you would not even have to say anything to them because they know you so well? This would be a person with whom you do life with consistently and it would not take long for them to look at you and say, "Hey,

ALL HEALING IS COMPLETED IN RELATIONSHIP WITHIN COMMUNITY.

something's not right." If you do not have such people in your life, get them. Think about who you have chemistry with, and begin to build a relationship with that person.

We are people who have a passion to transform the world. But God is all about relationship, and transformation comes out of relationship and a foundation of love. Building an intimate relational community takes time, effort, and work. A lot of people don't choose to live in a community of friends because it's really hard becoming one with a whole bunch of imperfect people. I fought community for a long time. I just didn't see its value. It always seemed so much easier to isolate and let it be just me and Jesus. But Jesus modeled life for us with His disciples—a close-knit community of friends.

---

[30]   See 1 Pet 2:5.

We often don't recall the backstory to Mark 16:15: "Go into the world and preach the gospel . . ." When Jesus said that, He was addressing His disciples, speaking to a group of men who had just spent three intense years together, just doing life. It was an incredible, intense, crazy, fun, exhilarating, frustrating, scary, stretching, stimulating, team-building rollercoaster . . . a three-year camping trip when they were rarely apart. Do you think at the end of those three years Jesus and His disciples might have been pretty close? Yeah, they were a tight-knit community.

Just imagine their campfire conversations . . . those times when they just sat around in the evenings as men shooting the breeze, talking about the events of the day. These conversations did not make it into the Bible. No possible way. I mean, come on . . . think about it!—men sitting around a campfire?! . . . No women around to temper anything. Trust me—they knew *all* about each other; in fact, probably more than they actually wanted to know. My point is . . . it isn't until they had spent over a thousand days together—day in, and day out—that Jesus said, "Okay . . . Go!"

We need one another, and we need to build a stronghold of friendships and community.

Four Benefits of Living in Community

1. Strength comes from community.

Proverbs 13:20 says:

He who walks with wise men will be wise . . .

There is supernatural strength with supernatural wisdom that a community of people provides.

Picture a guy who made a huge mistake in his life. I knew such a guy who made a horrible choice, and he was just disgusted with himself because of what he had done. Even his marriage was in jeopardy. This guy was definitely down in the dumps. Life was really not good at home. So I asked him, "With whom are you talking through all this stuff?"

"Well . . . no one." That's a bad choice, but it's one we men make all too often.

"Have you connected with anyone about this?" I asked.

"No one," he answered. "But hey, we've done the best we could do. I am doing the best I can, and she's doing the best she can. We know what to do, but it's just not working."

Buddy, it's not working because it's not set up to work. Our best is just not good enough. We *need* other people in our life. Personally, I need the best that the friends of my community— Dave, Tim, Magnus, Ryan and Shelby, Mark and Tammy, Keith, Bill and Kathy, and others—can give me. We need access to the best in others if we are going to make it through the really tough times. Yes, we have the Lord, and He's always our first go-to. In such extreme times of need we especially draw near to Jesus and we receive His love, His joy, His peace, His strength, His wisdom, and His revelation. Then, we get ahold of someone in our community with whom we have a deep trust and friendship, and they give us their best.

Community always works best.

2. Safety comes from community.

> *Where there is no counsel, the people fall; but in the multitude of counselors there is safety (Proverbs 11:14).*

> *Without counsel, plans go awry, but in the multitude of counselors they are established (15:22).*

> *For by wise counsel you will wage your own war, and in a multitude of counselors there is safety (24:6).*

These verses are talking about "wise counselors". You know, we can be really good at hearing the Lord, but sometimes we're not really good at understanding timing. Sometimes we hear clearly, but our emotions spin us, and that's why having a community that we trust—those who can contribute wise counsel—is so important.

Know this: when you make decisions inside of community, you are safe. Christians living within community are in a stronghold of safety.

3. God speaks through community.

Sometimes the answer you are looking for won't come directly from God. Sometimes He will speak it through someone in your community. God speaks through people. In 1 Corinthians 12, we have the nine spiritual gifts listed. If you look at them, you see that five of them are actually God speaking through people:

- Word of wisdom
- Word of knowledge
- Prophetic words
- Tongues
- Interpretation of tongues

God definitely speaks through community.

4. Encouragement comes out of community.

Now we who are strong ought to bear the weaknesses of those without strength and not just please ourselves (Romans 15:1, NASB).

I have learned from reading Brene Browne that there is not one person who doesn't have skinned elbows and knees, broken bones, and wounded hearts from falling and failing. Scars are easier to talk about than they are to show. It is very rare to see peoples' wounds when they are in the process of healing. The reason for that is the absolute terror they feel when they think of sharing. They believe if they do, people will no longer love and accept them for who they really are, and instead, they will move away from them and break relationship.

There is something about the way the world views success that does not fit well in Heaven, but unfortunately, it seems to fit well in the church. That has to change. People want to be associated with what the West preaches: image and success. So if you fail, or expose a weakness, people have a tendency to distance themselves from you really quickly. That's why we have such a hard time revealing our wounds. The fact is, we *need* one another . . . all the time.

If we don't feel safe in sharing our wounds, we will not step into the emotion of them and own our stories. What happens then? We hide the hurt, we bury the disappointment, and we deny the pain. We also set ourselves up for a destructive erosion of our community relationships.

- Instead of feeling the hurt, we act out our hurt.
- Instead of acknowledging our pain, we inflict pain on ourselves and on others.
- Instead of feeling disappointed, we choose to live disappointed.

The real cure for that is to belong to a safe community. The failures and weaknesses in the lives of those people around you are rich with possibilities for deeper connection, deeper friendship, and reconnecting people to the heart of their Father. When we step in and connect with people in their failures, disappointments, and weaknesses, and we love them and stand with them, they know they are truly loved. This provides for the best possible environment for healing.

I know the strengths and the weaknesses of those in my community and they know mine. I know the areas they do well and the areas where they struggle, and I unconditionally accept and love them. They do the same for me. I don't have to improve in my areas of weakness for them to still love me. I can reject all the Holy Spirit's attempts to help me be transformed in my areas of struggle, and yet, my friends in my community still love me and stand with me. They may be a bit frustrated with me, and they are working with me, but they still accept me, even if they do not approve of some of my choices. Because of that, I do not have to hide behind some wall or pretentious façade because of fear of abandonment if they know I'm still struggling with an area of weakness. No, I know I am loved and accepted, even as I'm overcoming my weakness.

Acceptance does that. Everyone should have the permission to be themselves, because that encourages honesty and vulnerability. We need to live in a culture of honor in which we can say, "Guys, I'm struggling with this still. I need help."

We absolutely need to be people who love authentically all the time. We need people who will stand with others in their failure for the sake of love.

Adopted into Community

In our key verse, Jesus is healing this Shulamite maiden. He knows that she needs people in her life to help continue this healing process, and so He tells her to reconnect with her community. God is obsessed with relationships. He loves intimate friendships. Everything the Holy Spirit does, He does out of intimate relationship. We were never meant to be alone or to live as orphans. We have been invited into a relationship with a Father, a Son, and a Holy Spirit. The Apostle Paul tells us that the Holy Spirit has many identities, and one of them is called the "Spirit of adoption":

> For you did not receive the spirit of bondage again
> to fear, but you received the Spirit of adoption by
> whom we cry out, "Abba, Father." (Romans 8:15)

Adoption is a process in which a person who was an orphan—one who has no family—legally becomes a part of a family. In the 1970s, the United States adopted the no-fault divorce, and what resulted was the acceleration of an onslaught against the family unit, so that many children grew up in "broken" homes. Some grew up in homes with only one parent around, and a generation emerged feeling orphaned. We are currently observing today how so many are manifesting orphan tendencies, in which they live isolated, overly protecting their hearts, and living a self-absorbed, self-protected lifestyle. They have no desire to enter into a spiritual community/family because they have no concept what that means and they have no grid for it. But then God comes and invites them into His family community and adopts them, He forever crushes that orphan spirit in them.

This whole idea of family is such an extreme beacon of

hope as the hearts of fathers and sons, mothers and daughters, mothers and sons, fathers and daughters are turned toward one another again.

Each one of us has these four needs—

- The need to be known,
- The need to be loved,
- The need to be accepted, and
- The need to be part of a family.

That's the way God created us, to be relational and to live in close relationship with others in the flock. In God's Kingdom, this is a big deal.

However, living in community takes a lot of work, and it has its risks. In community, you have to be willing to open your heart, become more and more vulnerable, and be willing to be transparent with a whole bunch of imperfect people. There's an intimate exchange that takes place in such a close community, and this can be difficult for some. But it is necessary if you are to make any substantial contribution to the community, as well as receive what you need. At the same time, the community involvement will never take the place of your intimate relationship with God; you need both! God will speak to you personally but He will also speak to you through your community. You need to develop a level of interdependency where you are also open to those in your community to speak into your life.

A community plays a vital role in our well-being. God never has us walk alone in this life; we are to live in community. He has situated us to live with neighbors, and to be a neighbor. He heals us, and then He gives us a community of people who encourage us, who love us and stand with us, and who help us walk out that healing. There are people all around us who are wounded, hurt, and devastated in some relationship. They need encouragement, and it will be your compassion and kindness that will release the fortitude they need. The Samaritan man in the gospels made the choice to help a wounded man, because when he saw him, he was overcome with compassion. That is one of the significant benefits of community; we release courage to those in need around us. So often we are not even aware of those who are emotionally wounded because we have become so good at hiding behind a façade. But as we become more sensitive to the Holy Spirit, we will be able to discern when someone just needs a kind word of encouragement. There have been so many instances where someone came and spoke such a timely word of encouragement to me, releasing courage that broke discouragement, loneliness, or depression off of me. That is the value of community, where we give, and receive what we need.

The Lollipop Moments of Life

I read a story recently about a man named Drew Dudley, who shared an encounter he had with someone on his college campus. In his final days as a college student, he described an incident he had with another student nearing the end of the school year.

This student approached him and began to share with him about her first day of school four years earlier, when she was scared to death and trying to decide whether or not to stay. Her parents were with her, and she was leaning more towards going back home.

That first morning as they walked on campus, this young lady turned to her parents and declared that she just didn't have the courage to stay and begin her college career. She was struggling with anxiety and fear and had come to the conclusion she would return home with her parents. At that moment, she went on to explain, "A man walked out of the student center wearing the most ridiculous hat I had ever seen with a big sign that read: "Students Fighting Cystic Fibrosis."

She added, "He was also carrying a bucketful of lollipops to hand out." Dudley approached the woman, stared at her for the longest time, then turned to a young man who just happened to be standing next to her and handed him a lollipop. As he did, he instructed him: "Give this lollipop to the beautiful woman standing next to you."

This young man, quite red-faced with embarrassment now, could barely make eye contact with the beautiful young woman, and just reached out his arm and handed her the lollipop.

The young lady felt so sorry for this guy who clearly was dying with embarrassment, that she quickly took the lollipop. The moment she did, Dudley looked at the parents and declared; "Look at that. First day away from home and she is already taking candy from a stranger."

All those who were standing nearby—twenty-feet in every direction—erupted in uproarious laughter. As the student is relaying this story to Dudley, she says, "I know this may sound kind of cheesy, and I don't even know why I'm telling you this story," she said, "but it was in that exact moment, I knew I should *not* quit college and give up on my dream."

She went on to say, "In that moment I just knew this was where I am supposed to be. This is my new home." It had become a benchmark moment that transformed her life.

She went on to tell Dudley that she had not spoken to him at all in the four years since that day, but she heard he was leaving, and realized she had to come and tell him that story just to let him know how much that one simple act had impacted her life.

The girl walked away, and Dudley stood there somewhat shocked. As the girl got about five or six feet away she turned around and said, "Oh, and by the way, you should probably know this. I am still dating the guy who handed me that lollipop four years ago."

The thing that so surprised Dudley is that he could not remember that day or that particular incident, even though he felt like he should, because it was a humorous and a profound encounter. "To think that perhaps the biggest impact I had on someone's life would cause them to approach me four years later and tell me what an important part I played in her life, and I can not even recall it, is startling."

I would imagine you and I have had many such moments

where we handed someone a lollipop, unaware of the tremendous impact we made with that act. I know that I have been the recipient of many such lollipop moments myself.

That's the beauty of community. We have opportunity after opportunity to step into lollipop moments. Community is *that* important. But if you remove yourself from community, you forfeit your opportunity to be a lollipop dispenser and a lollipop receiver.

Jesus talked about this when He told people how impacted He was when they gave Him water when He was thirsty, when they gave Him food when He was hungry, when they visited Him in prison.[31] The people were confused and asked, "When did we do those things?" Jesus responded by telling them, "When you did it to the least of these, you did it to Me." Lollipop moments happen within community and they really please the Lord.

Walk with Wise Men

Independence, isolation, and the Church simply do not mix. But the bond with believers within community works very well. This is where wisdom from Heaven is dispensed. The writer of Proverbs has much to say about walking with a circle of friends termed, "wise men".

He who walks with wise men, will be wise (13:20).

We need the wisdom of those in our community. When we do not have a community to help us with wisdom in situations, then we are totally dependent upon ourselves and our own level of revelation, insight, and wisdom.

Notice it does not say, "He who walks with Me . . ." It says, "He who walks **with wise men** will be wise."[32] Consider again these verses from Proverbs about the results of walking with the wise:

Where there is no counsel, the people fall; but

---

[31] See Matt 25:35-40.
[32] Emphasis added.

in the multitude of counselors there is safety (Proverbs 11:14).

Without counsel, plans go awry, but in the multitude of counselors they are established (15:22).

For by wise counsel you will wage your own war, and in a multitude of counselors there is safety (24:6).

The conclusion of Scripture is that there is **safety** in community: When you make decisions inside of community there truly is safety; making decisions outside of community is simply void of safety and wisdom.

Find Your Community

If you do not have a community of trusted intimate friends, get them. Find the people you have chemistry with and begin to build a deep relationship with them. Contribute well to your community and determine to be one who builds it up.

Because we are a people who have a mission and passion to transform the world, our community relationships strengthen us from a solid foundation of love that will transform the world around us. Wherever God sends us in this world, we go in the strength and love of a community who is *with* us and *for* us. This world needs the model of a strong and healthy community environment—a real family—where love and grace abound, adoption and acceptance is found, and forgiveness flows freely. You are very much a vital part in that community with specific gifts and skills to contribute and build His Kingdom.

So I ask you again, who is your community?

"The Strength of Community" Prayer

Thank You, Father, for the power and strength of community. I ask that You provide a loving environment of community for the reader to be an active participant and contributor to build Your Kingdom.

Show them who You have provided for them to just do life with. Thank You, that You put the lonely in families, and Your provision to strengthen us is within our community.

Father, I thank You that You walk with us through the good and the bad. Thank You for walking with us on the mountaintop and through the valley, and that Your commitment to us is never less than 100% because that is who You are.

Father, I ask that You touch the reader with Your Presence to experience You even in their senses in a tangible way. This is Your moment, Lord, to draw us deeper into Your heart. I ask that You, Holy Spirit, would come as Comforter. Would You come and touch their heart, emotions, and mind and replace a negative mindset about You with a better one?

Replace the incorrect mindset about ourselves with the one You have about us, so that the eyes of our heart will be opened. We want to really see just how You see us and how much You love us.

Amen.

ACTIVATION #5
The Strength of Community

Ask yourself the following questions and write down the answers in the space provided.

1. Who are you doing life with? (Consider those you interact with most often from your business, work, and spiritual community.)

Daily: _____

Weekly:_____

Monthly/occasionally: _____

2. Who is your most intimate friend(s) that you can easily share what you are struggling with? (Note: These are ones who know you and can easily read you. They are the ones who would say, "Hey, something's not right . . . How are you doing?" Who are those people you celebrate life with? (Note: these are ones on your inner circle and other friends.)

Birthdays, lunch/dinner out, coffee, etc.:

_____

Holidays:

_____

Theme parks, picnics, and day outings:

_____

Fishing, hunting, camping, hiking, etc.:

_____

Ballgames, golf, shopping, etc.:

_____

3. Who are your friends? (Note: these are on your outer circle list.)

_____

_____

_____

_____

4. How can you improve upon the way you contribute to your community?

_____

_____

_____

5. What are some practical ways you can demonstrate gratitude to your community family?

_____

_____

_____

_____

_____

_____

_____

_____

_____

SIX

Bridegroom Encounters

*I have compared you, my love, to
my filly among Pharaoh's chariots.
Your cheeks are lovely with
ornaments, your neck with chains of
gold.*

*We will make you ornaments of gold
with studs of silver (1:9-11).*

I n this chapter of the Song, we will see that the Bride is
going to discover another aspect of the nature and beauty of
her Bridegroom. The Holy Spirit is bringing another level of
revelation, another opportunity for the Bride to experience the
depth of love her Bridegroom has for her. The Holy Spirit is still
in the process of replacing her mindset with a better one; He
is moving her out of only seeing and reasoning with her mind,
because a mind that reasons without God at the center, wars
against truth and divine reasoning. As Bill Johnson says:

> *We do not submit revelation to logic and reasoning;
> we submit logic and reasoning to revelation.*

Tending our own Flock

Feed your little goats beside the shepherds' tents.

v 8b

The Shulamite is instructed to take care of her Holy Spirit-directed responsibilities—to feed her flock. Notice it is specific. It is not to tend the vineyards that others give her (to you). No, in this directive she must care for the flock as He instructed her to do. Now, you may have one direct assignment, but within that assignment, the Holy Spirit will also give you other responsibilities for ministry. Be sure to only do those assignments in which the Lord is specifically directing you.

For a number of years, I was the director of the school of the supernatural at our church. In that capacity I had a direct assignment, but there were often many opportunities in my role as director and pastor to minister to needs that surfaced. However, it was still very important for me to stay loyal to my assignment and only agree to other ministry opportunities within that assignment as I felt directed by the Holy Spirit. There were many issues that surfaced in the lives of the students, but not all of those were mine to carry. In every case, God raised up someone else on my team, or another student, to work through the situation.

The third directive for the Shulamite is to **do everything in submission to spiritual authority.** This is a significant directive for her because her anger toward the leadership in the church is what caused her to initially withdraw. Many Christians have church-hopped or left church completely because of the issue of being wounded by someone in leadership. In the wounding they make a determination in their heart to never put themselves into a position where they can be hurt by leadership again.

The Bridegroom is letting the Shulamite know that she must come to the place near the sanctuary of His shepherds—"besides the shepherds' tents"—because as she does, she will find the One she is seeking. As she responds in obedience, she will discover that the Lord will release His divine grace that will allow her heart to heal, and she will also discover that she is able to relate well to those in leadership. She will discover that the shepherds are the ones anointed by the Shepherd Himself to lead us into a deeper place of intimate experiences with our Beloved Jesus.

THE BRIDEGROOM AFFIRMS HIS BRIDE

To encourage her, the Bridegroom affirms her in three ways. As He always does, He begins His conversations with her by declaring who she is in His sight, and by letting her know just how deeply and passionately He loves her.

> *I have compared you, my love, to my filly among Pharaoh's chariots. Your cheeks are lovely with ornaments, your neck with chains of gold.*
>
> *We will make you ornaments of gold with studs of silver (1:9-11).*
>
> *My dearest one . . . Let me tell you how I see you— you are so thrilling to me. To gaze upon you is like looking at one of Pharaoh's finest horses—a strong, regal steed pulling his royal chariot. Your tender cheeks are aglow—your earrings and gem-laden necklaces set them ablaze.*
>
> *We will enhance your beauty, encircling you with our golden reins of love. You will be marked with our redeeming grace (vs 9-11, TPT).*

The Bridegroom comes to her once again in such tender love, compassion, and care and He reveals His heart overwhelmed with love for her. His affection toward us is so far beyond what we could ever comprehend. But God has never asked us to understand it, defend it, or explain it. He simply asks us to believe it, receive it, and live in His love.

"A Strong, Regal Steed"

He then says to her: "Let me tell you how I see you. You are so thrilling to me. To gaze upon you is like looking at one of

Pharaoh's finest horses—a strong, regal steed pulling his royal chariot."

The Bridegroom calls His beautiful beloved one a horse! In ancient poetry, the "horse" was always used as an emblem of beauty and inner strength, and in this instance, it is a symbol of strength and power. Historians write of the chariots of Pharaoh as being built with pure gold, and the horses of Egypt were known as the most powerful and most beautiful horses in the entire world. Because of Pharaoh's wealth, he had the most highly skilled and well-trained horses on earth and chose only the very best of these to pull his own personal chariot.

So this is the imagery used here. In this passage, Jesus is saying to His Bride:

> You are so beautiful to me; you are so powerful—so full of strength. I compare you to the chariots that carry royalty, and you have proven to me that you carry the King everywhere you go. You have carried the burdens of the Lord, you've been yoked to the very King Himself, and you have taken Him into every conflict, confrontation, and opposition you had to face.
>
> You have carried Me into the hearts of others with an amazing grace and love. You have carried Me into difficult situations, and because of that, I was able to release My power to set people free through you time and time again. Just because you have failed in some areas does not mean I have forgotten or will ever forget what you have done in My name.

He lets the Shulamite know that He remembers all that she's done in His name . . . forever.

> *For God is not unjust to forget your work and labor of love which you have shown toward His name, in that you have ministered to the saints, and do minister (Hebrews 6:10).*

Know this: as you have helped people and continue to help them, it does not escape Jesus' attention. He never forgets it. We have a tendency to say, "Oh that was nothing . . . it was no big thing." But we say that because we don't esteem the deeds we do in His name to the full extent our Father does. In Matthew 10:42, we are told that even a cup of cold water given in Jesus' name is valuable to Him, and He will remind us of it on the last day.

The Bridegroom is letting His beloved know that she has done so many wonderful things for Him that have been released out of her love for Him, and He will never forget it. She has a track record of love and compassion, and she needs to understand that she has proven to be a skillful "horse" who carries the burden of the Lord very effectively. She is so effective in reach the lives of others with the powerful love of Jesus, because she always put Him first. She loves Him above all others, and her love for Him—being drawn to Him—is what empowers her to love others and to spend herself in utilizing her gifts, talents, and abilities.

"Your cheeks are lovely"

The Bridegroom begins to talk about her emotions in the next verse.

Your cheeks are lovely with ornaments (v 10).

The Lord designed you and I to be emotional beings, and that is what this verse is speaking about. The "cheeks" throughout the Song speak of emotion. When you look at somebody's cheeks, you can usually tell if there is joy in their heart or if there is anger or sadness. Emotions are so often relayed through the cheeks, and the Bridegroom calls her emotions beautiful. Others may think you are strange when you express your emotions, but Jesus calls them beautiful, because He is the Creator. The Bridegroom is seeing that her emotions are being restored and rekindled towards Him.

God is the most emotional being in the universe, and He is awakening our emotions by touching us with the emotions He has in His heart for us. We are told to love God, love ourselves, and love others with all our heart, mind, and emotions. The reason God instructs us to love in this way is because that's the way He loves us. He loves us with His mind; His thoughts about us are always full of love. He loves us with all His heart, and He loves us with all His emotions.

I have discovered in my life as a Christian that many people, myself included, have a difficult time connecting with their emotions, or letting God or others into their emotions. I was raised in a home with a loving mother and father, an older sister, a younger sister, and a younger brother. I loved my childhood, I loved my family, and we enjoyed being with one another. But I don't ever recall being encouraged to connect emotionally. The most prevalent emotions in our home were anger, frustration, laughter, and excitement, especially when engaging in athletic events. But intimacy, the sharing of feelings, or the communicating of emotions was something we didn't do. So I developed a lifestyle where I either disconnected with those emotions or pushed them deep inside.

When I met Jesus and invited Him into my heart at the age of 25, I found myself in an environment that was emotionally charged, and I began encountering people who freely displayed their emotions. I found it very difficult to navigate my way through such emotional expressions.

For about twenty years I was part of the Christian community, but hiding most of my emotions from God and from people, until I had an experience one Sunday morning in our church, which started the process of transforming this area. I was worshipping in front of the platform with my good friend, Keith, right next to me. This friend of mine has no issue connecting with his emotions. He is a very demonstrative man and he was loudly expressing his love to the Lord with a lot of body movement. At some point I turned toward him and in my mind I was thinking, *Dude, I'm standing right next to you, and I'm not manifesting. I'm not yelling out loud.*

The moment I said that, I heard a voice in my mind say, "That's right, you're not . . . and that's too bad. Because I am taking Keith to places in the heart of My emotions and love that he has never experienced before. He is sensing and feeling Me in new ways physically, mentally, and emotionally. That is the reason he is responding so demonstratively. It's too bad you have chosen to level off."

Two days later I was having coffee with one of our students from the supernatural school who is also very much in touch with his emotions. He was even slightly crying because his coffee was too hot that morning. So I asked him about his emotions and how he was able to so easily connect with them, and he told me his story.

At the conclusion, he asked me if I wanted to know about my struggle with my emotions. I jokingly said, "No, because I am the teacher and you are the student!" We both laughed. But then he suggested that each time an emotion would arise within me that I identified and felt safe with, I would connect with that emotion. But any emotion that rose up within me that I did not recognize or that I did not feel safe with, I would immediately ward off by telling a joke. The moment he said that, I told a joke. It was then I realized I had an issue that I needed to confront.

After leaving that meeting, I had a conversation with the Lord where I opened my heart, my mind, and my emotions, and invited Jesus to touch me. He responded very quickly to my request, and I discovered feelings of joy, laughter, tenderness, tears, fears—all the emotions I had not allowed myself to engage with—begin to rise up within me and I responded to them. I began to understand that in His Presence I was safe to explore the emotions He created within me. I would be teaching and suddenly, tears would be filling my eyes. As a result of these encounters, I started to worship with a greater physical expression. I even began to dance a little in worship. I am not completely where I want to be in the development of encountering and releasing my emotions, but I am a lot further along than I was.

We were created as emotional beings, just like God, our Father. So all we have to do is open our emotions to Him and He will release the emotions He has for us, and the transformation begins.

Let me strongly encourage you to make a commitment to love God with *all* your emotions by opening your heart to allow Him to love you with all of His emotions. You will never be the same.

"With Ornaments"

*Your cheeks are lovely **with ornaments**.*[33]

Ornaments are created by the skillful work of an artist and they speak of our character. Jesus is the artist that has worked to beautify us. The Bridegroom saw those things in the Shulamite (and in us) that we are struggling with, but He also sees passion growing for Him deep within her.

"Chains of gold and studs of silver"

Your neck with chains of gold (v 10b).

The "chains of gold" speak of royal authority, for only a king in that time had chains of gold; they were very costly and most common people could not afford them.

The "neck" speaks symbolically of our will. The neck is what turns the head as it chooses which way to go—right or left. When a king triumphed over another nation, the conquering general put his foot over that defeated king's neck in an act of dominance.

We will make you ornaments of gold with studs of silver (v 11).

"Ornaments of gold" speak of divine character. The maiden will be Christ-like in her character. "Silver" speaks of redemption. She will be used to bring redemption to other people. She will be an ambassador of redemption and reconciliation.

---

[33]   v 10, emphasis added.

Ministry of Reconciliation

The Apostle Paul tells us that we have a ministry of reconciliation, defining all Christians with a role as an ambassador of reconciliation. An ambassador is an authorized representative.

> *Therefore, if anyone is in Christ, he is a new creation; old things have passed away; behold, all things have become new.*
>
> *Now all things are of God, who has reconciled us to Himself through Jesus Christ, and has given us the ministry of reconciliation, that is, that God was in Christ reconciling the world to Himself, not imputing their trespasses to them . . . (2 Corinthians 5:17-19).*

Right now, the whole world is reconciled to God. I am not saying the whole world is redeemed, but every person in the world is reconciled to God so that He is not counting their trespasses against them. We have to understand that God is not obsessed with sin, because it has already been resolved. When Jesus announced from the cross, "It is finished," He was talking about the sin issue. God is consumed with life, and His payment has already reconciled the world to God. That means that every pre-Christian you encounter has already been reconciled to God, and all they need to do is make it official by receiving the finished work of Jesus on the cross and inviting Him into their life. It is like having an unlimited dollar credit card, but you cannot use it until it is activated. Reconciliation activates redemption.

That's why we are not to judge or condemn anybody on this earth, because Jesus has been judged, and Jesus has been condemned, so we can let go of all our negative judgment. The One who is perfect has been judged. So anytime a word of judgment comes out of our mouth, we are completely undermining the sacrifice of the Lord Jesus Christ. There is just no place for judgment in the Body of Christ. There was Calvary, which was the judgment of sin on Jesus, and then there is the Day of Judgment, when all the books are opened. But between those two dates, all judgment has been suspended.

We are living in a prophetic season of grace, where miraculous salvations will take place every day because people are already reconciled to God in His heart.

> *And has committed to us the word of reconciliation (5:19b).*

That means every one on earth is a target for blessing, and God has given you and I the ministry of reconciliation.

> *Now then, we are ambassadors for Christ . . . (v 20).*

We are now ambassadors of a dimension of life that the world has never seen in its existence. We are ambassadors of a Kingdom that the world does not fully understand. We are the ambassadors of a nation of people so energized by love, so energized by mercy and grace and forgiveness, that we'll ruin anybody's appetite for sin.

So, what type of ambassador of the Kingdom of God are you? What are you an ambassador of? Unfortunately I see a high number of Christians who are ambassadors of negativity, or ambassadors of criticism and judgment. When we are ambassadors of the Kingdom and we are negative, critical, or judgmental, we are declaring this is what God is like, because I represent Him. Let's ask the Lord to forgive us of our critical spirit, get healed, and begin to be an authorized representative of a Kingdom that loves really well.

Reconciliation is a passion of God! In fact, it is such a passion of His that He seeks to share the work of reconciliation with us. His desire is that we would be as passionate about reconciliation as He is. God doesn't count people's sin against them, otherwise we wouldn't even be here today. Did you ever think of it like that? Walk down the street you live on and understand that every person on your block is already reconciled to God, and they simply need to know that good news. You could be the Ambassador of Heaven to notify them of this good news.

The "studs of silver" speak of redemption and reconciliation.

The Shulamite is reconciled and redeemed, and because of that, she will bring redemption to others.

"The King is at His table"

> While the King is at **His table**, my spikenard sends forth its fragrance. A bundle of myrrh is my beloved to me. . . . My beloved is to me a cluster of henna blooms . . . (1:12-14, emphasis added).
>
> As the king surrounded me, the sweet fragrance of my praise perfume awakened the night (v 12, TPT).

In these verses we have the second revelation of Jesus to the Shulamite. The "table" here is a picture of the cross. In 1 Corinthians 10:21, where Paul is teaching about communion, he speaks about the table of the Lord. The table of the Lord is a reference to the cross. The Lord is feeding the Shulamite's spirit on the revelation of who He is and what He did for her at Calvary. He wants her to know that out of this place of inexpressible love, and in the most brutal way imaginable, He was beaten and nailed to a cross, taking upon Himself all of her sins and failures. It was all for love . . . all for her . . .

> YOUR BRIDEGROOM IS PLANNING THE NEXT ENCOUNTER WITH YOU. YOU ONLY NEED TO RESPOND TO HIM.

When Jesus died on the cross, He died in my place—He died as me. When Jesus rose from the dead, He rose as me. For so long I heard that when the Father looks at me, He sees me through Jesus, and only because of that, He accepts me. It has not been that long since I realized that is not exactly correct. I mean, He put me into Christ, and He put Christ into me, and

I am seated in heavenly places in Christ—and that's all true. But when all that happened—when I was born again—I become a *new* creation, because Jesus died *as* me and He rose as me. His resurrection was *my* resurrection. I am a new creation, and so are you! So when the Father looks at you, it isn't that He looks at you in disgust and sees this weak, puny person that is covered over by Jesus. He doesn't look at you *through* Jesus; He looks at you as a new creation. He looks at you as a resurrected one . . . and that is the Good News.

"The sweet fragrance of my praise"

My spikenard sends forth its fragrance . . . (v 12b).

The sweet fragrance of my praise perfume awakened the night (v 12b, TPT).

The reality of what Jesus has done for the Shulamite because of His love rocks her to the core, and worship, praise, and adoration simply explodes out of her. As she feeds on everything Jesus has done for her, worship ascends effortlessly from her. It rises up as a spontaneous response from deep within her, which releases the songs of her heart as she experiences the depth of the love Jesus reveals to her.

Her perfume is released from the depths of her worship, and the fragrance of her perfume fills the atmosphere as the revelation of the cross begins to touch her heart. The depth of love and the radical sacrifice her Bridegroom made for her causes worship and praise to erupt from her and its fragrance ascend to God. That is exactly the picture of our worship. Each one of us has a fragrance, a wonderful perfume to share with our Beloved Jesus. When the aroma of our love, affection, and adoration rises to Him in worship, it comes right before Him in Heaven, and He breathes in the sweet-smelling sacrifice of our love. What a wonderful picture.

When you encounter love like that, when you receive the revelation of how deeply you are loved, worship is such an automatic response. We all worship at the level of our revelation.

If one desires an upgrade in worship, another encounter of the divine character of Jesus is all you need. Revelation is an invitation from the Holy Spirit to experience Jesus in a specific part of His nature. That fresh revelation of Jesus amps up your worship, and this is exactly what we see happening with the Shulamite here.

The Depth of Love

This kind of encounter with the depths of divine love not only happens in the spirit realm but is also manifested in the natural. For instance, when people step into your life at critical moments of need and love you sacrificially where it is purely for your benefit, you bond together with a high level of love out of gratitude.

When I was newly saved, just a number of months living as a Christian, I was navigating my way through this walk with Jesus and was still carrying a lot of baggage from my former life that included alcohol abuse and violence. One afternoon I had gone to the Sacramento River and spent the day with friends drinking and just messing around. At some point in the evening we had a confrontation with another group of young men that escalated from words to a full-on fisticuff event with about eight or ten of us. I remember getting dropped off at my house and staggering to the backyard and collapsing into a fitful sleep.

I woke up the following morning, with blood on my shirt, cuts under both my eyes, and one swollen-shut black eye. I also awakened to my head resting in the lap of my father-in-law, Cliff, who was crying and declaring over me, "If you do not stop this lifestyle, you will die."

I wish I could say that this was the first time something like this had occurred, but it wasn't. This kind of activity was becoming more and more common in my life. But Cliff, standing with me in the middle of yet another catastrophic failure, touched my heart in very powerful ways. He did not abandon me, though it would have been justified. Time and time again, Cliff was there, pouring out his love, believing in me, just being there for me, and it caused such a depth of love to well up in my heart for him.

I'll say it again: we love at the level of our revelation. My father-in-law, Cliff, demonstrated a deep love and value for me; it was a determination to stand steadfast and love someone who failed in the same area over and over, again and again. For certain, this level of love seems to be fading fast in the world today, and sadly, in the Body of Christ as well.

That evening, I had the first of many profound encounters with the Lord, and I owe that to Cliff, to whom I will be forever grateful. As I was on my knees before the Lord, the room was suddenly filled with a heavy fog. I could not see it, but I could feel it, and this incredible terrorizing fear caused me to fall upon my face. At the same time, however, there was an overwhelming sense of safety and love. I had never experienced anything like that before. The atmosphere was so thick with the Presence of God, and then I heard the voice of the Lord. It was not audible, but it was loud and clear in my spirit. What a wonderful experience.

I'm so thankful for fathers who will stand with us right on through to the much-needed breakthrough in our lives.

The Worship Response

When you receive a revelation of how deeply you are loved, it transforms you from the inside out, and causes you to respond with such gratitude and love. In the same way, God's demonstration of love and goodness, along with a fresh revelation of how much we are worth to Him, causes a deep spiritual response of thanksgiving and worship. We cannot help ourselves when we experience fresh waves of His manifested love in our lives in multiple ways. Genuine worship is the only response.

In the book of Revelation, we have a picture of worship in Heaven.

> Before the throne there was a sea of glass, like crystal. And in the midst of the throne, and

around the throne, were four living creatures full
of eyes in front and in back (4:6).

Around God's throne we see some pretty strange creatures that are completely covered with eyes. In fact, their whole body is covered with eyes. My friend, Dan McCollam, says because these creatures have eyes on every part of their body, they have unlimited perspective, which means, that in every position they find themselves, they behold a fresh revelation of the glory of God. In verse 8, we are told they never rest day or night, they never take a break, and they don't get tired or bored. The reason is because every time they make another cycle around the throne, with all those eyes fixed on the One seated on the Throne, they get another revelation of who He is. They see something about Him they have never seen before, and the automatic response is one of worship, where they declare, "Holy, holy, holy!" That is the only appropriate response!

The Shulamite is also getting another revelation of the passion of her Bridegroom. She's getting another revelation of what He has done for her out of His heart of love, and the revelation prompts another eruption of praise, worship, and adoration.

There are a couple of interesting verses in Psalm 145.

Every day [with its new reasons] will I bless You
[affectionately and gratefully praise You]; yes,
I will praise Your name forever and ever (vs 2,
AMPC).

Great is the Lord and highly to be praised; and
His greatness is [so vast and deep as to be]
unsearchable [incomprehensible to man] (vs 3,
AMP).

Every day, there are new reasons to bless and praise the Lord because His greatness is so vast and so deep that we will never be able to search it all.

In John 4, Jesus is speaking with a woman who has some questions about worship styles. She wanted to know which style is the correct style, and Jesus answered her with something like, "You Samaritans do not know who you are worshiping; you do not comprehend the one you are worshiping. But we worship who we know; we worship out of a place of knowing—from a place of revelation.[34]

And He follows that up by saying:

> Yet a time is coming and has now come when the true worshipers will worship the Father in the Spirit and in truth, for they are the kind of worshipers the Father seeks (v 23, NIV).

Worshiping in spirit and in truth means to worship with revelation of who He is, and with the revelation of what He has done for you on the cross. The Samaritan woman did not know where or how to worship because she did not know who to worship. But true worship comes out of revelation, and that's why it's important to continually press in to the Lord for more and more encounters with Him. You can only worship to the degree of your comprehension of who He is to you, and a fresh revelation of who the Lord is will always bring you to an upgrade of your worship.

The Bridegroom is revealing a new aspect of who He is to the Shulamite. He will continue to do so in the Song, and you will see her increasing in her worship anointing and release.

If we are not personally pursuing more of Him and spending quality time in His Presence—beholding Him, encountering Him in His Word, and hanging out in the Holy Spirit—we will discover that our worship times seem to be going to the same place over and over again. That may be a great place for you at present, but if you never move from there, you can level off in your worship experience and expression and end up bored. You may have reached a great place of thanksgiving, a great place of celebration, and find that it's a comfortable place for you, but there's more! The Holy Spirit desires to lead you into the "more" of fresh encounters and experiences with Him.

_____

[34] Based on John 4:22.

The Fragrance of Christ

Jesus is giving the Shulamite a revelation of Himself on the cross, and this revelation releases an upgrade in worship and she releases a new fragrance of worship. The New King James Version uses the word "spikenard." This was a costly fragrance imported from India enclosed in alabaster boxes and used only for special occasions to anoint guests. When the Shulamite realized the cost that Jesus paid for her, the automatic response is to break open her own sealed alabaster box and "waste" her life's savings in an extravagant worship expression upon Him. She releases the fragrance of costly worship.

When you find yourself embraced in this kind of love, there comes a deep passionate sense of thanksgiving that rises up from within you—a gorgeous fragrance that ascends into the very throne room of God. The Lord enjoys the fragrance emanating from our spirit as we focus on the provision of His table.

As His people, we are the fragrance of Christ to God. This is manifest in those overflowing with gratitude and love. The Apostle Paul writes about this very thing.

> *Thanks be to God who . . . through us diffuses the fragrance of His knowledge in every place. For we are to God the fragrance of Christ among those who are being saved and among those who are perishing. To the one we are the aroma of death leading to death, and to the other the aroma of life leading to life. And who is sufficient for these things? (2 Corinthians 2:14-16)*

In Luke's Gospel, we see the story of a woman who walks into the house of Simon the Pharisee because she heard Jesus was in the house.[35] She broke the vial of perfume upon His feet. The costly perfume that filled the room speaks of the fragrance Jesus saw in her . . . love. This was an extreme act of worship that came right from the deepest part of this woman's heart of thanksgiving and brokenness. The spiritual perfume, her worship, deeply touched the heart of Jesus. This

---

[35] See Luke chapter 7.

is emotion expressed. So often we allow issues like, fear of man, what others will think of us, or some type of religious spirit of conformity or dignity to rob us of the opportunity to release our raw passion with all its holy emotions.

Determine to love God and pour out your fragrant worship with all of its demonstrative expressions. Your Bridegroom is planning the next encounter with you. You only need to respond to Him drawing you into the secret place of His presence.

"Bridegroom Encounters" Prayer

Father, we are asking that You increase our capacity to receive more of the Spirit in our life. Fill us to overflowing, Lord. We want to be a people wholly filled and flooded with God Himself.

Make this your prayer:

Holy Spirit, You are so present with me even as I am reading these words, and I appreciate the reality that You never leave me nor forsake me. I so love hanging out with You every moment of the day. You are so refreshing to my soul. You always bring such energy, a zeal, a passion, and fresh levels of excitement to my life. I pray for a deeper release of extreme joy and enthusiasm that would wash all over me and through me.

You amaze me, Lord, and I love You so much. I love the way You make Yourself at home in my heart. I love the way You lead me to Jesus. I love the way You show me the Father. I love the way You love others through me. I love the joy You explode within my heart and I love the passion for life You have birthed within me. I just love the way You love me. I love the way You love me even when I'm not having a good day. I love the way You love me even when I fail. Thank You for always loving me.

I devote my heart to worship You with everything within me. Amen.

ACTIVATION #6
Bridegroom Encounters

As part of this activation, I want to recommend that you **read Revelation 4** where we have a picture of worship in Heaven as all of Heaven beholds the one upon the Throne. Likewise, as you behold God, we will always discover something new of Him. The Amplified version of Psalm 145:2-3 says this:

> *Every day [with its new reasons] will I bless You [affectionately and gratefully praise You]; yes, I will praise Your name forever and ever (v 2, AMPC).*

> *Great is the Lord and highly to be praised; and His greatness is [so vast and deep as to be] unsearchable (v 3, AMP).*

Every day there are new reasons to bless and praise the Lord because His greatness is so vast and so deep we will never be able to search it all.

Activation

Put on some worship music. As you worship the Lord, behold Him just like the creatures circling around the throne. Have an expectation God wants to encounter your heart and reveal new facets of Himself to you. Be aware of your response of worship and worship Him at the level of that revelation with abandon. Expect your worship to go to a whole new level.

Record in your journal what you have encountered and how it is transforming your life.

Prayer:

> Holy Spirit, as I worship, adore, and exalt You, I ask that You inhabit my praise. Capture and captivate my heart as I worship You. In Jesus' name, amen.

SEVEN

Revelation of the Cross

> *My beloved is to me a sachet of*
> *myrrh resting between my breasts.*
> *My beloved is to me a cluster of*
> *henna blossoms from the vineyards*
> *of En Gedi. How beautiful you are,*
> *my darling! Oh, how beautiful! Your*
> *eyes are doves. How handsome you*
> *are, my beloved! Oh, how charming!*
> *And our bed is verdant. The beams*
> *of our house are cedars; our rafters*
> *are firs. (1:13-17, NIV).*

The Shulamite is being overwhelmed with revelation that is taking her into deep encounters with the furiously, passionate love of her Bridegroom Jesus. As she does, her automatic response is one of worship, adoration, and thanksgiving.

> *A sachet of myrrh is my lover, like a tied-up*
> *bundle of myrrh resting over my heart. He is like*
> *a bouquet of henna blossoms—henna plucked*
> *near the vines at the fountain of the Lamb. I will*

hold him and never let him part. Look at you, my dearest darling, you are so lovely! You are beauty itself to me. Your passionate eyes are like gentle doves. My beloved one, both handsome and winsome, you are pleasing beyond words. Our resting place is anointed and flourishing, like a green forest meadow bathed in light. Rafters of cedar branches are over our heads and balconies of pleasant-smelling pines. (1:13-17, TPT)

"A bundle of myrrh"

A bundle of myrrh is my beloved to me, that lies all night between my breasts (v 13).

A sachet of myrrh is my lover, like a tied-up bundle of myrrh resting over my heart (v 13, TPT).

Myrrh is mentioned eight times throughout the Song and is always associated with suffering. The "bundle of myrrh" is a beautiful picture of the cross.

In ancient times, myrrh was used as an embalming fluid, and as a sweet perfume, it symbolizes the sweetness that comes out of His death. Only the very wealthy could afford myrrh, the most expensive of fragrant ointments. A "bundle of myrrh," suggests something very costly, a perfect representation of the extreme extravagant act of God's love in Jesus' death on the cross.

The "bundle of myrrh . . . between my breasts" is a picture of what it means to meditate upon such truths and receive revelation. Wealthy women in the ancient world often wore a tied-up bundle (or large necklace) of myrrh sprigs to bed at night to provide a sweet fragrance as they slept. The Bride's statement that "myrrh lies all night between my breasts" is a declaration that she is beholding Him in her heart, and the revelation she receives causes her to "see" the extreme cost of suffering Jesus endured in His death on the cross. When the Shulamite declares her Beloved is a "bundle of myrrh", she's saying that she understands (at least in part) His great suffering—how He endured such tremendous anguish just for her. Thus, with an impassioned heart she's beginning to see her worth to Him, and His worth to her. With it comes the understanding of just how costly it will be to follow her King. As she meditates upon this all night long, the "bundle of myrrh" begins to deeply penetrate and permeate her whole being until His love transforms her.

One of the greatest statements about our value is what Jesus endured for us: God became a man of like passions and was crushed by the wrath of God for you and for me. This unfolding revelation of the depth of His suffering upon the cross then releases in her extravagant worship. As this reality hits the Shulamite, she determines that the suffering love of Jesus will be held close to her heart for the rest of her days, and worship erupts from within her: "The suffering You endured in dying on the cross for me is like an abundance of this costly myrrh."

With this she declares that no one else holds the greatest place of affections in her heart.

Progression of Inheritance Statements

The Holy Spirit is feeding this maiden at the table of Jesus, and as she meditates on His suffering, spontaneous worship gushes forth as she cries out, "My Beloved is to me . . . !"[36] That is such a significant statement, because it begins a succession of inheritance statements the Shulamite declares over the course of the Song, each one revealing a higher level of her ongoing maturity progress. At the beginning of her salvation, her life in God is all about her and what she can get out of it: all the blessings, and all the benefits of being in relationship with Jesus. Then she declares: "My Beloved is mine and I am His."[37] It is still her first, then Jesus, but with greater encounters, affirmational encouragement, and revelation, she adds a new dimension of His ownership over her life, "I am His." In 6:3,

---

[36] v 13.
[37] 2:16.

the Shulamite ultimately declares: "I am my Beloved's and He is mine." So there it is: Jesus is finally first, then her—a significant reversal from her first declaration. Finally in 7:10, the Bride says: "I am My Beloved's and His desire is towards me." Here she is declaring that it is all about Him: "I am His! I am His!" She is filled with the reality of her love toward Him and His total ownership of her as she finally discloses: "I belong to Him, and His desire is all I really care about."

At this point in the Song, the Shulamite is right in the midst of this journey toward spiritual maturity of the Lordship of Jesus.

Returning to verse 14, the maiden declares:

> *My beloved is to me a cluster of henna blooms in the vineyards of En Gedi (v 14).*

> *He is like a bouquet of henna blossoms—henna plucked near the vines at the fountain of the Lamb. I will hold him and never let him part (v 14, TPT).*

Henna is a shrub, a small little tree that has beautiful fragrant flowers on it. Here the Shulamite likens the pleasure of her Beloved to a cluster of fragrant henna in full bloom. It symbolizes that Jesus is not a burdensome God or a harsh taskmaster as the spirit of religion suggests. Rather, He is as delightful as a fragrant full-blooming henna bush. It's like she is saying, "Jesus is sweet . . . everything about Him is so pleasing to me." The fragrance of His love is so enjoyable, the Shulamite can but only worship Him.

Affirming Words of Love

With these declarations of the Shulamite, the Lord responds:

> *Behold, how beautiful you are, my darling, behold, how beautiful you are! Your eyes are dove's eyes (v 15, AMP).*

Look at you, my dearest darling, you are so lovely!
You are beauty itself to me. Your passionate eyes
are like gentle doves (v 15, TPT).

These words of Jesus are just stunning. He doesn't just say, "You are lovely;" He says, "You are *so* lovely . . . beauty itself." What He's saying is: "You are so beautiful . . . you are My love. You look so good to Me . . . I really like you." Over and over and over He speaks that to our heart. As the Shulamite hears these words again and again, she is coming to understand that she really is His favorite. Eight times in the Song the Bridegroom describes His beloved maiden as "beautiful" or "lovely".

The Bridegroom is desperately trying to get us to upgrade our image of who He is and our value to Him. He needs to break the lie of the enemy that keeps us locked in that place of, "I am dark," so that we don't ever believe His heart of love for us to be able to say, "I am lovely in God's eyes." We have a natural religious resistance to this truth. Even though we love the idea of it, it is still too difficult for us to grasp and take to heart. It is really critical that the Shulamite accept the reality of the truth that she is, indeed, beautiful to Him before she is able to progress any further. We must come to that place where we can say from the core of our being with sincerity: "I am beautiful to You, Lord." It sounds so good, but it lives in the heart with a lot of difficulty. We are too convinced that our sins and failures are what dominate the mind and heart of God, when in reality, He is focused on our heart that is determined to love, serve, and please Him all of our lives. It's very difficult when we always feel such guilt over the wrong things we've done, and then when we hear that we are beautiful to God, we say, "Yeah, well, I doubt that is true for me . . . especially now. Look at what I did!"

This is something that only God Himself can reveal to you, and He will—until you understand. We only need to hear His affirming words again and then make a choice to believe Him from our hearts. Only then are we able to progress to the next level of maturity.

Success is Measured by Faithfulness

Remember this: God never measures success; He measures faithfulness. To illustrate this, consider the life of Ezekiel. God tells Ezekiel that He is commissioning him as a prophet to the nations by sending him out with words of warning. However, He also tells Ezekiel that the people He is sending him to will not listen to one thing he says. In fact, they will *reject* everything he prophesies. For over twenty years Ezekiel faithfully gives out the prophetic word of the Lord to these nations knowing full well that they will not listen or respond appropriately.

So then, how do we measure Ezekiel's success with virtually no verifiable proof that his message bore fruit? His success was measured by his faithfulness to the Lord in obedience.

God doesn't measure success by results, either. He measures it by the faithfulness we display day in, and day out, week after week, month after month, year after year. So few of us really understand the incredible power in being faithful to what we know we are called to do. Allow the Lord to speak to you about the faithfulness He sees in your heart. It's there. He sees your desire to please Him, and any failure in your life has not caused Him to negate His feelings of love towards you by any means.

Faithful Love

You have heard this before, but here's a reminder: there is nothing you can do to cause the Lord to love you more than He does right now, nor is there anything you could do that would cause Him to love you less than He does right now. It would be really helpful, therefore, if we would abandon all activities that attempt to win His love and approval. God's faithful love is unconditional, so there is absolutely **nothing** that could ever separate us from His love. The Apostle Paul assures us of that.

> So now I live with the confidence that there is
> nothing in the universe with the power to separate
> us from God's love. I'm convinced that his love will
> triumph over death, life's troubles, fallen angels,
> or dark rulers in the heavens. There is nothing

in our present or future circumstances that can weaken his love.

There is no power above us or beneath us—no power that could ever be found in the universe that can distance us from God's passionate love, which is lavished upon us through our Lord Jesus, the Anointed One! (Romans 8:38-39, TPT)

Here's my own version of these verses:

Nothing in the universe has the power to diminish His love toward us. Troubles, pressures, and problems are unable to come between us and heaven's love. What about persecutions, deprivations, dangers, and death threats? No, for they are all impotent to hinder omnipotent love. Nothing in the universe has the power to diminish His love towards us.

You see? There is nothing in Heaven or Hell that would ever cause Him to renegotiate His covenant of love with you. So it would be really helpful if we stopped beating ourselves up over sin. Remember, God already dealt with our sin at the cross; you're forgiven. It's **all forgiven** . . . and forgotten. The power of the enemy's lies accusing you has been broken by the blood of Jesus that cleanses you. Time to move forward into what He's **doing** and not back to what you did. He's forever freed you from the weight of all of that.

God's **present** and **future** focus is on the provision for all you need to live an **abundant life** in great joy. Make that your focus, too, and listen for His tender words of faithful love affirming you today.

"You have dove's eyes"

After affirming the Shulamite again, the Bridegroom tells her the qualities He loves about her:

You have dove's eyes (1:15).

Your passionate eyes are like gentle doves (1:15, TPT).

There are a number of things that He is saying to her here. First of all, the "dove" is a picture of the Holy Spirit throughout Scripture, beginning in Genesis with Noah. He is allowing you to see into the Spirit by giving you His eyes of revelation, wisdom, and knowledge; the Holy Spirit is consuming you.

> A FRESH REVELATION OF THE CROSS AND HIS EXTRAVAGANT LOVE UNRAVELS OUR TIDY LITTLE WORLD AND LEAVES US SIMPLY UNDONE.

I have learned that doves do not have peripheral vision; they can only see straight ahead, so they don't get distracted by what's all around them. A dove also has another unique dimension; they are very loyal and mate with only one its entire life. When its mate dies, it does not mate again. The Lord is saying to the Shulamite, "I see you as loyal. You have eyes only for Me . . . your heart is wholly devoted to Me. I love that about you."

The Shulamite is still very early in her journey and has much more processing to go. She is still going to fail along the way by making some poor choices (as we'll see before the end of the Song), of which her Bridegroom is aware. Yet, it's as if this incredible God says to her: "You are the one I love . . . Your spirit totally gets it . . . and now your mind is starting to get it. I see that your image and identity of Me is growing, and so I am going to help you upgrade the image you have of yourself. You are beginning to believe you are beautiful in My sight; you see that I not only love you, but I *like* you. You see that you have weak flesh—you are "dark"—but you also have a great willing spirit. You are beautiful to Me, My love!"

The Dance of Divine Romance

At this point, the Shulamite is so overwhelmed, she gives a three-fold response to this truth about her beauty as He just described to her.

> *My beloved one, both handsome and winsome, you are pleasing beyond words. Our resting place is anointed and flourishing, like a green forest meadow bathed in light. Rafters of cedar branches are over our heads and balconies of pleasant smelling pines. (1:16-17, TPT).*

The Shulamite then begins a dance of divine romance. She starts out by talking about her total fascination with Jesus. There is an exchange of deep affection that is going on back and forth between them. They are communicating their love to one another with a spontaneous flow of His heart toward her and her heart toward Him. This is Holy Spirit-birthed romance at its finest. The Holy Spirit loves it when we adore Jesus, and at the same time allows us to experience the deep adoration and love of the Lord. God, the Holy Spirit, is empowering the Shulamite to feel His love for her, and He is empowering her to love Him back. She is feeling God's enjoyment of her and she's releasing her enjoyment of Him. That's what's happening here.

You are handsome . . . (v 16).

The Shulamite is telling Him, "I love you . . . I'm amazed that You love me like You do. I am fascinated with You. I love walking with You, I love living with You . . . I just love being with You, Lord."

She proclaims to Jesus, "You are handsome, my Beloved." In other words, "You are beautiful, God, and I love You." The more of Jesus' beauty she sees, the more she loves Him, and the more spiritual pleasures she experiences in her walk with Him.

Abiding Brings Rest

Our couch is green (v 16, YLT).

The Shulamite lays down to rest on a "luxuriant couch," a bed made of the meadow grasses. Beds and couches speak of deep places of rest and stillness. The Shulamite is at a renewed place of hope in her life. She understands that abiding in Jesus' love brings a refreshing rest and confidence in her life. Her heart is overwhelmed with His love and she realizes He has become her safe and secure hiding place.

Green always means abundance. The Bride is saying, "I am experiencing deep, deep rest here in this place." She has lived in such chaotic unrest for so long, but now she is immersed in the endless *shalom* of God. Notice that she declares it to be, "our bed." Luxuriant fertile fields with dense growth were often referred to as "green" meadows. The couch-bed of the Spirit of God is ample, verdant, and teeming with life, leading us into a season of abounding refreshment, relaxation, and quietude.

The Shulamite speaks of the deep, growing intimacy between her and the Bridegroom:

The beams of our houses are cedars, our rafters of firs . . . (v 16, YLT)

Beams and rafters provide the structure for a house, which are hidden. Cedar and fir were the most permanent, expensive, beautiful, and fragrant wood used as building material. In King Solomon's day, cedar and fir trees were used in building the temple so that its structure would not decay. Wood in the temple is a picture of humanity. Jesus paid the full price as the ultimate act of His immeasurable love for all humanity upon a cross made of wood. Our hearts can only respond in return with worship and love.

The Shulamite is still dwelling in this secret place of Jesus' Presence, choosing to abide with Him in an eternal house of intimacy, safety, protection, and security. It has become her secret hiding place of rest and confidence.

His love for us is so outrageous, so stunning, that it almost borders on insanity. It's nearly impossible to articulate such love. A fresh revelation of the cross and His extravagant love manifested to our hearts unravels our tidy little world and leaves us simply undone.

I have determined to abide there.

"Revelation of the Cross" Prayer

Holy Spirit, the revelation of the cross has impassioned my heart and causes it to erupt in worship. My greatest heart cry is for a greater intimacy with You, and I know You put it there, Lord, and I thank You for that.

God is saying to you:

Beloved, a wide-open space is before you—a life-giving place of rest and refreshment. You have this brilliant opportunity to simply step into My heart and cross over the borders of your previous territory and step deeper into the land of My promises.

Take My hand, and let's walk together into that place.

ACTIVATION #7
Revelation of the Cross

With the greatest demonstration of God's love, we need to let the truth of His message penetrate our mind, our emotions, and our soul. Hear His beautiful words of love and affirmation to you and take them to heart.

ACTIVATION: A Declarative Prayer

Take time to pray this as a declarative prayer out loud and engage with the Holy Spirit. Let the power of this truth penetrate your heart and mind for its full transformational effect.

> Father, thank You for a fresh revelation of the cross and all You have provided for me. You amaze me; You astonish me, Lord. Of all the places You could have lived, you chose to live in me. Thank You for choosing me, for valuing me, for seeing something in me that perhaps no one ever saw. And thank You, that I am learning to see that in myself as well. I am beginning to perceive myself in an entirely new way, and I am learning an entirely new language when I talk with myself about me because of what You have said about me—the person you see me to be.
>
> Thank You, Lord, for Your love and eternal faithfulness towards me. It is transforming my life, and continues to transform me.

Make these declarations aloud:

I am being transformed by Your love, God.

You are faithful towards me every single day.

I am thinking about myself in a whole new way; I no longer view myself as being rejected or being "less-than", but I now live in a joyful quiet confidence that **I AM MY BELOVED'S AND HE IS MINE.**

You are teaching me to live every day with **real joy**, with an expectation of Your goodness washing over me, and with a confidence that **I am truly the Beloved of my Father in Heaven** whose heart is ravished over me.

I am learning how to walk in the tremendous **favor of God**. And the biggest question I will ask today is: "What will I do with all the favor that the Lord is bestowing upon me?"

Thank You for Your love that is so wonderful, so incredible, so amazing, it causes me to **live astonished**. My prayer today is that You would grant me the grace to live a life that is **full of wonder and astonishment.**

Thank You, Lord.

Amen.

EIGHT

Our Truest Identity

I am the rose of Sharon, and the
lily of the valleys (Song 2:1).

I am truly His rose, the very theme of
His song! I'm overshadowed by His
love, growing in the valley! (2:1, TPT)

With this verse, the Shulamite is declaring her truest identity by referring to herself as, "the rose of Sharon." In poetic language she declares herself to be the inheritance of Jesus. At one time she declared she was unworthy of His love, but now she understands that she has fully won His heart and that she is His beloved rose, a lily of the valley. In this exchange with the Lover of her soul, she discovers a deeper dimension of who she is, and makes her second confession: "I am a beautiful rose to Him." Her first confession was, "I am dark, but I am lovely." This is definitely progress in accepting her identity as the Lord sees her.

The Rose of Sharon

The rose of Sharon is a low-lying meadow flower that is extremely fragrant. It symbolizes that the beloved one is the most intoxicating and the most beautiful rose of them all. There is only one rose Jesus longs for, and she is the one—the rose that exhilarates and captures His heart. So the maiden declares, "I am *the* rose—the inheritance the Father has promised His Son." The Shulamite is finally discovering aspects of her truest identity of how she is known in Heaven. She is beginning to understand her true identity. This identity statement has gone up a significant level from, "I look good to You," and "You like me."

This is what I mean when I say this journey is a progression; it's an ongoing process. Because of the maiden's continual encounters with a God whose heart is ravished over her, she is coming to know that *she* is the inheritance the Father promised Jesus.

Declaring Our True Identity

The Shulamite then declares what she sees in her Bridegroom as her own identity: "I am the beautiful lily of the valley." Lilies always represent purity, and valleys are the low and dark places of this fallen world. What the maiden is saying is: "When God looks over all the earth, He sees only one pure thing of beauty in the dark valleys of this world, and that is His redeemed people." She says, "I understand that I am the choicest lily of the valley—His redeemed one. I am a bright light in a dark world."

The Shulamite knows that all the darkness in her heart is not entirely gone. She understands that she is still very immature and developing, but she does not focus on this negative. She feels clean, innocent, and pure before Jesus. She is making a prophetic declaration that is not yet her reality. She is saying, "I am the rose—the one He waits for, the one who intoxicates Him. I am the lily that is clothed in purity, faith and trust, and abandonment."

She's beginning to step into agreement with her truest identity as the Beloved bride of Jesus. The Shulamite is making good progress in this process, because prophetic identity—stepping into your truest identity—is all about the process.

It is discovering who God says we are in Scripture and who Heaven says we are. We are discovering who God says we are by hearing the Holy Spirit. And, we are hearing who we really, truly are through the prophetic ministry as the Lord speaks out our identity through others.

Everyone has an identity in Heaven, and Heaven sees you in a very specific way. But here's the thing: when we hear our truest identity spoken out, we have a really hard time believing it usually. The problem for us is that when God shows us how we are known in Heaven, we have issues with it, because we try to take it on in our natural identity. Now our spirit believes it and knows it to be true, but our mind begins to talk us out of it.

We see that with Moses. When God called Moses and told him he was raising him up as a deliverer, he responded with his natural identity:

- "I cannot do that."
- "I'm not capable."
- "I am not able to properly speak to these people."
- "I don't have the ability to lead these people."

All of it was rooted in his natural identity. But God came and spoke to his **truest** identity—how he was known in Heaven: a Spirit-empowered deliverer. Even though he didn't feel very powerful, God told Moses that He was going to make him like God to Pharaoh. In order for that to happen, however, Moses needed to see himself as Heaven viewed him.

A focus on our natural inabilities is common to us all, but this has the potential to halt the forward momentum of our process-journey. It really takes a Holy Spirit intervention with a heavenly revelation to see it fully for what it is and walk courageously in that revelation.

Gideon

Another biblical character who focused on his natural inabilities was Gideon. God showed up one day and announced to him: "You are a mighty warrior." We read in Judges that Gideon was sitting in a winepress threshing wheat. Life was really pressing in on Gideon and he was really feeling that pressure. When we are under pressure, we have a tendency to whine. Gideon had very low self-esteem, and when you are in that two-fold pressure cooker, you start to *whine*, "Oh, poor me!" When the squeeze is on us from every side, self-pity can really take hold. So here's Gideon in the "whine-press," and then an angel shows up and they have this conversation.

> *And the Angel of the LORD appeared to him, and said to him, "The LORD is with you, you mighty man of valor!"*
>
> *Gideon said to Him, "O my lord, if the LORD is with us, why then has all this happened to us? And where are all His miracles which our fathers told us about, saying, 'Did not the LORD bring us up from Egypt?' But now the LORD has forsaken us and delivered us into the hands of the Midianites"* (6:12-13).

Don't you love this? God shows up with one agenda: to get Gideon to see himself from Heaven's perspective and change his identity from the natural to a heavenly one. And Gideon— whining and complaining—doesn't even flinch while the angel is standing there **talking** to him! He's really feeling the pressure of life right now—I get it; he's pressed on every side and it's producing a pitiful whine. He can't even hear what the Lord is saying, and he even tries to change the subject.

But God totally ignores these attempts. Have you noticed that about God? He's got something on His mind for you . . . He's speaking to you about an important issue, and you desperately want to change the subject. But it's not going to happen. God totally ignores all of Gideon's whining negativity. He doesn't say, "Yeah, dude, I know . . . You have issues. Life's so tough." God never gets down to our level of complaining or gives it a response.

Instead God says, "Ahhh . . . just forget all that, Gideon.

I am here to tell you who you *really* are. In Heaven you are known as a 'mighty warrior' . . . a 'mighty man of valor' . . ."

In this earthly realm, you can become known as a mighty man because you do all kinds of "mighty" things: you win battles, you show tremendous courage, and you build a reputation as a mighty man. In the Kingdom of God, however, you are known as a mighty man because God *says* you are a mighty man. That's how you are known in Heaven. This is your authentic true identity, because the Kingdom of God is based on your God-given identity, not on what you do . . . not by how well you perform. In the kingdom of man you are defined by your performance. In the Kingdom of God you perform by how you are defined.

When Heaven confronts us with our true identity, we are going to have difficulties with it because it contradicts who we think we are in the natural. In the kingdom of man, you only become something by what you do, and then you have a performance-based identity. In the Kingdom of God, you have an identity based on who God says that you are, and you do because you are. When Gideon stepped into the person God said He was—a mighty man with valor full of Heaven's favor—he delivered his nation.

Aligning with our true heavenly identity is a huge issue on the heart of the Father.

The Refreshing of the Lord

> *Like an apple tree among the trees of the wood, so is my beloved among the sons. I sat down in his shade with great delight. And his fruit was sweet to my taste (2:3).*

> *My beloved is to me the most fragrant apple tree—he stands above the sons of men. Sitting under his grace-shadow, I blossom in his shade, enjoying the sweet taste of his pleasant, delicious fruit, resting with delight where his glory never fades (v 3, TPT).*

The apple tree represents that which refreshes, and we see

it again in the fifth verse of this chapter, where the Bride makes a request of her Bridegroom.

Refresh me with apples, for I am lovesick (v 5).

There is only One who refreshes the human spirit at the highest level. When we receive the revelation of Jesus as an apple tree—the primary source that satisfies our heart—then we seek Him with all our heart.

I sat down in his shade with great delight, and his fruit was sweet to my taste (v 3).

Notice it is "his shade." The Shulamite is not standing on her own religious efforts. She didn't produce the shade by anything she did—by her own labors. She stands in *His* shade. She is not striving here in this place. She is not trying to motivate God to like her through her good works. She is *sitting* down in His shade. It's a place of rest and refreshment.

"His Fruit"

His fruit was sweet to my taste.

Notice as well that it is "his fruit" that she was enjoying. Paul writes about the fruit of the Spirit.

> But the fruit of the Spirit is love, joy, peace, longsuffering, kindness, goodness, faithfulness, gentleness, self-control. Against such there is no law. And those who are Christ's have crucified the flesh with its passions and desires. If we live in the Spirit, let us also walk in the Spirit (Galatians 5:22-23).

Again it is the fruit of His Spirit, and He is the One responsible for producing it in our lives. It does not say "the fruit of a disciplined life," although having a life of discipline will certainly help you partner with the Holy Spirit in developing His fruit. It does not say it is "the fruit of all our hard work," or "the fruit of a mature Christian." It actually says "the fruit of the Spirit." It is not our responsibility to produce the fruit, because it is not ours. We are not producing the fruit; the Spirit is the producer of the fruit. If we *could* produce it, we would not need the Spirit.

Look at the Amplified version of Galatians 5:22:

> *But the fruit of the [Holy] Spirit [the work which His presence within accomplishes] is love, joy (gladness), peace, patience (an even temper, forbearance), kindness, goodness (benevolence), faithfulness (AMPC).*

The New Century translation reads like this:

> *But the Spirit produces the fruit of love, joy, peace, patience, kindness, goodness, faithfulness . . .*

The New Living Translation says:

> *But the Holy Spirit produces this kind of fruit in our lives: love, joy, peace, patience, kindness, goodness, faithfulness . . .*

It is obvious that the Spirit is the one who produces this fruit in us. Even though we don't produce it in our lives by our own efforts, we do have a responsibility to guard it, grow it, and protect it in our lives.

In John 15:5, Jesus tells us what fruit-bearing in the New Covenant is all about.

> *I am the vine, you are the branches. He who abides in Me, and I in him, bears much fruit; for without Me you can do nothing.*

The vine does not have to do anything to produce fruit except to stay connected to the branch. You stay connected to Jesus, you live in Him, abide in Him, and He produces the fruit in you. He is the life-giving substance flowing in and through you producing the fruit of His very nature within you.

It is really important that we abide in Him, because while it is good fruit, it develops in rough soil. Think about the fruit of patience. It is developed, matured, and strengthened in you when you find yourself in a circumstance or situation where you are anxious. How does the fruit of peace develop in you? When you are in a situation that challenges your peace. If you remain, abide, and stay in your spirit-man, yielding to the Holy Spirit, He will produce the fruit of patience in you. However, if you respond out of your own spirit and take the external circumstances on board in your soul, in your mind, and in your emotions, you will produce fruit evidenced by your choice, such as anxiety, worry, stress, and doubt.

If you use every opposition in your life as a vehicle to carry you into the Presence of God—into that internal castle of Him abiding within you—and you yield to the Holy Spirit, He will produce the fruit of joy, peace, patience, kindness, goodness, and self-control through you.

"House of Wine"

He brought me to the banqueting house, and his banner over me was love (2:4).

Suddenly, he transported me into his house of wine—he looked upon me with unrelenting love divine (2:4, TPT).

I love this vivid picture describing the Holy Spirit picking up His beloved one, carrying her into His "banqueting" hall—a "house of wine"—with the intention of overwhelming her with His unrelenting love where, once again, she will be intoxicated on the love of Jesus!

The Moffatt Translation paints a beautiful picture by calling this a "chamber of joy". I think "chamber of joy" really conveys God's intentions here. The maiden is transported into this palatial room of unbridled love raining down from the highest heights, its walls vibrating the rhythms of His passion—a virtual heavenly atmospheric joy-chamber. Wow. I can just imagine her being led by the Holy Spirit into the private chambers of His unrelenting passion, and seeing God's beloved people exuberantly dancing, singing, and shouting in response to such an outpouring of impassioned love.

184

One of the Hebrew words for "praise" is *halal*,[38] and it's used over 150 times in the Bible. There is no other word used as many times as this one particular word for "praise." *Halal* most vividly describes praise as: to "shine brightly;" to "make a show; to rant"; and "to rave foolishly", and "to go crazy for God". I think this pretty well describes what is going on in the King's "house of wine".

> WHEN HEAVEN CONFRONTS US WITH OUR TRUE IDENTITY, IT CONTRADICTS WHO WE THINK WE ARE IN THE NATURAL.

So the Shulamite is lovingly carried into that deliciously joyous environment. It is the atmosphere of the Kingdom of Heaven itself—singing, rejoicing, shouting, dancing—a jubilant celebration of its redeemed and lavishly loved-on citizens. The King is welcoming her into His world. He is letting her know: "This is where you belong; this is what you were created for. This is the place of favor, blessing, protection, and the place to receive the all-captivating, all-consuming love I have prepared especially for you."

Connecting to the Heart of God

The Holy Spirit is so passionate and so persistent in His efforts to connect your heart with the ardent love of Jesus. Revelation is to help us live with an experiential connection to the affections of the heart of God so we can truly know how He **feels** about us. When His passionate loves connects with our heart, it is so startling, so powerful, so captivating that you feel it throughout your whole being: physically, mentally, and emotionally. I am convinced that we humans are addicted to love. We would give anything to encounter such

---

[38] See *Strong's Hebrew Lexicon*, #H1984, *"halal"*.

authentic passionate love. When we have been hurt, offended, disappointed, we use those events to give up on love. But in the process, we also give up on hope, joy, and to some degree, passionate desire.

I read a wonderfully written book by Erwin McManus called, *Soul Cravings,* where he speaks about the human drive for love.

> *We cannot live unaffected by love. We are most alive when we find it, most devastated when we lose it, most empty when we give up on it, most inhumane when we betray it, and most passionate when we pursue it. The human story seems more driven by the insanity of love than the survival of the fittest.*[39]

The Shulamite found herself in such a place where she had a powerful need to belong, to be accepted, and be connected to passionate authentic love. The Lord knew that, and He began the healing process by releasing waves of His pure love into her heart, which transformed her.

I want you to know, dear reader, that Jesus is romancing you. The Holy Spirit longs to pick you up and carry you into His house of wine. It is His personal invitation for you to follow Him into a new revelation and fresh encounters with His intoxicating, unrelenting, unbridled love and joy. With it will come an understanding of your truest identity as Heaven knows you.

He is waiting for you there.

---

[39] McManus, Erwin. *Soul Cravings.* Published by Thomas Nelson/ Harper-Collins, 2008.

"Our Truest Identity" Prayer

> Father, thank You. I ask that You would continue to connect the reader with Your deep affections. Continue to encounter their heart and awaken it to Your healing love.

Pray this with me:

> I thank You, Father, that You are pursuing me, that You are after me, Lord, because not only do You love me, but You like me and You want to hang out with me. I invite You, Lord, to please come and touch me today. Come bless me and speak into my heart Your beautiful affirming truths that show me how You see me.

> Father, reveal my truest identity as Heaven sees me. Help me to walk in this with You.

> I am ready to run towards You afresh today, responding to the romancing drawing of Your Spirit, Lord. I am opening my heart and exploring this atmosphere of Your love—Your house of wine, Your chamber of joy. This place where you are leading me is a land full of joyous laughter and fruitfulness, and I am ready to run towards it and dwell there in it, abiding with You.

> Holy Spirit, teach me to receive. I've never lived in this kind of love before, so help me Holy Spirit, to see myself as Jesus sees me. Help me to receive this love that is so beautiful and incomprehensible. Strengthen me to receive this revelation today. May Your love continue to transform me and produce "His fruit"—the fruit of the Holy Spirit—in my life.

ACTIVATION #8
Our Truest Identity

Prayerfully read this word from the Lord and listen carefully as the Spirit loves on you. Record how His word and His love is transforming your heart.

> You are My beloved, and you occupy a high place in My affections.
>
> My intention is always that you will be the beloved of My heart. **Never** think of yourself outside of romance.
>
> One of the goals of your life should simply be to enjoy your encounters with My glory that leave you slack-jawed with astonishment, celebrating unashamedly out of thanksgiving—even dancing wildly as the citizens of the Kingdom of Heaven do.
>
> I am really stressing this to you, My beloved, because it has to be My perception of you that must govern your heart all the days of your life. My appraisal of you will make your heart glad and renew your mind.
>
> I have such a huge heart for you. I have this all-encompassing compassion for you. I see your struggles, I understand your weaknesses, but I want you to have an even greater understanding of My love, My grace, and My mercy than you do for your struggles. You see, in My great love for you, I have set aside an ocean of grace and peace for you to personally experience. Let this overwhelm you, for it is the only way you can understand Me. I always give much more than what is needed. I adore abundance. I love

outrageous grace. I AM the peace that passes all understanding.

Get this: **You** are **My** beloved, and as My beloved, it is your duty, your joy, and your delight to be overwhelmed by this love. You are dear to Me. I have pursued your heart, and now I seek to captivate you.

The more extravagantly you will allow yourself to receive My love, the more you will become My beloved; the stronger your passion for Me becomes, the more extravagantly I will receive it and respond.

Come up higher, beloved. Come up higher. Come to the place of your elevation. I am the One lifting you up. I am lifting you to new heights. Let go, and allow Me to take you there.

My indulgence is surrounding you right now.

You are the seed of Heaven, and I am planting you in the soil of My heartfelt indulgence, and watering the seed of your heart with passion. I shall give you all that you need to grow, to be fruitful, and to multiply.

I am releasing to you right now My romantic love. I have activated it in this place where you are at this moment. Allow it to touch you. Allow it to shape your destiny. Allow My romantic love to transform your heart.

Do **not** say, "I am not good enough . . . This is too much," because I say you are My love and I will not be denied, and I will deny you nothing. So rise up, My beloved, and see yourself as the supreme object of My affection. For I have set My heart on you. I want to take your breath away.

Yes, you will be so astonished at this.

Understand that you are entering into this place by My divine permission, not your own performance.

The Father so wants you to get this . . .

That desperation in your heart for a deeper, abiding sense of His love—that hunger to experience a greater depth of His love, *all* that longing—I put that into your heart, says the Lord.

God is saying to you—

My longing, My passion, My desire as well . . . your longing for *Me*— is evidence of My *longing* for you, says the Lord.

Live before Me as someone who has outrageous blessing on them.

So, rise up and see yourself as My beloved. I'm speaking about *you* . . . Yes, *you* are the one. I have set My heart on *you*. I have set My heart so powerfully on *you*.

Expect My favor. I want to take your breath away. I want you to be astonished and live that way. I want you to be amazed. This is an affair of the heart that I am calling you to, so you must think from your heart, not your head.

And understand, beloved, you can only enter into the depths of My heart of affection by permission! It is never by *performance*. Walk towards Me—seeing, believing and yielding—and you *will* encounter My huge heart for *you*!

NINE

Waves of Refreshing

Sustain me with cakes of raisins,
refresh me with apples, for I am
lovesick.[40]

Revive me with your goblet of wine.
Refresh me again with your sweet
promises. Help me and hold me, for
I am lovesick! I am longing or more—
yet how could I take more?[41]

As we open this chapter, we see the Shulamite experiencing another wave of the passionate heart of Jesus. The Holy Spirit has allowed her to experience and encounter another chamber of His heart of love and she is being rocked to her very core.

She cries out, "Revive me again! Refresh me again! Hold me again! I am lovesick. I don't know how I could take any more, but I am hungry for more." That's the way of the Kingdom. In the Kingdom of God we eat, and then we are famished again. In

---

[40]   2:5.
[41]   2:5, TPT.

the world we get hungry, so we eat and we are filled up; but in the Kingdom we are hungry for more, and we partake of more, and it stimulates another level of hunger.

I have been at The Mission Church since 1999 where I am privileged to serve as a pastor. I did not assume my role until 2009, however, so I had a ten-year break between my previous pastoral position and the one I stepped into. When I resigned my pastoral position in 1999, I was physically, mentally, emotionally, and spiritually bankrupt. I needed a break, and I needed some serious healing. The Holy Spirit ushered me into a five-year season of what my friend Graham Cooke labels a time of "hiddenness and manifestation." This is a time where the Lord brought me close to Himself and released over me wave after wave after wave of His refreshing love, joy, and Presence. It was an extended season where He simply loved on me and let the refreshing gentle winds of His Spirit wash away my weariness and heal the depths of my pain and woundedness. Because the Lord went so deep to heal wounds, hurts, and offenses, I really needed this long period of time to access His intensive love treatments. Even today, I discover that this place of hiddenness and manifestation is readily available to me whenever I need the refreshing wind and waves of His Spirit to wash over me once again.

"Lovesick Longings"

The Bride's cry for more—to be revived again—reminds me of Psalm 84:

> How lovely is your dwelling place, LORD Almighty!
> My soul yearns, even faints, for the courts of the
> LORD; my heart and my flesh cry out for the living
> God (v 1, NIV).

This Psalm was penned by the sons of Korah, who were a group of priests under the Old Covenant on a passionate pilgrimage into the Presence of God. They were so driven in their desire for His Presence, they literally felt that passion in their physical bodies. These priests were not "born again" because the blood of Jesus had not yet been shed. They did not have the

Holy Spirit *in* them, but they definitely had the Spirit *on* them and all over them. Reading on in the next verse, it says:

> *So deep within me are these lovesick longings,*
> *desires and daydreams of your Presence of living*
> *close to You, living in deep intimacy with you*
> *that when I am near You my heart and my soul*
> *sing with worship and joyful songs and my body*
> *aches for you (v 2, TPT).*

That is passion and it is the same cry of the Shulamite with her request: "Revive me! . . . refresh me . . . help me . . . hold me . . . for I am lovesick. I am longing for more." The dictionary defines the word "passion" as: "a strong and barely controllable emotion." I would say that definition describes these priests. They are declaring that their hearts are set on pilgrimage—a journey to go deeper. They are stating, "God, I have set the course for the remainder of my life to know You intimately, to worship You only, to adore You, to have an intimate friendship with You . . . I'm so desperate for it, that I feel this ache for You in my spirit, my soul, and my body." Everyone who calls themself a Christian should have that same ongoing ache in their heart and soul as these guys. There should be a passion burning in all of us—a strong, barely controllable emotion—for the Presence of God. We were born to burn with a passion for God.

The Bridegroom's Embrace

> *His left hand is under my head, and his right*
> *hand embraces me (2:6).*

> *His left hand cradles my head while his right*
> *hand holds me close. I am at rest in this love (v*
> *6, TPT).*

The Shulamite understands God's twofold activity in her life: the right and left hand of God. The **left hand of God** speaks of the activity of God that we cannot see. It is under the head, therefore, it is out of view. The Lord does many things for us that we do not see: He withholds and releases many things to bless, provide, and protect us. He spares us from troubles that we are not ever aware of—the indiscernible. For example, He delivers and protects us from potential accidents and mishaps we could never prepare for ahead of time.

The **right hand of God** speaks of the visible (the discernible) activity of God. The idea is that Solomon stood in front of the Shulamite to embrace her. She could see and feel it. This speaks of the sweet, manifest presence of God that can be felt and discerned. At times, we feel our heart tenderized by the working of God's right hand.

Psalm 16:11 gives us a description of the right hand of God directly linked to His presence:

> In Your presence is fullness of joy; at Your right hand are pleasures forevermore.

In Psalm 48:10, we learn that by God's right hand, there is always victory and triumph. In 2 Corinthians 2:14, it says the Lord always leads us in triumph. Triumph is different than victory. In Colossians 2:15, we are told that Jesus disarmed *all* principalities and powers, and He made them a "public spectacle," triumphing over them at the cross. The word for "disarmed" that is used there is a military term. Look at this verse in *The Message Bible*:

> He [Jesus] stripped all the spiritual tyrants in the universe of their sham authority at the Cross and marched them naked through the streets (MSG).

This verse, and the image Paul portrayed here, would have been understood by those of the New Testament era. It is describing what happens at the end of a battle when the generals of both armies—the victorious army and the defeated army—would meet. The general of the defeated army would surrender his sword and all weapons over to the triumphant general, who would then **strip** the awards and symbols of victory off of the losing general's uniform. Then the victorious general would take this general and all his officers, strip them naked, chain them together and attach it to the back of the chariot of the victorious general. He would then lead his chariot and this procession through the streets, making a "public spectacle" of this thoroughly defeated foe.

Paul used this common military practice familiar to those reading his letters to illustrate what happens in the spirit: At the cross, Jesus triumphed over our enemy Satan, and all the powers and principalities of his realm. He has been defeated, stripped naked, and chained to the back of Jesus' chariot, if you will, and you and I are sitting next to Him in the chariot, because He always leads us in triumph. Now Jesus' triumph is manifested through our lives so that the enemy is nothing more than a spectacle of a thoroughly defeated foe.

The Voice of the Accuser

But here is where we often encounter difficulties. Even though we know in our minds that the enemy is defeated and stripped of all his power and authority, he still has a voice. Unfortunately, we hear his words and allow him to influence us.

One of the names of Satan is the "accuser of the brethren";[42] when we listen to him and succumb to his lies, he lives up to his name. He begins to accuse us. He tells us things like, "You shouldn't be in that chariot next to Jesus," citing some failure, some poor choice, a bad thought, a sin in our life. Because we are listening to his voice, the one who has no power has just been given power by our invitation. His accusing voice hits its mark, because his voice is releasing the demonic power twins: guilt and shame. His goal is that we allow our failure to progress from an action into an identity. Here is an example of what happens in our mind.

> You are not even worthy to be in that chariot, and you know it. You are a façade—hiding behind what you want people to think you are. You know as well as I do that you shouldn't be sitting up there with Jesus.

---

[42]   See Rev 12:10.

> You know God's disgusted with you because you fail in the same areas over and over, and then you always tell Him, "I am going to do better," and for a while, you do, but then you fail again. God is just disgusted with you . . . yeah, He's pretty well done with you.

Suddenly, we agree with the enemy's assessment of us and our actions, and we find ourselves getting out of the chariot, chaining ourselves to Satan, and walking *behind* the chariot. It's time to silence that accusing voice! As we are sitting in the chariot with Jesus, this enemy of ours *is* defeated, broken, powerless, stripped naked, and chained, being dragged behind the Lord's chariot.

When Satan begins his accusational assault, make this your response: "Yeah . . . you're right. But my failures do not affect my relationship with Jesus or my position in Him."

WE WERE BORN TO BURN WITH A PASSION FOR GOD.

Remember, in your failures, Jesus does not move away from you in anger or disappointment. Rather, He draws in close. He loves you, and He speaks to the treasure in you. It is always His goodness and His kindness that will break your heart, leading to repentance and turning back to Him wholeheartedly. This is when you must determine to stay *in* His chariot—engulfed and surrounded by His immense and overwhelming love. In His full embrace, He assures us of His ongoing protection from the power of the lies of the enemy and deliverance into victory. His right hand holds you close. His right hand leads you all the way into triumph.

The Charge of the Bridegroom: "Do Not Disturb!"

In this place of intimacy, love, and contentment, the Shulamite finds such peace, stillness, and rest. Her Bridegroom says:

> *I charge you, O daughters of Jerusalem, by the gazelles or by the does of the field, do not stir up [disturb] nor awaken love until it pleases (2:7).*

> *Promise me, brides-to-be, by the gentle gazelles and delicate deer, that you'll not disturb my love until she is ready to arise (v 7).*

The Bridegroom is telling the Daughters of Jerusalem not to disturb this Shulamite in this place of extreme rest and peace He has provided for her. He wants her to receive everything He has intended for her in His special treatment rooms of refreshment and rest. He is warning these Daughters not to judge her fervency or not to criticize her for not being involved in some area of service in the church. He is telling them, "This Shulamite is in a season of hiddenness. She is being refreshed and she is being healed. Her journey is causing her heart to be captured and captivated once again by the love of Jesus.

It is for a season, but the season is not yet over.

"Waves of Refreshing" Prayer

Dear Reader, hear the word of the Lord to you:

Do not be weary, for I have sent My Presence here to strengthen you and to renew you in My Spirit. I have come to lift you up.

I am the God of the sudden breakthrough. I know you are hungry and crying out for more and have come to a place of weariness in the battle. Do not stop asking; do not stop seeking; do not stop knocking; for I AM the God who comes and opens the doors suddenly for that which you have been praying.

I AM saying to you, even those words, those dreams, those passions that you have given up on and let die, I AM the God that brings that back to life because I AM the resurrection and life.

Beloved, there are some things that you have given up on and let go of that I would have you pick back up. I AM asking you to resurrect those dreams in your heart and bring these things back to Me.

I understand, beloved, you are growing weary. Please do not cease to cry out for the higher realms and desires I have put into your heart and your spirit, for you will reap, in due time, if you do not grow weary; instead, allow the refreshing wave of the Spirit to wash over you.

I have brought you to another season of refreshing of My Presence. For this is the rest I prepared for you and know you so desperately need. Stay in this place without agitation or restlessness, and receive all I have prepared for what is yet ahead.

ACTIVATION #9
Waves of Refreshing

There are times, when we are facing situations alone, and there is no one around to help strengthen and encourage us. We need times and seasons of refreshing, and the Lord knows this, and He always provides for these. Do you have a strategy and plan in place on how to strengthen and encourage yourself in the Lord? Use the following Activation as a guide to make your own personal Action Plan.

Activation

In this activation, the intention is to develop a plan of how to strengthen yourself in the Lord. Sit with the Holy Spirit and take some time to develop your own action list and strategy steps that will both encourage and strengthen you during a difficult time. The result will be a season of refreshment to your soul.

- Review all the prophetic words given to you, especially those speaking on identity.
- Listen to messages and read books that speak courage and encouragement to you.
- Review your own past journals of God's words spoken to you personally.
- Make a list of action steps focused on your identity that you can implement immediately that give you a boost to nourish your soul.
- Make sure you are properly positioned for encouragement. What do you need to step away from and/or step into that will bolster encouragement to your soul?
- Think of an encouraging and affirming friend or family member you could

contact that you know will speak hope into your life at this particular time.

- Take careful note of the forward advancement—no matter how small those steps are. Celebrate them, and record its progress in your life.
- Remind yourself of your history with God who always brings you through difficult times into triumph. Review those victories, and thank God for them.

As you walk through these steps, allow praise to God to flow freely. Praise and thanksgiving always paves the way into a time of refreshment and rest and initiates forward momentum.

TEN

Out of Hiding

*The voice of my beloved! Behold, he
comes leaping upon the mountains,
skipping upon the hills (2:8).*

*Listen! I hear my lover's voice. I
know it's him coming to me—leaping
with joy over mountains, skipping in
love over the hills that separate us, to
come to me (v 8, TPT).*

This chapter marks the beginning of a significant turning in
the maiden's life. In Chapter One,[43] she prayed and asked
the Lord to draw her, and she would run after Him. Now
He is answering her prayer. He has drawn her, and she has had
stunning times of revelation and transformation. He is about to
fulfill the "running together" aspect of her prayer request.

The Sovereign King

This is the third revelation of Jesus in the Song. He is
revealing Himself as the sovereign King. The Shulamite is able

---

43   See Song 1:4.

to clearly discern the sound of her Beloved's voice and has learned to be sensitive to it, She even recognizes the sound of His coming and she responds by saying, "I hear the voice of my Beloved!"

I find it so interesting that she is still in the early stages of her process—her journey into full-bridal partnership—and yet she is about to compromise her relationship. Even still, she calls Jesus, "my Beloved." He comes to her, "leaping upon the mountains" and "skipping upon the hills". Jesus is coming to the Shulamite in a way she has never seen before from Him. She has only really known Him as a Shepherd and as an affectionate Father who feeds her while she is sitting comfortably at His table.

Facing our Fears

The Shulamite is confronted with her second spiritual crisis: fear. She's in a comfort zone, and the Lord is calling her out of it into a place of risk, but she's afraid to move forward.

We don't know how much time elapses between these two seasons of her life (between verses seven and eight) but we know that they are two different seasons in her life. She likes where she is currently living in her intimate relationship with her Bridegroom. She feels safe and sees no reason to move from this place of safety and comfort. So often in our own minds we believe it is safer to be in the boat without Jesus than on the water with Him. The question is: Is it safe to be with Jesus outside of our comfort zone? Is one hundred percent obedience really safe? It seems so costly. *Can I trust Him? . . . Will He protect me and keep me safe if I abandon myself completely to Him?* These are often internal questions we ask ourselves in such times. It is very important to God that we abandon ourselves to Him in order to place our trust fully in Him—that He is believed against all other fear-based probabilities. It is at this juncture we run the risk of compromise.

The Lord is calling the Shulamite to a deeper place of trust in Him. To help her come to that place, Jesus brings an entirely new revelation of Himself. He shows her a sovereign King who easily conquers every single thing that would oppose her. He comes leaping upon mountains, effortlessly skipping over the rocky crags and hills, conquering all the highest mountains and deepest valleys (symbolic of human hurdles and hindrances, demonic traps, and the obstacles of life itself). The Lord is making it very clear that the enemy does not faze Him in the least. He is modeling for His beloved one the confidence He has within Himself. She is getting her first view of Jesus as the King of kings and Lord of lords. He is the Lamb of God, but He is also the great and mighty King. He's not just the Lamb; He's also the Lion of the Tribe of Judah—the Almighty King, the Lion who conquers all.

The Lion and the Lamb come together in this verse, and He's showing the Shulamite, "There is nothing that can conquer Me . . . have confidence in Me . . . put all your trust in Me. Have confidence in My intentions toward you." It is important to take to heart that we serve a very confident God. The Bridegroom is letting His beloved know that there is nothing that can keep Him from her. There is no discouragement, or difficulty too great. There is no failure or poor choice; there is absolutely nothing that can keep Him from coming to her. He can speak to *all* the mountains in her life, and they will be removed.

Remember when she asked her Beloved to draw her to Him so they could run together? But when He came to answer her request, she was not ready and she did not go. He knows that one day she *will* run with Him, and at that time He will allow nothing and no one to stand in opposition to her decision.

He is the King preparing His queen.

The Bridegroom Stands Readied For Action

> *My beloved is like a gazelle or a young stag. Behold, He stands behind our wall; He is looking through the windows gazing through the lattice (2:9).*

> *Let me describe him; he is graceful as a gazelle— swift as a wild stag. Now he comes closer, even to the places where I hide. Now he gazes into my*

soul, peering through the portal as he blossoms within my heart (v 9, TPT).

Notice she does not call it "her" wall, but "our" wall. Initially, He put her behind the wall—hidden away from everyone—to make her lovesick. But now the wall has become a wall of self-protection—a place of self-imposed isolation. It has even become a barrier that has come between her and her Bridegroom. She is not as close to Him as she has been because she has withdrawn into an isolated place of hiding. It has become her comfort zone, and Jesus has come to challenge that comfort zone as He stands behind the wall looking through the windows.

Jesus is pictured here as **standing** ready for action. Often in Scripture, He is pictured as sitting in rest and victory with His feet upon His enemies.[44] But when Jesus stands, powerful things are about to happen. For instance, when Stephen died, the Lord stood up to receive him.

> *But he, being full of the Holy Spirit, gazed into heaven and saw the glory of God, and Jesus standing at the right hand of God, and said, "Look I see the heavens opened and the Son of Man standing at the right hand of God" (Acts 7:55-56).*

When the Lord stands, it is because He is about to intervene in some dramatic way. He stood up to receive Stephen as he was martyred, and then He immediately initiated a world-changing action: He poured out a great revival. The remainder of the Book of Acts records the results.

We also see Jesus standing in the book of Revelation.

> *Behold, I **stand** at the door and knock. If anyone hears my voice and opens the door, I will come in to him and dine with him, and he with me (Rev 3:20, emphasis added).*

When He stands and knocks, He is saying, "I want in . . .

---

[44] See Ps 110:1.

and I desire a new level of intimacy and ownership!" He is saying that He wants to enter the life of this Shulamite in a new way, and so He reveals Himself to her as King! Jesus looks through her windows, communicating His desire to draw her into a deeper relationship with Himself. He is challenging her comfort zone. Likewise He challenges the comfort zone in our lives in many ways: our present spiritual plateau, our relationships, ministry and church-related endeavors, our work, recreation activities, etc. The challenge her Beloved presents manifested the fear in her heart. She does not want to climb up to the heights of the mountains where her Beloved is because she is content where she's at; the bottom line is, she's afraid to go.

"He gazes into my soul"

He gazes into my soul, peering through the portal as he blossoms within my heart (2:9, TPT).

For the first time there is a wall between her and the Lord. She sees that she is no longer that close to Him because of her wall of self-protection. He pierces her heart with His gaze and sees that she is immature and tentative; He knows she is not coming with Him. She wants to stay in the comfort of her own house, rest under the shade of their favorite apple tree, but He is calling her out of all that and up into the mountains.

Jesus looks right into our soul in these moments and sees all those hidden areas. Yet, all we see in His gaze is love, acceptance, and patience.

My beloved spoke, and said to me: "Rise up, my love, my fair one, and come away" (2:10).

The one I love calls to me: "Arise, my dearest. Hurry, my darling, Come along with me! I have come as you have asked to draw you to my heart and lead you out. For now is the time, my beautiful one" (2:10, TPT).

With His piercing gaze, He sees within her heart the fear that causes her to say "no" to His call. He can hear in her thoughts she is not ready—that she would rather simply sit and enjoy His companionship under the shade tree. Even so, He calls to her . . . urging her to come to Him out of her isolation and hiddenness.

The Divine Romance urges us to "Rise Up"

The divine romance of the Bridegroom is ongoing and undeterred. He speaks to her in love. He affirms her identity by calling out to her—"My beautiful one . . . My love." Again every step of the journey He calls her either "beloved" or "beautiful." He uses endearing language to motivate her. He communicates His passion for her, "You are so precious to me. You mean so much to me. I want to rule and reign in partnership with you right at My side."

He speaks tenderly to her and urges, "Rise up!" but it is always paired with, "You look good to me, and I like you . . . so arise, My beautiful one." When Jesus challenges us to come out of a place of comfort, He always says, "I like the person you are. You are *so ready* for this. Wait until you see what I have prepared for you! Now, come . . . come with Me." He is not saying, "I **command** you as My servant to come and **do** [these things]." His passionate beckoning to us is never a demanding order. The Bridegroom is communicating to the maiden that she is the one He loves and desires. She is the one He longs to gaze on, and so, He romantically beseeches her, "Rise up, My love!" He does not condemn her in her state of fear and refusal. He is not pointing to any area of rebellion in her life. He is not telling her that she is self-absorbed, threatening that she will be making a *huge* mistake if she doesn't come with Him *right now*. Rather, He is gently persuading her with all of His tenderness to go up into the heights of greater intimacy.

Take the Risk

The Bridegroom is speaking tenderly to the Shulamite to arise and come with Him high up on the mountain heights. He wants her to get off the bed, out from behind the wall, and away from the comfort of sitting under the shade tree. Her resistance—and very often our resistance—centers around this one word, "risk." He is asking her to take huge leaps in trust and faith, and faith is often spelled, R-I-S-K.

Recalling His Faithfulness

The Lord then begins to remind the maiden of His faithfulness to her, and that her season of guilt, shame, and failure is over. He says to her:

> *Arise, my love, my beautiful one, and come away, for behold, the winter is past; the rain is over and gone. The flowers appear on the earth, the time of singing has come, and the voice of the turtledove is heard in our land. The fig tree ripens its figs, and the vines are in blossom; they give forth fragrance. Arise, my love, my beautiful one, and come away (2:10-13, ESV).*

> *The season has changed, the bondage of your barren winter has ended, and the season of hiding is over and gone. The rains have soaked the earth and left it bright with blossoming flowers.*

> *The season for singing and pruning the vines has arrived. I hear the cooing of doves in our land, filling the air with songs to awaken you and guide you forth. Can you not discern this new day of destiny breaking forth around you? The early signs of my purposes and plans are bursting forth. The budding vines of new life are now blooming everywhere. The fragrance of their flowers whispers: "There is change in the air" (vs 11, 12b-13, TPT).*

Notice, again, that Jesus is speaking to the Shulamite with tender love and affection by calling her His "dearest", His "darling", His "beloved", and He always reminds her of her beauty. He continues to beckon her with such tender love. "Awaken, My dearest," He says, "I have come to answer your prayer. You asked Me to draw you so we could run together." My goodness, when you hear Jesus call you "beloved", "dearest", "beautiful", and you realize you are the one that fascinates Him, it is very easy to come out from behind your protective wall. With such terms of endearment, your heart is willing to take any risk.

And yet, she listens more to the reminders of her failures and her fears than she does to the voice of the One who is enraptured by her. Jesus is prophetically reminding the Bride of His faithfulness to her. He is saying, "Remember, the season of guilt, shame, and failure is over. You can arise now, because My love for you is so much more powerful." He encourages her by recalling how He has been so faithful to her in the past winter seasons of her life. He lets her know that He was with her in those winter times; they are still together, and they are still in love.

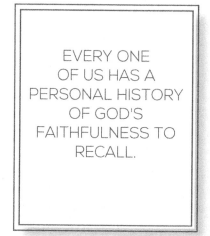

EVERY ONE OF US HAS A PERSONAL HISTORY OF GOD'S FAITHFULNESS TO RECALL.

The winter seasons of our life are trials, misunderstandings, death of dreams and visions, the emptiness we sometimes experience; it is dark, cold, and difficult. Even still, these seasons of "the north wind" strengthen our root systems as we develop a personal history with and in God. We discover characteristics of the nature of God in the dark winter seasons that we would not at other times.

The Lord looks at the Shulamite and says, "I was with you in the winter, wasn't I? You made it through, even though you didn't think you would last through the bitter rains and the dark, cold winter season. You didn't believe you would make it . . . but look! You did! You came all the way through that season! Here we are . . . we still love each other. You trust Me . . . you love Me, and I love you. Look back at the struggles, the disappointments, the discouragement . . . was I not there with you? Now the winter is past, and your heart is still alive to Me."

The Lord appeals to His dealings with us in the past seasons of our life. He says, "Remember those times? Remember My faithfulness to you?" What He is doing is calling up our personal history in His faithfulness.

Look back over the years of your own life and recall the times of breakthrough that were brought by Jesus. He says to you even now: "Recall each of those times . . . and let My faithfulness to you in those instances play again in your mind. . . . All I provided for you, those desperate moments I showed up for you, the times My goodness was manifested so generously."

Every one of us has a personal history of God's faithfulness to recall. We only need to remember all those times He came through on our behalf which caused our faith to grow, our trust in Him to increase, and our mindsets to be transformed according to His greatness. We need to draw on that history of His faithfulness to us as we look toward our future in order to courageously confront the obstacles we face at this present time. Recalling His faithfulness strengthens faith to trust Him once again, and combats all our fears. It is in the recalling of His faithfulness we come to realize that none of those things we feared were actualized, and that alone is a faith booster.

The Coming Harvest

In the Song, the Bridegroom then gives the Shulamite signs of the coming harvest. He says:

The flowers are appearing on the earth.

In the natural, blooming flowers are a sign of the next fruitful season and the coming harvest. The flower emerges on the vine just before the fruit appears—a picture of God's abundant provision and loving care. Jesus is pointing out that the signs of the harvest are all around her—the flowers are budding everywhere. He is saying, "The beginning stages of the harvest have already begun. I will care for you in this new season. There is absolutely nothing to fear." This is also true as we consider the time and season that we find ourselves presently in. We only have to look around and see the signs of His care are as obvious as the coming harvest already in bloom and ripening on the vine.

The Holy Spirit uses these prophetic seasons to teach us how to respond appropriately in trust and obedience when He calls us up, regardless of what our external circumstances and situations look like, or anything that would oppose His directive. It will require greater levels of trust and faith. And as the Lord reminds her of His past faithfulness to her, she grows in these levels of faith to trust Him more.

"The Voice of the Turtledove"

> *The voice of the turtledove is heard in our land (2:12).*

> *I hear the cooing of doves in our land filling the air with songs to awaken you and guide you forth (2:12b, TPT).*

Hearing the "cooing of the dove" is a message of a coming harvest. The "voice of the turtledove" is heard in the Land of Israel at the time of harvest, and everyone knew this signified its soon coming. The Lord says, "Can't you see what hour you are in right now? You need to open your eyes, look around, and see what is really happening."

Then He repeats His offer to her: "Rise up, My love, My beautiful one, and come away. Rise up . . . You look good to Me, and I like you . . . follow Me now . . . in obedience." He repeats a second time His call for the Bride to arise and come out of her comfort zone. She has come through a season of testing. She's come through seasons of failure, and she has been in a season and place of Holy Spirit-arranged isolation and hiddenness, but now it is time for her to get up and get going. We can make it to Heaven living a 'comfort zone'-Christianity lifestyle, but it will not bear the fruit necessary to co-labor with God and "run" with Him on the heights.

Eight Prophetic Signs of the New Season

There are eight prophetic signs that the Holy Spirit is giving the Shulamite here to encourage her to come out of her comfort zone.

#1- The season has changed; the bondage of your barren winter has ended.

The Bridegroom was faithful in her wintertime, and He will be in this next season as well.

#2- The rains have soaked the earth.

The Shulamite was in a dry, dull place, but the Word of God has brought pools, streams, and rivers of refreshing to her, preparing her heart for the springtime of flowers and blossoming vines.

#3- The blooming of flowers produced by the rain means that the fruit is not far behind.

With it comes His urgency in responding to the call to "come out" and "rise up", because the harvest is soon upon her.

#4- The season of pruning the vines has come.

Vines are pruned as the season changes from winter to spring and indicates that a new season is upon us.

#5- I hear the cooing of doves in the land.

The dove is a picture of the Holy Spirit singing to our spirits and awakening a greater love and deeper affection for Jesus.

#6- The air is filled with songs to awaken you and bring you forth.

There is a time of celebration and joy breaking forth. You may have just passed through a season where you had no joy and you could not even bring yourself to sing. Yet the Holy

Spirit is announcing a new season has come where everything will shift.

When you sing and rejoice in times of barrenness, you are seeding the ground for your breakthrough. In Isaiah 54, we read:

> *Shout, O barren, you who have not borne! Break forth into singing, and cry aloud (v 1).*

Here we see an amazing principle in action: shout for joy while you are barren. Anyone can shout for joy when she is pregnant. We can all shout for joy when great things happen, but there is such power and authority released when you can shout for joy *prior* to your breakthrough. It is that joy you release in those moments that causes things around you to alter and change. Your joy being released is what shifts atmospheres, but it must be released. Sometimes it is released through faith and with trembling, but joy has to find expression for its full powerful effect; it cannot be quietly contained in the heart. Joy is one of those things that *must* be demonstrated.

Let out a joyful shout, you who are barren, because your faithfulness is about to produce a supernatural increase.

#7- Can you not discern the new day of destiny breaking forth?

A new song is released, aligning our hearts for the coming breakthrough. It has been our unbelief that has held us back. But no more, for my trust level in Jesus has gone to another level. I trust in my testimony of who Jesus is and how much He loves me and cares for me beyond anything I see in my circumstances.

#8- The budding vines of new life are blooming everywhere.

This is all about a profusion of new fruit bursting through our life. It is a new season of fruitbearing multiplicity.

So now, beloved, because of these eight prophetic signs, it

is time to follow Him. It's like He is saying to you, His beloved one:

> Can you not discern this new dawn of destiny breaking on the horizon? The early signs of My purposes and plans are bursting forth around you. The budding vines of new life are in full bloom everywhere. The captivating fragrance of their flowers whispers My message: "There is a change in the air." So, I say again to you: Arise, My love, My beautiful companion, and run with Me to the higher place. Now is the time to come away with Me.

He poetically communicates the season's transition, which signals the urgency of the hour. But He sees in her heart that she is not going to respond to His pleading; yet He continues to call her to come. This is the second time He presents her with His challenge.

"Secret places of the cliff"

The Bridegroom urges the Shulamite to step out in faith and come and partner with Him.

> *O my dove, in the clefts of the rock, in the secret places of the cliff, let me see your face, let me hear your voice; for your voice is sweet, and your face is lovely (v 14).*

> *For you are my dove, hidden in the split-open rock. It was I who took you and hid you up high in the secret stairway of the sky. Let me see your radiant face and hear your sweet voice. How beautiful your eyes of worship and lovely your voice in prayer (v 14, TPT).*

The Lord reveals His tender heart of affection for her as He declares her beauty in her struggle with fear. He knows she is going to refuse His offer, but He is telling her the same thing He told Peter, "I know that your flesh is weak, but I also see the willingness in your heart." The Bridegroom can see in the face of the One He loves that she is not in a place right now that will allow her to choose to leave her comfortable place. Knowing that she is driven by fear and not being rebellious, He reveals His tender heart of affection for her. The "secret places of the cliff" and being hidden in the rock is a call to intimacy—those up-close and personal encounters with Him. He is saying, "Come hide in Me; find that place of rest in Me." He wants to see the Shulamite's face and hear her voice in close proximity. He says to her, "Your voice is sweet . . . your face is lovely. I know what you are thinking. I see the fear in your heart, and I know you are going to deny Me in the future.[45] But right now, here in this place, I want to hear your voice. Don't draw back away from Me . . . press in to Me . . . let Me hear the sweetness of your voice with your face uncovered. I love to hear your worship; so don't draw back from Me."

He is saying, "Come on! Stand in that crevice of the rock (in Jesus) I've provided and ask Me for help." I love the verse that references "the secret places of the cliff." The King James Version reads, "in the secret places of the stairs," and *The Passion Translation* says, "in the secret stairway of the sky." He's talking about stepping into a steep, inaccessible place. He is calling the Shulamite into new places of intimacy in Him, up to new heights. The Hebrew word for "cleft" is *chagav*,[46] meaning, "a place to be hidden; a place of refuge." The rock is a fortress, and in that fortress, we hide in Jesus.

"Let me see your face"

Then He says:

> Let me see your face, let me hear your voice (2:14b)

> Let me see your radiant face and hear your sweet voice. How beautiful your eyes of worship and lovely your voice in prayer. (2:14b, TPT)

He's speaking prophetically to her, because He knows she's

---

[45] See verse 17.
[46] *Strong's Hebrew Lexicon*, #H2288, "*chagav*".

going to say "no." Don't turn away from Him in your sorrow of failure. What we need to do, instead, is stand with confidence in the cleft of the rock—in Jesus. Hear what He is really saying:

> You are My dove. You are My pure one. I see your heart that loves Me. I see the desire in your heart to say "yes." Don't let guilt, shame, or condemnation deceive your heart into believing that anything you have done has diminished My passion and love for you. It has not. You love Me. You are beautiful to Me; so let Me hear your voice. Cry out to Me for help. Do not draw back with shame. Cry out for My help. You will have all you need.

He also calls her, "My dove." He says that her eyes are like loyal, gentle doves. He sees her as a dove who has this ability to fly so gracefully onto His shoulder and land there and stay. The eyes speak of the ability to see, and He knows that she is beginning to see with eyes of faith. But in this moment, she's simply allowing fear to win the day.

"Catch for us the foxes"

In response to the call of her Bridegroom—"Let Me hear your voice . . ."—she cries out for His help:

> *Catch us the foxes, the little foxes that spoil the vines, for our vines have tender grapes (v 15).*

> *You must catch the troubling foxes, those sly little foxes that hinder our relationship. For they raid our budding vineyard of love to ruin what I've planted within you. Will you catch them and remove them for me? We will do it together (v 15, TPT).*

She immediately responds to Him by crying out for help and deliverance from the little areas of her life that trigger fear and cause her to compromise. She's saying, "I'm not able to go forward where You're leading me. . . I just can't move on with You because of these little areas of weakness and failure in my life. I want to, but I just can't."

Foxes are cunning little animals that have the potential to destroy the vineyards under the cover of the night. They are not bold like strong lions that attack during the daylight hours. They are quick, subtle, crafty, and hard-to-catch animals, sneaking around when no one can see them. They go after the fruit in our lives.

Foxes represent the compromises that lie hidden deep in our hearts. They are areas where we have not yet allowed the victory of Jesus to come in—those secret issues in our life that keep us from where the Lord desires to take us, such as habits, weaknesses, and compromises that give access to the enemy. These "little foxes" the Shulamite is talking about are fears, unclean speech, an unclean thought-life, and all the little attitudes that we just kind of shrug off with, "Oh well. I'll deal with all those one of these days." The little foxes are more like those areas that we know are not really right, but they don't seem that big to deal with; therefore, they just lie undercover, and continue to do their destructive work a little at a time. By ignoring their potential, we don't actually deal with them properly. We reason, "These are just minor annoyances, so I'll let them sit here in my mind and influence my thought patterns until I have the energy to deal with them."

The Shulamite knows that these little foxes hinder intimacy and she also recognizes that she cannot deal with it alone. She needs Jesus to reveal these hidden areas of compromise—these blind spots in her life. She is asking Him to help her go after the subtle sins of her life that spoil their intimacy: her fears, habits, weaknesses, and insecurities she struggles with. She asks for His help, and He says, "We will do it together." It becomes a team project. Her Beloved will put His finger on those things that need to go.

The Negativity Exchange

The way He deals with these "little foxes" is through a divine exchange. There was a time in my life when I was such a negative person. You could easily have built a case for me possibly being the most negative person on the planet. I admit I am a recovering "negativist." The sad thing about that is, in this particular season, I was pastor of a church, yet I was so judgmental. I had a critical spirit, and I was very negative in every aspect of my thought life.

Not surprisingly, I found myself surrounded by people exactly like me, many of them were local pastors. We would meet for coffee on a regular basis and it almost seemed like we tried to out-do one another in our negativity and judgmentalism. It was horrible. Looking back on it makes me want to grab an airline flight sick bag. Seriously. Such a sad season in my life, and it started to really wear on me physically, mentally, emotionally, and spiritually. My wife quickly tired of it and did her best to pull me up and out. One day I proudly declared to Karissa, "I am going on a negativity fast!"

She was not as impressed as I thought she would have been, and replied: "Big deal. Why don't you make it a lifestyle instead?"

I thought about it, and then said, "I can't. I'll lose all my friends!" I was joking, of course, but I felt the Holy Spirit come so powerfully upon me. He told me, "This negative attitude is not going to travel well where I am taking you, Gary. So why don't you give Me your negativity and I will give you My joy in exchange? Joy is just what you need where we're going."

I call it the "divine exchange moment" between me and the Holy Spirit. It was one of the best decisions of my life.

The Holy Spirit shows you what would not be beneficial in this new land of inheritance where you're headed. But in exchange, He has something that *will* be beneficial and will fit perfectly well in that place where He's leading. To help this exchange process, He floods us with an overwhelming sense of His love, His mercy, and grace, and we use the flow of His glorious presence to simply yield and make that exchange.

"My beloved is mine, and I am His"

The Shulamite speaks of His ownership over her for the first time.

> *My beloved is mine, and I am his. He feeds his flock among the lilies (2:16).*

> *I know my lover is mine and I have everything in you, for we delight ourselves in each other (v 16, TPT).*

She is declaring that she belongs exclusively to Jesus. She knows she has not lost that deep place of love and affection in the heart of God. Even in her weaknesses and struggles He is the One she desires, and she knows she is the one He desires.

Notice the order of relationship that the Shulamite defines in her statement: "My beloved is mine and I am His." Her only focus is her inheritance in Him and how He blesses her. It is her first, and then Jesus. She does add a new dimension of His ownership of her life. She now realizes that she loves Him because she is His inheritance. However, this is secondary to her. Her life in God is still very self-referential. At this point, she is still the most important person in the relationship. She talks about what He is to her without much awareness of what she is to Him.

The Painful Compromise

> *Until the day breaks and the shadows flee away, turn, my beloved, and be like a gazelle or a young stag upon the mountains of Bether (2:17).*

> *But until the day springs to life and the shifting shadows of fear disappear, turn around, my lover, and ascend to the holy mountains of separation with me. Until the new day fully dawns, run on ahead like the graceful gazelle and skip like the young stag over the mountains of separation. Go on ahead to the mountain of spices—I'll come away another time (v 17, TPT).*

In this verse, she tells her Beloved to go on; she is not coming with Him after all. The Shulamite tells Him, "No," she does not want to go to the high places; she's afraid of the heights. Refusing His invitation is all cased in fear. More often than not, it is fear that immobilizes us to progress spiritually. It is not rebellion; it is spiritual immaturity and a choice that becomes her compromise—all because of fear. To her, walking by faith is heading into the mysterious unknown, and that is just too risky, scary, and takes a lot of trust that she doesn't possess. And at this point in her walk in her new journey with God she responds to her Beloved by saying, "No, thanks." Even though she loves Him so much, her fear is overriding all the affections she has for Him.

Fear and faith are the exact same emotion; they are just running in opposite directions. Faith moves you toward God, while fear moves you away from God. Not all fear causes you to move away from God, but this particular fear—obeying the Lord's request to come out—does.

Experiencing the "Hiddenness" and "Manifestation" of God

But the Bridegroom is not going anywhere; He never leaves without you. He's that committed to the relationship. In that moment I am convinced that He rolled out a plan to draw the Shulamite closer to Himself: the "hiddenness" and "manifestation" strategy. We begin to see God's intentions as He withdraws a sense of His Presence from her, even though He's still very much there. He's readily available to her faith, but not available at the moment to her emotions, her soul, or her physical senses. It seems that this strategy is used in two different ways in the life of the Shulamite. The plan here is to cause her to search for her Beloved, exercising and developing her faith. This maturity of faith will obliterate fear as His love overshadows her. Later in the Song we will see Him use this strategy again so she can see how far she has progressed in her passion and intimacy with Jesus.

Graham Cooke applies Hosea chapter 2 as the basis for what he calls a period of Holy Spirit-initiated "hiddenness". About His beloved the Lord says:

Therefore, behold, I will allure her, I will draw

> *her. I will bring her into the wilderness, and speak kindly to her (v 14).*

Here is where the Lord leads you into a "wilderness" and has you hidden away all to Himself. There, He withdraws a sense of His Presence, which is shocking to the Shulamite, because He has been so readily available to her emotions their entire relationship. But in this wilderness place, she cannot even find Him.

> *By night on my bed I sought the one I love; I sought him, but I did not find him (Song 3:1).*

It seems the Lord is unveiling His ultimate plan here for the Shulamite. He withdrew a sense of His presence, but He has not *left* her. Feeling God is far away is not a punishment, by any means. In such times of hiddenness when you can't sense His presence, He is still there. He is simply hiding, but He is hiding in plain sight. He is just teaching you to look for Him in a *different* way—to look for Him with the eyes of your faith, not your feelings.

> *Night after night I'm tossing and turning on my bed of travail. Why did I let him go from me? How my heart now aches for him, but he is nowhere to be found! (3:1, TPT)*

For the first time, she has told her Beloved to go on without her. She is tossing and turning at night upon her bed. But she isn't supposed to be in her bed in this season of her life; she is supposed to be on the mountains with her Bridegroom Jesus. Mystics call this season the "dark night of the soul." It is a time when she feels her Bridegroom has left her completely, but she still calls Him "the one I love", not "the one who left her." In reality though, He has not left her; He is only in the shadows, because He promised to *never* leave. He is continually there with her even when she can't feel Him. He will never leave His beloved . . . but she does not know that yet.

Seeking Him and Finding Him

This is a new experience for her, to seek Him without

finding Him immediately, because all through chapter 1 and 2 of the Song, we see that every time she sought Him, she found Him. But now she seeks Him and she can't find Him. Notice the wording here: "By night on **my** bed . . ." It is now **her** bed. Where it had been **their** couch . . . **their** bed,[47] now it is hers. It seems they are not in deep partnership right now. Compromise has caused a breach in their relationship. He is absent; she feels alone. But still very much in love with Him, she seeks out the One she loves, because she is still very sincere in her love.

Not long before this[48] she had proclaimed to Him, "I am my Beloved's and He is mine." She never loses her spiritual identity as a lover of God, even in this challenging time. That's who she is . . . that's who we are. This is a statement of identity: "Throughout this difficult season, I am still passionately in love with God, and He is still passionately in love with me." Her praise of Him is unceasing, and this becomes a declaration of faith that arises within her . . . a budding faith that begins to trust Him in this wilderness period.

Two times she states, "I sought the One I love . . . I sought Him." The disappointment of losing His Presence motivates her to rise up off her bed and leave behind her comfort zone. She is saying, "I just can't live without Him." As she seeks Him, she is appropriating all the means that worked in the past that secured her connection with Him, but it's just not working. She does not realize she is in a God-initiated strategic season of hiddenness with her Bridegroom. This immature, lovesick Bride announces during her time of distress:

> *"I will rise now," I said, "and go about the city; in the streets and in the squares I will seek the one I love." I sought him, but I did not find him (3:2).*

> *So I must rise in search of him, looking throughout the city, seeking until I find him. Even if I have to roam through every street, nothing will keep me from my search. Where is he—my soul's true love? He is nowhere to be found (3:2, TPT).*

---

[47] See Song 1:16.
[48] See 2:16.

We do not know the time frame between verses 1 and 2, but we see it is the disappointment of losing His Presence that motivates her to arise and go search for Him. It is her love and ardent passion for intimacy with Jesus that gets her up off her bed. She finally realizes she is addicted to Him, and her love for Him conquers her fears. She's determined to seek Him and to find Him.

The "city" represents the Church. I find it really interesting that this is the place where she goes to find Him. Why? Because Jesus dwells among His people. When we isolate ourselves, we lose that corporate part of Him. And when our hunger finally reaches the point that we cannot stand our self-imposed isolation any longer, the Spirit of the Lord will always draw us to the Church.

She also looks for Him in the streets and town squares—the places where people work, interact, and just hang out.

> *The watchmen who go about the city found me; I said, "Have you seen the one I love?" (v 3)*

> *Then I encountered the overseers as they encircled the city. So I asked them, "Have you found Him—my heart's true love?" (v 3, TPT).*

The "watchmen" are elders who are responsible for overseeing the affairs of the city. These elders, or spiritual shepherds, are entrusted to watch over the activities of the Church. The Shulamite humbles herself, once again, to the spiritual authority of the Church through these elders, even though she has been "hurt" and offended by them in the past. This is a huge risk for her, but she is so desperate to find her Beloved.

But the risk provides the result she desperately sought:

> *Scarcely had I passed by them, when I found the one I love. I held him and would not let him go, until I had brought him to the house of my mother, and into the chamber of her who conceived me (3:4).*

> *Just as I moved past them, I encountered him. I*
> *found the one I adore! I caught him and I fastened*
> *myself to him, refusing to be feeble in my heart*
> *again. Now I'll bring him back to the temple within*
> *where I was given new birth—into my innermost*
> *parts, the place of my conceiving (v 4, TPT).*

Suddenly the Lord manifests His presence to her. A renewed resolve to never let Him go is the resounding cry of her heart, and she fulfills this commitment, as we will see later in the Song. The Shulamite then embraces her Beloved in a bold new way, demonstrating her maturing faith and passion as a result of her painful experience of not sensing His Presence. She then commits to bringing Him into the deepest recesses of her heart. This is where true intimacy really happens. The Holy Spirit carried her into the depths of the heart of Jesus, and now she's inviting Him into the most concealed places of her own heart. She is enraptured and captivated to a whole new level with her Beloved.

"Do Not Disturb!"

Then the Bridegroom comes back onto the scene and tells everyone not to bother her.

> *I charge you, O daughters of Jerusalem, by the*
> *gazelles or by the does of the field, do not stir up*
> *nor awaken love until it pleases (v 5).*

The Lord puts up a very clear "DO NOT DISTURB" sign over His beloved one. She is in a season of renewed intimacy and He does not want the Daughters of Jerusalem—those who are less mature and less passionate in their pursuit of Jesus—to influence her in this season. Very often, Christians, whose hearts are in the right place, respond to our life challenges and difficulties with sympathetic sentimentality, which actually may be the exact opposite to what God is doing in our life at that moment. They mean well, but sometimes people want to rescue us out of something where God clearly desires that we pass on *through* it with the grace He provides. That's why He posts a "DO NOT DISTURB" over her. She must be left alone to walk through it **with** Him.

The Bride's Security Detail

> *Who is this coming out of the wilderness like pillars of smoke, perfumed with myrrh and frankincense, with all the merchant's fragrant powders? Behold, it is Solomon's couch, with sixty valiant men around it, of the valiant of Israel. They all hold swords, being expert in war. Every man has his sword on his thigh because of fear in the night. Of the wood of Lebanon, Solomon the King made himself a palanquin: He made its pillars of silver, its support of gold, its seat of purple, its interior paved with love by the daughters of Jerusalem. Go forth, O daughters of Zion, and see King Solomon with the crown with which his mother crowned him on the day of his wedding, The day of the gladness of his heart (3:6-11).*

> *Look! It is the king's marriage carriage. The love seat surrounded by sixty champions, the mightiest of Israel's host, are like pillars of protection. They are angelic warriors standing ready with swords to defend the king and his fiancée from every terror of the night (vs 7-8, TPT).*

When He says to her, "Arise and come away, let us go to the mountains," what He did not tell her was, "You do not have to walk up that mountain. I am going to carry you in the safety of the marriage-carriage. I never intended that you would have to walk up the dark mountain trail in your own strength." This beautiful imagery is about the Holy Spirit and His caring provision and powerful protection in our lives. Jesus is revealing Himself to His beloved as the safe Savior.

The Holy Spirit asks the Shulamite a rhetorical question and then He gives her a two-part answer. She then communicates this two-part answer to the Daughters of Jerusalem. The first answer we will see in verses 7-8 is spoken in ancient military terms, and the second answer is seen in verses 9-10, using the language of a royal kingly procession. Both reveal how safe the people of God are under Jesus' leadership and the Holy Spirit's protection. The Shulamite ends by sowing more seeds into the hearts of the Daughters of Jerusalem by revealing to them her secret for overcoming fear. Then she exhorts them to press in more and more into the Beloved.

This Scripture says it is "Solomon's couch" coming out of the wilderness with "sixty valiant men" surrounding it. The king's couch was a chariot used in his royal wedding processions. It was carried on the shoulders of the royal guard. In the Eastern world during Solomon's time, a bride on her wedding day would be carried on mens' shoulders on a chair (or couch) surrounded by a carefully selected group of the most-feared, the strongest, most-trusted, well-trained bodyguards of the king as they escorted the young bride back to the palace. These highly-trained guards were vitally important for this task as thieves would often try to ambush the royal wedding procession and steal the wedding gifts and gold, and in most cases, kill everyone in the wedding party.

This picture of "sixty valiant men" is clearly speaking of the Bridegroom's ability to deal with any enemy—all thieves—who would try to take them out. In the natural, Solomon's bride would be sitting right next to him in this elevated place, riding upon the shoulders of the royal guard. In the spiritual interpretation, it is a picture of the Bride of Christ being escorted by the Holy Spirit to King Jesus.

Security through the Prophetic Gifts

The Shulamite is not afraid of an enemy ambush as she sits on this marriage couch, because she is surrounded by fearless, valiant, experienced soldiers who are well trained, and each one expertly armed.

> *Every man has his sword on his thigh because of the fear in the night (v 8).*

These skilled soldiers are not novices; they are seasoned warriors with veteran warring abilities—all "hold swords", and each one skilled in the use of their weapon. These warriors were not hired hands or mercenaries who would flee if the pressure got too great. They were native-born bodyguards who love and willingly serve their king with an intense loyalty. In fact, they would lose their lives before they would see the king lose his, and so they provide elaborate and extensive protection on the way to the wedding feast. The enemy seeks to ambush us, but Jesus is on guard.

This verse says that "every man has his sword on his thigh" because of the "fear" in the night. This is all about the protection of the Holy Spirit. One of the ways the Holy Spirit protects us is by releasing to us prophetic words, dreams, or visions about the strategy of the enemy. We see such a great picture of this in 2 Kings.

> Now the king of Syria was making war against Israel; and he consulted with his servants, saying, "My camp will be in such and such a place." And the man of God sent to the king of Israel, saying, "Beware that you do not pass this place, for the Syrians are coming down there." Then the king of Israel sent someone to the place of which the man of God had told him. Thus he warned him, and he was watchful there, not just once or twice.

> Therefore the heart of the king of Syria was greatly troubled by this thing; and he called his servants and said to them, "Will you not show me which of us is for the king of Israel?"

> And one of his servants said, "None, my lord, O king; but Elisha, the prophet who is in Israel, tells the king of Israel the words that you speak in your bedroom." (6:8-12)

This Syrian king is so angry because every time they make plans to invade and crush the Israelites, the Israelites are waiting for them—fiercely armed watchmen. It's obvious to him that someone in their camp is a traitor and is giving the enemy their battle plans prior to each invasion. But finally one of the prophets corrects him and says, "Uh, excuse me, sir. But there is no traitor in the camp. It's actually Elisha, the prophet. The Holy Spirit is revealing to him your battle plans, and then he's telling the king of Israel."

That's one of the ways the Holy Spirit protects us, by releasing words of knowledge. Prophecy absolutely destroys oppression in our lives. The devil loves to oppress us. He looks for ways to afflict us, cause us to be consumed with worry, terrorize us with anxious thoughts, be depressed about circumstances, and overwhelm and crush us under the weight of life's concerns and difficulties. The prophetic word of the Lord, however, is destructive to the plans of the enemy and the powers of darkness. He delivers us from all such attempts.

Another way we see the protective heart of the Holy Spirit is when He stirs the heart of someone to intercede on our behalf, or He may release warring angels to come to our defense. Holy Spirit is brilliant at His job to shield you, and your protection is driven by His passionate love.

The Shulamite has come to a very secure place with her Bridegroom and she is making progress on her journey. With His loving encouragement, the Bridegroom will beckon her onward into full bridal partnership.

"Out of Hiding" Prayer

I want to pray Psalm 121 from *The Message* over you and into your spirit. It is about the keeping power of God in your life.

> *I look up to the mountains; does my strength come from mountains? No, my strength comes from GOD, who made heaven, and earth, and mountains.*
>
> *He won't let you stumble, your Guardian God won't fall asleep. Not on your life! Israel's Guardian will never doze or sleep.*
>
> *GOD'S your Guardian, right at your side to protect you—shielding you from sunstroke, sheltering you from moonstroke.*
>
> *GOD guards you from every evil, he guards your very life. He guards you when you leave and when you return, he guards you now, he guards you always (vs 1-8).*

ACTIVATION #10
Out of Hiding

In this chapter, we saw the stunning keeping-power of God over our lives. Psalm 121 gives such a marvelous description of the keeping power of God. Let's look at it again.

> *I will lift up my eyes to the hills—from whence does my help come from? My help comes from the* LORD, *who made heaven and earth. He will not allow your foot to be moved; He who keeps you will not slumber.*
>
> *The* LORD *is your keeper . . . the* LORD *shall preserve you from all evil; He shall preserve your soul. The* LORD *shall preserve your going out and your coming in from this time forth, and even forevermore.*

There are so many great promises to us in this. The Psalmist tells us that God is our keeper. He never sleeps; why, He doesn't even nap. Instead, He watches over you so you don't slip and fall; He makes sure your feet won't stumble over something. He promises to keep you from every evil intention that comes against you. You are blessed when you go and equally blessed upon your return . . . from now through eternity.

The words, "keep," "keeper", and "preserve" are all the same Hebrew word, *shamar,*[49] which means, "to guard, have charge of, keep watch over, protect, be a watchman, observe, to keep safe, to restrain, to make aware, to pay close attention to and to treasure."

God keeps you safe because you are His treasured possession. This is very personal. Take it to heart: The Lord, Himself, is your keeper (*shamar*).

---

[49]   *Strong's Hebrew Lexicon, #8104, "shamar".*

Activation

Take time to meditate on this Psalm until the truths that the Spirit of God wrote here are deeply rooted and established in your heart, your mind, and your soul. Record these thoughts in your journal. Do a study of this word, "*shamar*", and see how its fuller meanings pertain to you personally and your present situation. Consider the other Scriptures where this word is used as well.

ELEVEN

The Bridegroom Beckons

Behold, you are fair, my love!
Behold, you are fair![50]

The Lord challenged the Shulamite to arise in chapter two of the Song, but she disobeyed because of fear. These are some of the first words that the Lord speaks to her after this season of hiding His manifest Presence. He breaks the silence in His usual way by affirming her, nourishing her, and declaring how much He cherishes her. He begins to speak about the treasure and virtues He sees within her. She responds by saying how she is even more captivated hearing she is His inheritance. His words absolutely stun her heart as they do ours every time we hear how passionately He loves us.

Let's look what the Bridegroom says to her.

> *Behold, you are fair, my love! Behold, you are fair!*
> *You have dove's eyes behind your veil. Your hair*
> *is like a flock of goats, going down from Mount*
> *Gilead. Your teeth are like a flock of shorn sheep*
> *which have come up from the washing, every one*
> *of which bears twins, and none is barren among*
> *them. Your lips are like a strand of scarlet, and*

---

[50] Song 4:1.

your mouth is lovely. Your temples behind your veil are like a piece of pomegranate. Your neck is like the tower of David, built for an armory, on which hang a thousand bucklers, all shields of mighty men. Your two breasts are like two fawns, twins of a gazelle, which feed among the lilies. Until the day breaks and the shadows flee away, I will go my way to the mountain of myrrh and to the hill of frankincense.

You are all fair, my love, and there is no spot in you. Come with me from Lebanon, my spouse, with me from Lebanon. Look from the top of Amana, from the top of Senir and Hermon . . . (4:1-8).

Affirming the Budding Virtues

Jesus is prophetically affirming the budding virtues He sees in this young maiden's life. Even in this place of weakness and immaturity, the Lord speaks to her as if she was already walking in that place of full-bridal partnership.

From the lions' dens, from the mountains of the leopards. You have ravished my heart, my sister, my spouse; you have ravished my heart with one look of your eyes, with one link of your necklace (vs 8b-9).

Before we take a deeper look at each of the virtues, let's identify the symbolism used in these verses.

Dove's eyes: Eyes of single-minded devotion and revelation.

Hair like goats: Dedication to God.

Teeth like shorn sheep: Chewing the meat of the Word.

Lips like scarlet: Speech that is redemptive.

Kisses of the mouth: Intimacy with God.

***Veiled temples (cheeks/countenance)*:** Emotions impacted by the grace of God.

***Neck like David's tower*.** Setting our will to obey God.

***Breasts like fawns*:** The power to edify and nurture others.

The Bridegroom knows what's next for this Shulamite on the road to full bridal partnership, so He is going to point out the treasure He sees in her. He does this by defining eight treasures—distinct virtues—of her beauty that He sees emerging from her. His intent is to strengthen and equip her.

He begins, as always, by letting her know how beautiful she is to Him.

> *Behold, you are fair, my love! Behold, you are fair! You have dove's eyes behind your veil. Your hair is like a flock of goats, going down from Mount Gilead (4:1).*

> *Listen, my dearest darling, you are so beautiful—you are beauty itself to me! Your eyes glisten with love, like gentle doves behind your veil. What devotion I see each time I gaze upon you. You are like a sacrifice ready to be offered (v 1, TPT).*

The Lord has a big smile on His face and says to her, "My love! You are absolutely beautiful to Me! You've captured my heart." This is the romance of the Gospel! This is the reality that will give us the power to ascend the highest mountain and challenge any obstacle.

Outrageous Faithful Love

Through all the obstacles of life we face, this is something that we simply have to get: the outrageous love of God. He is the most faithful Person I have ever met in my life. He is tenacious in His faithfulness towards me and towards you. Even when I am faithless, He remains faithful. His faithfulness is one part of Jesus' nature that the Holy Spirit has personalized and used to apprehend my heart. Every time I was faithless, every time I failed and started to withdraw, the Holy Spirit flooded my heart with the faithfulness of Jesus.

When the Holy Spirit tells you that He is going to be something for you, He is that for you, tenaciously. He is my faithful Beloved. The word for "faithful" in the Hebrew is *hesed,* and it means, "a fixed and determined love." God has a fixed and determined love in His heart towards us at all times.

Jesus has an immense and eternal compassion. His compassion obliterates sin in my life, because His compassion is much more powerful. He is full of mercy that is so strong, it crushes all shame.

He has neverending patience. He is full of extreme enthusiasm and never-ending energy in His radical pursuit of me. His love is enthralling, captivating, and designed to overwhelm all of my fear, worry, guilt, shame, and every bit of low self-esteem.

Eight Virtues of the Bride

There are eight virtues listed in these verses. These are eight things that make the Lord's heart glad when He sees us grow in them, and they make our hearts glad as well. They are, in fact, prophetic declarations over the Bride's life.

1) Dove's Eyes. The Bridegroom tells her that she has eyes that glisten with love—they are like gentle doves behind her veil. Eyes refer to faith and revelation. He is saying she walks in high levels of wisdom and revelation. She has the eyes of understanding.

"Dove's eyes" also speak of purity and loyalty, which we covered earlier. "Behind the veil" also speaks clearly of her humility. Humility comes out of that place of brokenness before God. It comes from a place of being poor in spirit—the realization that everything in life comes from God. All the fruit of your gifts, service, and ministry that touches the lives of people comes out of your understanding that God gives you credit for what He does through you.

2) Hair. Hair is symbolic of beauty and consecration. The Bridegroom is bragging about her dedication and commitment to Him and to His Kingdom. Part of a Nazarite vow of the separation of purity was that they would not cut their hair. Samson was a Nazarite, and we know his long hair was the secret of his strength,[51] but it also symbolized his consecration to God. The result was extraordinary power.

3) Teeth. Teeth have the idea of digging into the Word of God—chewing and meditating on His word.

> *When I look at you, I see how you have eaten my*
> *fruit and tasted my word (4:2a, TPT).*

There are two ways I see in Scripture that the word comes to us. One is called the milk of the word, and the other is the meat of the word. Both are necessary for us to strengthen ourselves in our spirit.

The **milk** of the word is nourishment you get from someone else—like a child gets milk from his mother. It is that word which comforts and soothes, and also brings hope and comfort. We love it when someone comes to us and speaks an especially encouraging word in a timely manner. God loves to bring encouragement to us in this way.

The **meat** of the word is what you get when you hunt. This is the word that goes deep and provokes change in us. It is the word that brings correction, often addressing areas that need to be yielded to the Lord. The meat of the word brings about transformation in our lives.

The milk-word confronts things in my life that are contrary to the Kingdom, and the meat-word exposes that which affects my walk and my intimacy with the Lord. When that meat-word hits my spirit and soul, I stop right there and have a dialogue with the Holy Spirit about it. This word struck a chord in my heart and the truth of it convicts my heart; I am *not* going to leave it or pass over it. I will enter into a time with the Holy Spirit with it because it is *provoking* transformation in me.

---

[51]   See Judg16:17.

We need both forms of His word: the **milk** and the **meat**. I want to encourage you to read your Bible every day. There are so many good translations out there now, so find one you like. Read it until the Holy Spirit speaks to you, because this is one way you will become strong in the Spirit. Develop a hunger for His word and allow the Spirit of God to transform you. The more you eat His word, the hungrier you'll get. You'll receive fresh encounters with His word that releases new levels of faith, hope, and encouragement.

As you read His word, the Holy Spirit is going to show you something about yourself that you don't like—something that frustrates you—and at the exact same moment, He is going to show you something about Himself that you will love, and it is going to absolutely overwhelm you. God only challenges you on that part of your life where He has a plan for transformation. As you read the Word and the Holy Spirit convicts of sin, He is also *convincing* us of the love of God. Remember, God will never point out your sin and leave you to wallow in it. He's just not like that. You see, every time God challenges you, He has the solution ready to reveal to you. Then He says, "Can we get started today?" At the exact same second the meat of the word convicts you, the Holy Spirit shows you part of His nature that you need, and His love overwhelms you and you make an exchange with Him. In this intimate moment, a displacement is going to take place.

4) Lips. When He says to the Bride, "Your lips are lovely . . ." He is speaking about mercy and grace. Lips speak of speech—our verbal communication. Under the blood of the Lamb, she does not use her words to tear people down, nor are her words used in negativity or gossip. Instead, she uses her words to bless, to edify, and to strengthen others.

5) Kisses. The fifth virtue of kisses speak about her intimacy with God. In 1:2, the Bride calls out to her Bridegroom to come and kiss her, which is intimacy with God. Throughout the Song, the lips speak of speech as the mouth speaks of intimacy. Kisses intimately communicate the intentions and emotions of the heart between lovers and God wants to establish this same deep intimacy as a way of life with us.

6) Cheeks. These are the "veiled temples" of the Bride, which defines how her emotions are impacted by the grace of God. Our emotions are expressed by our countenance—through our cheeks. Like I said earlier, we can see anger, joy, gladness, and sadness on the cheeks—clearly evident on the countenance of a person. The cheeks are like windows into a person's emotions.

The Bride's godly emotions were like a piece of sweet pomegranate—something very sweet to God.

7) Neck. This virtue is like the tall imposing strength of David's tower. The neck is always symbolic of our free will. The Bride is choosing to set her will towards her Bridegroom by intentionally pressing in and embracing this next season of risk and upgrades. She has set her will to say "yes" to Him, and everything within her is moving to that end.

8) Breasts. The breasts speak of the power to edify and nurture others. This is a quality in her that is especially attractive to Him—her nurturing nature is the very nature of God Himself.

The Bridegroom recounts the treasure He sees in His Bride by describing these appealing virtues that are so attractive they are to Him. His cherishing words nurture and strengthen her.

The Shulamite's Love Response

When God speaks to the treasure in you, and you realize how He sees you and how He truly feels about you, that reality absolutely rocks you to your core so that you are simply undone. In this fresh encounter with the Beloved, we are transformed to new levels of intimacy with Him that directly affects our ministry to others. It also provides a resolve in our heart to go deeper in Him no matter the cost.

That's exactly what happens with the Shulamite; then we see her response:

> *Until the day breaks and the shadows flee away,*
> *I will go my way to the mountain of myrrh and to*
> *the hill of frankincense (4:6).*

I've made up my mind. Until the darkness disappears and the dawn has fully come, in spite of shadows and fears, I will go to the mountaintop with you—the mountain of suffering love and the hill of burning incense. Yes, I will be your bride (v 6, TPT).

The Shulamite has to experience Calvary. As His co-crucified partner, we must embrace the fellowship of His sufferings.[52] The Shulamite is saying "yes" to the cross here. This is the turning point in her life and in the Song. She is saying "yes" to the marriage contract.

After hearing these eight prophetic affirmations over her life, the Shulamite is ready to leave her comfort zone, and she makes a life-altering declaration. Life for her will never be the same from this moment on as she commits to embracing the cross—the mountain of myrrh—her fears, and anything that hinders her obedience. She announces: "I will go. I want to be Yours exclusively. I will go on my way now up to the mountain of myrrh." This is the very thing she said before she would not do. She told him, "No." Now she is saying, "Yes, I will go to the mountain!" And everything in the Song shifts right here. She calls it the "mountain of myrrh" and the "hill of frankincense." When she says, "I will ascend . . . I will go up to the mountain of myrrh," she is saying this: "There is not one issue in my life that I am saying 'no' to You: my time, my money, my speech, my thought life, all my resources, all my gifts, my ministry, my sex life—everything in my life is Yours, my Bridegroom." There are no areas of her life—not one issue—that she is not turning over to the Lord. His love has totally captured her. Perfect love has cast out all her fear and in its place is a steely determination to follow Him wherever He leads. She realizes who she is in Him, and that He is all-powerful; therefore, she is safe. I'm not saying she's mature at this point, but she is definitely making a significant faith declaration by stating her desire and the intentions of her heart.

This is a **mountain** of myrrh, not a small amount of myrrh. It is very costly to radically obey God. But when you compare it

---

[52] See Gal 2:20; Phil 3:10.

to what you get, the cost comes into perspective and you realize its full worth. Notice it is a mountain of myrrh, but only a **hill** of incense. Incense speaks of prayer. Even a small amount of prayer prepares us to embrace even the greatest of life's obstacles. The mountain of myrrh would be too high without living on the smaller hill of frankincense. Obviously I am not minimizing prayer; it is of significant importance in our life. What I am saying is that the Lord rewards even a little effort so well. Even a short period of communion in His presence makes a huge eternal impact.

The maiden makes a firm decision to leave the comfort zone, to go up the mountain, and to walk in all of God's will without fear. "I will go!" she says. How glorious these words are to God!

She refers to it as "my way." We must follow the unique path God has chosen for us. God calls each of us on our own tailor-made journey. Our unique pathway to the mountain of myrrh involves difficulties unique to God's purpose in our life.

The Shulamite commits to continue on the mountain of myrrh until all compromise is gone: "Until the day breaks and the shadows flee away," she says. The "shadows" speak of the areas of weakness or compromise, like the little foxes.

Then her Bridegroom responds:

You are altogether beautiful, my darling (4:7, NIV).

Every part of you is so beautiful, my darling (4:7, TPT).

Again He calls her beautiful, and He is saying the exact same thing to you right now. You are altogether beautiful to Him.

Moving into Bridal Identity

It is at this time that the maiden is upgraded to bridal status. She now will begin to enjoy the identity as the Bride as He beckons her forth:

*Come away with me to Lebanon, my **bride,** come with me from Lebanon. Descend from the crest of Amana, from the top of Senir, the summit of Hermon, from the lions' dens and the mountain haunts of leopards (4:8, NIV, emphasis added).*

Now you are ready, bride of the mountains, to come with me as we climb the highest peaks together. Come with me through the archway of trust. We will look down from the crest of the glistening mounts and from the summit of our sublime sanctuary. Together we will wage war in the lion's den and the leopard's lair as they watch nightly for their prey (v 8, TPT, emphasis added).

This is the first time in the Song where she is called His Bride. She has said "yes." She is walking in a higher level of intimacy and maturity at this point.

Here we also see the fifth revelation of Jesus in the Song as He reveals Himself as a heavenly Bridegroom. He has answered her call to "draw" her and to "run together" with her.

When He tells the Bride that they will "wage war in the lion's den and the leopard's lair as they watch nightly for their prey,"[53] He is talking about taking on the spiritual forces of evil in the spiritual realms. The Bride is seated with Him in heavenly places, co-laboring with Him, as she takes her place at His side in this war against the enemy. She cries out for intimacy, and the result of their intimate encounters is that she is equipped as a warrior Bride.

The Bride is now a living sacrifice, and she is no longer counting the cost of following her Bridegroom to the highest heights—wherever that leads, whatever the risk.

[53] TPT.

"You have ravished my heart"

The Bridegroom turns to speak to His Bride and tells her:

> *You have ravished my heart, my sister, my spouse; you have ravished my heart with one look of your eyes, with one link of your necklace. How fair is your love, my sister, my spouse. How much better than wine is your love, and the scent of your perfumes than all spices! Your lips, O my spouse, drip as the honeycomb; honey and milk are under your tongue; and the fragrance of your garments is like the fragrance of Lebanon.*
>
> *A garden enclosed is my sister, my spouse, a spring shut up, a fountain sealed. Your plants are an orchard of pomegranates with pleasant fruits, fragrant henna with spikenard, spikenard and saffron, calamus and cinnamon, with all trees of frankincense, myrrh and aloes. With all the chief spices—a fountain of gardens, a well of living waters, and streams from Lebanon (4:9-15).*
>
> *For you reach into my heart. With one flash of your eyes I am undone by your love, my beloved, my equal, my bride. You leave me breathless—I am overcome by merely a glance from your worshipping eyes, for you have stolen my heart. I am held hostage by your love . . . (v 9, TPT).*

The word "ravished" connotes intense delight; to be captured. Listen to His message: He is talking about you! You are the one who has conquered and ravished His heart. Hear His words to you:

> You have ravished My heart, My sister, My bride.
> You have ravished My heart with one look of your eyes.

He is saying, "Every time you simply glance at Me, my heart skips a beat . . ."—with just one glance! Can you imagine what you do to His heart when you look full-on at Him with gratitude and love in your heart? If you have ever wondered what Jesus really thinks and feels about you, here is your answer. You thrill His heart . . . you ignite His emotions. This all-powerful God who declares that there is no other power that could ever overcome Him has to pause and declare, "Oh wait! There is one who can overcome me: My Bride. She overwhelms me. I am a prisoner of her love."

Beloved, I cannot talk you into this. Your spirit knows this is true. Don't let your mind talk you out of this truth; let your spirit be refreshed and renew your mind with the understanding that you are the beloved of God. Jesus' heart is filled with a furious love towards you and nothing can ever change that. Nothing. He is simply overcome with emotions of joy and delight every time you come to His mind . . . which is constantly.

"Let My love nourish your heart"

Listen to these words of Jesus from the Gospel of John:

> I love each of you with the same love that the Father loves me. Let my love nourish your hearts (15:9, TPT).

The dictionary defines "nourish" as, "to provide someone with food that is needed to live a healthy life; to cause someone to develop and grow stronger; to promote growth, to increase passion." Hear the words of Jesus once again: "Let my love nourish your heart." God is giving you a deep message here. Your heart needs the nourishment of His love today. So hear this: You are passionately, overwhelmingly loved by a Father in Heaven whose heart is ravished over you simply because of who you are. I understand that you may be much more comfortable with conditional love than unconditional love. We seem to be okay with statements like:

- "I love you because you are so smart—so gifted."
- "I love you because you are so creative."
- "I love you because you have such a servant's heart."

- "I love you because you lovingly help people, compassionately pray for people, and tenderly care for people.
- "I love you because you are so passionate."

The fact is, God is relentlessly, outrageously committed to you exactly in the place where you are right now. His unconditional love is divine and cannot, therefore, be compared to the unreliable earthly relationships you've experienced in your lifetime. Does He want you to change—to be transformed? Absolutely. He loves you way too much to allow you to stay in the place where you are. But He *loves* you right now just as you are. He's not worried about what you are not. He lives with you in the present, but He has designs on your future. And He says, "We will simply solve all this 'stuff' as we go." God loves you to walk with Him in your brokenness, in your pain, in your suffering, and in your weaknesses. He doesn't disappear in any of those moments. No. We are the ones who disappear and hide from Him. But He is the one who draws nearer and says to us, "Keep walking close with Me," because the closer you walk with Him, the more you walk *out* of those things and into the territory that He has established for you.

Seriously, I can make a list of all the things I want to change in my life at this very moment. But I am happy with where I am right now. I'm planning to change, but I like myself in the process of what I am becoming. I like myself in what I have become. I like myself where I am right now, and I like myself in the process of who I am becoming. You cannot go anywhere in Christ unless you are absolutely clear about where you are right now.

Please listen to these words . . . let them wash over you: You are the beloved of God. I want to repeat what I've said earlier: He's not obsessed by your sin or what you've done. He's already dealt with it. He's consumed with giving you life—an abundant sustainable life. His abundance of grace will wash over you every single day of your life. There is never going to be a moment when He is not—or will not—be merciful to you. There is never going to be a moment when He is not full of kindness and generosity toward you.

Remember this: He is not embarrassed by any of your

failures. God is love, kindness, mercy, grace, and goodness towards you, and eternally committed to a relationship with you. Commitment is who God is to you regardless of the circumstances. When you get that, the doorway will open wide into intimacy. You know, there is not one person who isn't broken in some area of their life. We all have areas of weakness. We all have areas of struggle. So with that in mind, please receive this prayer as I pray it over you:

> Father, I thank You that You walk with us through the good and the bad, You walk with us on the mountain and in the valley, and Your commitment is always 100% because that is Your character.
>
> Would You come and touch my heart . . . touch my emotions . . . touch my mind . . . and replace the mindset I have about You with a better one? Replace the mindset I have about myself with the mindset You have about me so that the eyes of my heart will be opened and I can really see who You desire me to be and just how much You love me.
>
> I ask You, Father, in the name of Jesus, would You give me a spirit of wisdom and revelation in the knowledge of Jesus that I might know who God really is for me and what He has planned for me at this time?
>
> Holy Spirit, speak these truths to my mind: that God could not love me any more than He does right now. Father—let this truth **resound** in my mind so I get it. And for all of this I want to simply say, thank You, Lord. Amen.

"Better than Wine"

The Lord makes another stunning statement when He says:

How satisfying to me, my equal, my bride. Your love is my finest wine—intoxicating and thrilling. And your sweet, perfumed praises—so exotic, so pleasing (4:10, TPT).

Back in Song 1:2, the Bride had asked to know the kisses of His Word because she knew His love is better than wine. Now Jesus is taking the very thing that she said to Him, and turning it around and saying, "You know what? Your love is better than wine to Me as well!" Jesus is essentially saying that our love is better—and even more beautiful—than all the splendorous works of His hand. Out of all of His creation, He is basically saying, "I would rather have your love. Your love moves Me more than all I have created with My hands." The love of all the angels together cannot be compared to your love as it is released to Him, and your worship comes up to Him as the sweetest fragrant perfume. Your worship and your love minister deeply to His affections. You delight Him like no other in all of His creation—no one can give what you give Him.

"A Garden Enclosed"

A garden enclosed is my sister, my spouse, a spring shut up, a fountain sealed (4:12).

My darling bride, my private paradise, fastened to my heart. A secret spring are you that no one else can have—my bubbling fountain hidden from public view. What a perfect partner to me now that I have you (v 12, TPT).

This "closed garden" is talking about our heart. The heart of the Bride is the private garden of King Jesus. At the time of the writing of the Song, a closed garden was a private garden in contrast to a public garden. In the public gardens of that day, the animals would come and pollute the water source of the garden; they defiled it. So the king would put a fence around his private garden. Therefore, an "enclosed garden" means a garden with a fence around it. The purpose of the king's garden was for his pleasure and rest. The purpose of the common garden was to grow food for survival. Only the king had enough money, servants, and the amount of time it took to cultivate a garden for his own pleasure. Very few people had such gardens.

Beloved, we are the garden of pleasure in which Jesus seeks to find His rest. When our life is consecrated to the Lord and wholly devoted, we are as an enclosed garden; our heart is locked from the spirit of compromise and from the defilement of the world. We become the garden of pleasure where the Lord comes and rests in our midst for communion and fellowship. We cry out to Him, "My heart is Yours; my mind is Yours. I am living for You as a place of Your pleasure—a place where you can rest." It is a place where you can rest in agreement together. It is like when the Apostle Paul prayed that the Holy Spirit would come and make Himself comfortable and at home in our heart.[54] When does the Spirit of the Lord feel most comfortable in our hearts? When He is not being grieved and quenched; when He is hosted really well; when He feels loved; when He is surrounded with peace and love—the atmosphere of Heaven itself. That is when He can settle down and make Himself at home.

He is saying this to His Bride, "You are a garden enclosed to Me," because she created such an environment of rest, peace, and love for Him. This is one of the highest things that Jesus could ever say about us. Our hearts are locked to the world and reserved exclusively for the King: the internal castle where the Presence of God dwells, where His private chamber lives within us, is locked and reserved for Him alone. Psalm 91 calls this a "secret place", because when we live there, remain there, and abide there, and when we keep it locked to everyone but the Lord, the enemy cannot find us. This secret place is only open to Jesus. And as we live in that secret place, developing a private history with Him, the fruit of our passionate intimacy is released through our every action.

Expressions of Worship

This secret place of our inner world is a fruitful garden for His pleasure alone.

---

[54]   See Eph 3.

> *Your inward life is now sprouting, bringing forth*
> *fruit. What a beautiful paradise unfolds within*
> *you. When I'm near you, I smell aromas of the*
> *finest spice, for many clusters of my exquisite*
> *fruit now grow within your inner garden. Here*
> *are the nine: pomegranates of passion, henna*
> *from heaven, spikenard so sweet, saffron*
> *shining, fragrant calamus from the cross, sacred*
> *cinnamon, branches of scented woods, myrrh, like*
> *tears from a tree, and aloe as eagles ascending*
> *(4:13-14, TPT).*

The Bridegroom lists nine fruits and expressions of worship that flow through the Bride, and I will comment on a couple of them.

"Pomegranates of passion": The pomegranate contains some very sweet morsels of juicy fruit. But to get to them, one has to break the tough outer shell. That is such a great picture of the fruit that is within us. As we yield to the Holy Spirit who produces His fruit through us, we will see love, joy, peace, patience, kindness, goodness, faithfulness, gentleness, and self-control enrich the lives of others around us.

"Henna from Heaven": Henna speaks of forgiveness. As we have received forgiveness, so we freely extend it in mercy.

"Spikenard so sweet": Spikenard is a very costly spice, and was also the fragrance that Mary poured out on the feet of Jesus.[55]

"Saffron shining": This is a lover's perfume, which was also very costly.

The love of God is like a river flowing to us.

> *Your life flows into mine, pure as a garden spring.*
> *A well of living water springs up from within you,*
> *like a mountain brook flowing into my heart!*
> *(4:15, TPT)*

When we return that love to Him, we are like a river of love flowing right back into His heart. Our garden contains a

---

[55]   See John 12:3.

refreshing spring that is released in a continual flow of worship, praise, and adoration back to the Lord.

Risking the North Winds

The Bride is so encouraged and emboldened by the fact that Jesus delights in her and deals so tenderly with her, she has the courage to cry out this very significant prayer:

> *Awake, O north wind, and come O south! Blow upon my garden, that its spices may flow out. Let my beloved come to his garden and eat its pleasant fruits (4:16).*

> *Then may your awakening breath blow upon my life until I am fully yours. Breathe upon me with your Spirit wind. Stir up the sweet spice of your life within me. Spare nothing as you make me your fruitful garden. Hold nothing back until I release your fragrance (v 16, TPT).*

Oh my, what a prayer. The Bride is in such a safe place of peace, trust, and faith in the Lord, that she asks Him to release the harsh winter north winds into her life. She's saying that she is ready to participate in the sufferings of Jesus as she calls for the bitter north winds of adversity, crisis, and difficulty to come into her life. She is willing to embrace difficulty if that is what she needs to produce sweeter fruit and a more robust fragrance of His Presence in her life. She is saying, "I am not afraid of hardships. I am not afraid of saying "yes" and going through adversity to know You, my Beloved, in a deeper way."

She also prays for the south winds to come. The south winds are the winds of refreshing, the cool breezes of His Presence, His grace, and His favor. We all have a tendency to love the south winds and we cry out for those. The north winds, however, are the challenging times that bring us to a new place in Him. Now the Bride says, "I am not afraid of the north winds," because earlier in her journey, when He called her to the mountaintop, she *was* afraid. Now she is saying, "I am *not afraid* of anything that You will call me to because You love me.

You evaluate me with such kindness. I long to be closer to You."
She understands that this wonderful fragrance of His Presence
is really a combination of both the north and the south winds.
Only God has enough wisdom to know the combination of
north and south winds that is required in each unique season
of our life. I do not know what my life needs right now. I always
lean toward the south winds, but God allows the north winds
because it is the perfect combination of both that bring the
garden of my heart into its fullest, most pleasing fragrance.

The Bride has grown into a place of great trust. This
is another significant turning point in her journey as she
embraces new levels of faith. Another really important part of
this moment is that she now sees the garden as belonging to
Him instead of her. Remember in the first four chapters of the
Song, it was all about her inheritance and *her* garden. From
this point forward, it is all about her life being His inheritance
and His garden. This is where the Holy Spirit is bringing us;
He does this by affirming us and revealing the beauty He sees
when He receives our love. He always expresses the way He
truly feels about our love. The Holy Spirit is producing courage
and a resolve to not draw back from the seasonal changes of
either the north or south winds in order that our garden will
mature and truly become His garden.

Let's look at 5:1 in three different translations as the
Bridegroom answers:

> *I have come to my garden, my sister, my spouse;*
> *I have gathered my myrrh with my spice; I have*
> *eaten my honeycomb with my honey; I have*
> *drunk my wine with my milk (5:1).*

> *Come walk with me until I am fully yours. Come*
> *taste the fruits of your life in me. I have gathered*
> *from your heart, my equal, my bride. I have*
> *gathered from my garden all my sacred spices—*
> *even my myrrh. I have tasted and enjoyed my*
> *wine within you (v 1, NIV).*

> *I have gathered from your heart, my equal, my*
> *bride, I have gathered from my garden all my*
> *sacred spices—even my myrrh. I have tasted and*

*enjoyed my wine within you. I have tasted with
pleasure my pure milk, my honeycomb, which
you yield to me. I delight in gathering my sacred
spice, all the fruits of my life I have gathered from
within you, my paradise garden. Come, all my
friends—feast upon my bride, all you revelers of
my palace. Feast on her, my lovers! Drink and
drink, and drink again, until you can take no
more. Drink the wine of her love. Take all you
desire, you priests. My life within her will become
your feast (5:1, TPT)*

He responds to her with His invitation: "Come into my
garden, my Bride, my co-partner." Notice all the times He
uses the word "my": "My garden", "My myrrh", "My spice", "My
honeycomb", "My honey", "My wine".

The last line from *The Passion Translation* brings an
important point: "Take all you desire, you priests. My life
within her will become your feast." Jesus invites others to come
eat and drink of this love. The Bride becomes the banqueting
table—a feast for the nations. She becomes that feast because
she is the exact representation of Him.

The Lord responds to her cry for the north and south winds
by releasing wave after wave of His Presence. He intoxicates
her again with His passion and Presence. This is a very sweet
moment of intimacy as the Bridegroom is preparing His
Bride. He answers her cry for the north winds of adversity by
beckoning her into the fellowship of suffering. This is all part
of the spiritual maturity continuum. As we take up our cross
and follow Him, it propels us into a new season, which always
begins with a fresh revelation of who Jesus is for us.

Withdrawing a Sense of His Presence

Every new season has its own version of testing. This test
includes a withdrawing of a sense of His Presence once again.
This happened to the Bride earlier in response to her refusing
to go up the mountains with Him. At that time He withdrew a

sense of His Presence as a way of her realizing that she could not live without Him.

This new test is a little different for the Bride because it will reveal exactly where she is on her progress into full bridal partnership. We read in Deuteronomy that these tests[56] are not for God; they are for us so that we can determine by our response what is our present level of maturity. Will the Bride continue to radically pursue, trust, and love the Lord when all the prophetic promises don't seem to be happening or even look like they will never happen? Will the Bride continue to love and pursue her Bridegroom when her ministry is gone, or when she is being opposed, resisted, hurt, and wounded by those she loves? Will the Bride continue to love Jesus with all her heart, mind, soul, and strength when she cannot even locate Him or sense His Presence? When she feels lonely, alone, and abandoned, can she still say, "My Beloved is mine, and I am His"?

> CAN YOU IMAGINE WHAT YOU DO TO HIS HEART WHEN YOU LOOK FULL ON AT HIM WITH GRATITUDE AND LOVE IN YOUR HEART?

He withholds His presence from her to see if she will be true in love without the benefit and pleasure of feeling good. Will she do that for Him? Or is she only seeking Him so that she can experience the pleasures and joys of His presence? Is Jesus a means to an end for her? Or is He the goal? Is He only for the end of her life?

The north winds of adversity begin to blow in the life of the Bride and the Lord begins to withdraw a sense of His Presence

---

56   See Deut. 8:2.

from her . . . for only a brief season. That is the first part of this test.

The second part of her test comes when we see her spiritual leaders strike her, wound her, and take her veil away—her covering. She loses her function, her place, and the anointing of her ministry in the Body of Christ. The reason this is so big is because at the very beginning of the Song, she only had two great prayers:[57] She wanted to experience His Presence and prayed, "Draw me after You;" she wanted to be effective in ministry and implored Him: "Let us run together"—a reference to ministry. Her life vision consisted of these two primary goals: "I want to **experience** Your Presence, and I want to **partner** with You in bringing the power and goodness of God to others." That is a great life vision—to experience God, and then to bring that experience to other people by the power of the Holy Spirit and in partnership with Him.

What Jesus is going to do is the two things that she cares most about: He is going to cause them to be temporarily withheld from her. His question to her is this: "Are you serving Me so that you can feel good in My Presence?" It's a valid question for all of us. Don't you love to feel the powerful and loving Presence of God? I know I do. There is nothing better than feeling loved by God and sensing the power of His Presence to love Him back. That is the most dynamic reality the human spirit can experience—feeling God's love, expressing love, and feeling His love in return. What a pleasurable delight. The Bride goes on and on about that in the Song of Solomon, "His banner over me is love . . . I am at His banqueting table . . . sustain me . . . refresh me . . . I am lovesick. . . ."[58] The Shulamite was in such a great place—sitting in the shade of the Lord, reading her favorite books, being hand-fed bon-bons by her Beloved. Life is amazing! At this point in her walk with God, the life of the maiden was really all about her. The two things that she wanted most were to feel and experience His Presence, and to be useful—to have an anointed and meaningful, fruitful function in the Body. And now, in this two-fold test, both of these are temporarily withheld from her. There again is the thrust of this

---

[57] See Song 1:4.
[58] See Song 2:3-4.

particular test: "Are you in this relationship for Me, or only for you? As long as you feel My Presence, your ministry is going good, and circumstances are working out right, that's when you will worship Me? Or will you continue to passionately pursue Me even if all that is stripped away?"

This is the question He asks in such times as well. We hear Him calling to us . . . will we follow Him?

The Beckoning Bridegroom

I sleep, but my heart is awake; it is the voice of my beloved! He knocks, saying, "Open for me my sister, my love, my dove, my perfect one; for my head is covered with dew, my locks with the drops of the night." I have taken off my robe; how can I put it on again? I have washed my feet; how can I defile them?

My beloved put his hand by the latch of the door, and my heart yearned for him. I arose to open for my beloved, and my hands dripped with myrrh, my fingers with liquid myrrh, on the handles of the lock. I opened for my beloved, but my beloved had turned away and was gone. My heart leaped up when he spoke. I sought him, but I could not find him; I called him, but he gave me no answer. The watchmen who went about the city found me. They struck me, they wounded me; the keepers of the walls took my veil away from me. I charge you, O daughters of Jerusalem, if you find my beloved, that you tell him I am lovesick! (5:2-8)

The Beloved Bridegroom comes speaking to the heart of His beloved, and calls her to arise in the dark of night, which means the north winds must have already begun blowing into her life. He is calling out to her to open up and trust Him even if she cannot sense or feel Him with her through this season of difficulty. The Bridegroom opens the chapter by calling out to her with four different names:

- "My sister"
- "My love"
- "My dove"
- "My perfect one"

All four of those names are significant, so let's explore their meanings.

"My Sister"

When He says, "my sister," I believe He is declaring to her that He relates to her as a human being. Everything Jesus did, He did as a man in intimate, right relationship with the Father. Because Jesus was human, He understands me. Yes, He is the Son of God—the eternal Son of the Father—not a created being. But He set His divinity aside and lived His life here on earth as a man, making Himself completely vulnerable and dependent upon His Father. Philippians tells us:

> When the time came, he set aside the privileges of deity and took on the status of a slave, became human! Having become human, he stayed human. It was an incredibly humbling process. He didn't claim special privileges. Instead, he lived a selfless, obedient life and then died a selfless, obedient death—the worst kind of death at that—a crucifixion (2:7-8, MSG).

Jesus humbled Himself beyond our comprehension. He lived and modeled the life of a person living in complete dependence upon the Holy Spirit. If Jesus came and did everything He did as God, we would marvel; but that would not have been an example for us of *how* to live our life. But because He was 100-percent man, I not only admire Him, I also have an example of how to live an abundant life in complete dependence on a heavenly Father who passionately loves me as much as He loves Jesus.

Because Jesus was human, He experienced everything His Bride is experiencing: deep wounding, rejection, hurt, pain, disappointment, and loneliness. The more we grasp His humanity, the more we will find Him to be someone we can approach, know, love, trust, and adore. Jesus' favorite title for Himself was the Son of Man. Jesus felt what you feel. He had longings . . . you have longings. Jesus wept . . . you weep. Jesus laughed out loud, a lot . . . you also laugh. The One who created the human heart—His own heart is so kind and so vast—felt deeply. Jesus knew loneliness. This One who created love and friendship longed for the same.

The Bride—so hurt, so rejected, so wounded, so isolated, alone, and lonely—is in the presence of One who knows what it's like to spend time with people who didn't care enough to really get to know Him. We see this in His exchange with Philip when he said: "Lord, show us the Father."[59] And Jesus responded by saying:

> *Don't you know me, Philip, even after I have been among you for such a long time? Anyone who has seen me has seen the Father. How can you say, "Show us the Father"? (John 14:9, NIV)*

You can hear and almost feel the pain in Jesus' heart. He spent three years with these guys, opening Himself up at the deepest level, pulling back the veil, exposing all of who He is, and they did not even try to get know Him as He had hoped. Yes, Jesus truly *understands*. His very humanity causes me to fall in love with Him even more.

"My Love"

He motivates us by His tender love to affection-based obedience. Every time He speaks love, it creates love, it releases love, it captivates and captures you, and it transforms your life. All through this Song He has been love for her, and He releases that reality again.

"My Dove"

As we have mentioned earlier, the dove speaks of the single-mindedness of loyalty, and it also speaks of the Holy Spirit. He is reminding the Bride that the Holy Spirit is the One who will provide the comfort and be her strength in this time of testing.

---

[59] See John 14:1-9.

"My Perfect One"

With this name, He speaks again to her truest identity—who she is to Him. He reminds her, that to Him, she is His beloved Bride—the one who has ravished His heart again and again. She is His beautiful Bride for whom He chose to lay down His life. She is perfect to Him and He is radically and passionately in love with her.

Jesus always reveals Himself as such a source of compassion, love, and tenderness. He knows that this Bride has given her entire heart and life to Him. She has finally said "yes", and she has asked for the north winds of adversity to come. So He encourages her with another wave of heavenly identity, letting her know who she really is. He then points to another aspect of who He is by coming to her as the Jesus of Gethsemane, the one who endured the dark night of the soul. He now invites her to join Him in the fellowship of His suffering. He stands outside her door—knocking and inviting her to embrace the cross as He did. As He comes before her, He asks her to open her heart to Him as He reveals Himself. Her response is critical, because there is a dimension of God that we cannot experience unless we respond correctly. It is the desire of the Lord that we continue all the way with Him to the highest level of passionate love as described in chapter 8 of the Song,[60] but there are many Christians who choose to level off, hovering under the banner of love as described in chapter 2. That is such a great place to be, and that place is always a part of our journey. But we cannot simply camp out there—under His love banner. We hold that place dear in our hearts, but we *must* journey on. We must embrace the Jesus as revealed in chapters five through eight.

Surrendered in Total Obedience

The Bride responds now in complete and total obedience.

> *I have taken off my robe; how can I put it on again? I have washed my feet; how can I defile them? (5:3)*

---

[60] See Song 8:6.

I have already laid aside my own garments for
you. How could I take them up again since I've
yielded my righteousness to yours? You have
cleansed my life and taken me so far. Isn't that
enough? (5:3, TPT).

She thinks about it, and when she hesitates to ponder it instead of leaping up and going with Him, Jesus withdraws His Presence. The Bride is not compromising or argumentative. She responds obediently. She asks: "I took off my robe . . . should I put it on again? I have already washed my feet, should I get them dirty again?" She is not complaining about the inconvenience of getting out of bed. She is not resisting Him. Her heart is completely His, and she says, "I got up . . . I obeyed You. I opened my heart for my Beloved. I rose up and opened my heart to You—exactly what You asked of me. My hands were dripping with the fragrance of myrrh from the door handles."

The Bride instantly arises in obedience and declares: "I took off my robes and put on Your robes. I am taking off my old life, and putting on Your robe of righteousness." She is making a statement: "I will never ever go back to living in compromise."

My beloved put his hand by the latch of the door,
and my heart yearned for him (5:4).

My beloved reached into me to unlock my heart.
The core of my very being trembled at his touch.
How my soul melted when he spoke to me! (5:4,
TPT)

"Now the hand of God, my Beloved, Jesus," she says, "is at the door of my heart and it leaped for joy." Jesus is putting His hand upon her heart, releasing the grace of God upon her. Her heart is touched and stirred to assist Him; she is convicted. He came in grace to touch her heart, and she is preparing for the forthcoming two-fold test.

"I sought him, but I could not find him"

I arose to open for my beloved, and my hands

> *dripped with myrrh, my fingers with liquid myrrh, on the handles of the lock. I opened for my beloved, but my beloved had turned away and was gone. My heart leaped up when he spoke. I sought him, but I could not find him; I called him, but he gave me no answer (vs 5-6).*

> *My spirit arose to open for more of his touch. As I surrendered to him, I began to sense his fragrance—the fragrance of his suffering love! It was the sense of myrrh flowing all through me! I opened my soul to my beloved, but suddenly he was gone! And my heart was torn out in longing for him. I sought his presence, his fragrance, but could not find him anywhere. I called out for him, yet he did not answer me. I will arise and search for him until I find him (5:5-6, TPT).*

Here we have the first test of the "north winds" as she rises to greet her Beloved, but He is not there. She cannot find Him. This is an entirely new experience for her when she is living totally for Him with no level of fear or compromise in her life. These "north winds" are the hardships, trials, and difficulties that we all go through called life. There are things that God, in His wisdom, allows into our life for a greater purpose. God is love and He does not bring harm to His children; life does. But these times of adversity only serve to strengthen us because of His grace.

Whenever the Bride sought the Lord, she always found Him. She did what He said. She was not disobedient on any level. She's not compromising at all, and yet, she's absolutely shocked that she cannot find Him. This has happened to her before. She has not been disobedient to the Lord and so she knows this is not His discipline. In fact, she has been fully obedient to Him and remains in a posture of fully responsive love. She remembers that He will sometimes temporarily remove a sense of His Presence as a way for her to pursue Him more ardently.

In times like these we know that our Beloved is with us because there is never a time when His Presence—the Holy Spirit—is not living in us. His eyes are always attentive to us;

He is carefully watching over us at all times. However, there are those times when we cannot discern His Presence. He is not readily available to our feelings. But even in those moments He is stunningly available to our faith. The times when He hides can be part of His strategy to mature our love and faith. That is what is happening with the Bride at this time.

"O daughters of Jerusalem"

> *The watchmen who went about the city found me.*
> *They struck me, they wounded me; the keepers*
> *of the walls took my veil away from me. I charge*
> *you, O daughters of Jerusalem, if you find my*
> *beloved, that you tell him I am lovesick (v 7-8).*

I love that she became desperate to find Him. She is absolutely lovesick, and she walks throughout the city looking for her Beloved Jesus.

> *Nevertheless, make me this promise, you brides-*
> *to-be: If you find my beloved one, please tell him*
> *I endured all travails for him. I've been pierced*
> *through by love, and I will not be turned aside (v*
> *8, TPT).*

Though she is distraught, look how she responds, "I will **not** be turned aside." She has a fixed determination to find her Beloved, no matter what it costs her. In her amazing humility, the Bride goes to the "Daughters of Jerusalem"—the immature Christians—and she says, "If you find my Beloved, please tell Him I miss Him so much." What an amazing response. She's not offended. She does not let discouragement settle into her heart and cause it to fill with unforgiveness, bitterness, or offense. She is being unjustly mistreated, yet she responds with fruits of the Spirit deeply rooted within her: peace, patience, goodness, kindness, faithfulness, etc. So desperate is she to find Him, she tells this group of people who are not pursuing the Bridegroom Jesus with the same ardent passion to the degree she is: "If you see Jesus, please tell Him that I am lovesick for Him. Tell Him, 'Even if I do not see You again, I am in this until the end.' I love Him."

Stripped of Everything

The humility of the Bride is revealed as she asks for help from the spiritually immature Daughters of Jerusalem. She is in a time of divine testing as everything is stripped away from her—

- possessions
- ministry
- favor
- authority
- intimacy with Jesus
- feeling the woundedness and rejection by those she loves and trusts

And yet, she loves her Bridegroom Jesus despite what is happening in her life. She is no longer in this life with Jesus for herself. In this place, she declares: "No matter what anyone does to me, no matter if I have a ministry or don't have a ministry, no matter if I can sense Your Presence or not, I am not leaving You. I am not offended by all this . . . I want You . . . I am lovesick."

She tells the Daughters, "If you see Jesus, please tell Him I love Him more than ever. None of these difficulties affect the way I feel about Him. Tell Him I am not mad . . . I am not offended at anyone or anything."

"What love is this?"

This unusual expression of love astounds the Daughters of Jerusalem so much, they must know for themselves what kind of person is her Beloved. So they pried her with questions:

> *What love is this? How could you continue to care so deeply for him? Isn't there another who could steal away your heart? We see now your beauty, more beautiful than all the others. What makes your beloved better than any other? What is it about him that makes you ask us to promise you this? (5:9, TPT)*

Twice they ask, "**What** is this guy to you?" Not *who!* They believe they know *who* He is: He is the way to Heaven. But they do not know *what* He is to her that makes their relationship with Him differ so dramatically. They are asking her, "What is your Beloved more than another beloved . . ." because they have a lot of other loves in their life—money, pleasure, sin—things they love more than the Lord. So they are stunned by her exclusive love to this one she calls her "Beloved" and ask her, "What is He to you? What is He more than all the other loves of life?" The issue that provoked these spiritually dull, passive Christians was the Bride's deep love for Jesus more than ministry, more than giftings, more than notoriety—more than anything else they desire in life. What is so evident with this Bride is her passionate exclusionary love for Jesus. Such singular love is a stark contrast to nominal Christians and it certainly contrasts the worldly affections and attachments of immature believers.

From the obvious devotion the Bride has only for Jesus, they came to the conclusion: "She must know something we don't know." They can't even imagine such passion for Jesus, so they ask her: "How can you be so dedicated to Him when He seemed to treat you so unfairly? Please . . . tell us your secret. We follow Him too, but not like you do. We saw that He was hiding His Presence from you, He allowed you to be rejected at church which caused you to lose your ministry, so why are you still so tenaciously loyal to Him? What do you know about Him that we don't?" These daughters just don't understand this kind of steadfast devotion . . . they don't understand this kind of wholehearted dedication to one Lover. They just cannot grasp it because they have no grid for it. So they inquire of this Bride with an earnest desire to truly know, "What is your Beloved? We've got to know what it is that motivates you. What kind of person is He? What do you know that we don't know? Seriously, why aren't you offended at how you've been treated? Look at all you've given up for your Beloved! Look at all you do for Him . . . and this is how He repays you? How can you **not** be offended?" These questions are really the beginning of fervency being awakened in the hearts of these dull-hearted believers. What they're really asking her is, "What is He more than all the other loves of your life?"

They also call her, "O fairest among women," or as many versions translate it, "O most beautiful." We see the deep respect the Daughters have for the Bride. They describe her as more beautiful than all the ones with whom they are acquainted, even all the people of the earth. With her devotion, godliness, and purity, she outshines them all as the "most beautiful." Very often it is the fervency in us that will awaken in others and cause them to see God's character being manifested in our lives. This Bride is so full of Jesus—her heart is so saturated with the love of God and His Presence—she just leaked! And this is God's intention with us!

The Bride's Testimony: "My Beloved is . . . "

Because of this, the Daughters of Jerusalem ask her, "Tell us what you see in Him! What is He really like?" In response, the young Bride gives one of the most powerful descriptions of Jesus, and one of the most incredible expressions of worship found in the Word of God. This is the one time in the Song where she pours herself out in worship to the King. It really is a magnificent, poetic unveiling of the splendor of Jesus Christ. Though reading this passage with its poetic language may seem a little awkward at first, we need to sit with the Holy Spirit and go over it time and again. Here the Holy Spirit uses metaphors of the human body to convey ten descriptive attributes of the personality of Jesus. The first one is a general statement, and then she lists ten distinct attributes of God, with her last statement being a summary. The full meaning is somewhat obscure, but it is meant to be poetic. These are dynamic statements about the glory of God through which the Holy Spirit will give us a powerful revelation about the beauty of Jesus' character and personality.

> *My beloved is white and ruddy, chief among ten thousand (v 10).*

> *He alone is my beloved. He shines in dazzling splendor, yet is still so approachable—without equal as he stands above all others, waving his banner to myriads (v 10, TPT).*

She starts out by saying, "Jesus is my Beloved . . . I love Him with all my heart." She goes on to say, "He is white," or as the NIV says it, "He is radiant." Other translations say, "He is brilliant." The Hebrew word translated as "white" means, "radiant, dazzling, brilliant, or shining white." It would be like looking directly into the brightness of the sun. This verse reminds me of the manifestation of Jesus' glory on the Mount of Transfiguration.

> *And He said to them, "Assuredly, I say to you that there are some standing here who will not taste death till they see the kingdom of God present with power." Now after six days Jesus took Peter, James, and John, and led them up on a high mountain apart by themselves; and He was transfigured before them. His clothes became shining, exceedingly white, like snow, such as no launderer on earth can whiten them. And Elijah appeared to them with Moses, and they were talking with Jesus. Then Peter answered . . . (Mk 9:1-5).*

The "white" described here is an unearthly, supernatural brilliance. This is the description of our Bridegroom.

I also love the last phrase in this section that says, "Peter answered." What did he answer? There was no question asked. Peter said to Jesus:

> *Rabbi, it is good for us to be here; and let us make three tabernacles: one for You, one for Moses, and one for Elijah—*

When Peter talks about a tabernacle here, he's not talking about a large building; he's talking about a tent. Luke also covered this story in his Gospel.

> *As he was praying, the appearance of his face changed, and his clothes became as bright as a flash of lightning (9:29, NIV).*

As Jesus was praying, His face "changed". Remember when

Jesus was walking in Emmaus[61] with two men who did not recognize Him? These two guys were walking with Jesus but they did not know who He was because His face had changed.

In this story Jesus' face changed in the same way; it transformed into something else. But these guys saw it happen, so they knew it was Jesus. As the Kingdom comes in glory, the appearance of things will change—altered into its heavenly state. Standing with His disciples on the mountain that day, Jesus' clothes transfigured with radiating brightness, like the brilliance of a flash of lightning. In Luke's version of this story, we are told the disciples were really, really sleepy before this and were falling asleep; but as Jesus transfigured before their very eyes, they were fully awakened.

That word "transfigured" is the same word used in Romans 12:2, where Paul tells us:

> *Do not conform to the pattern of this world, but*
> *be transformed by the renewing of your mind . . .*

The wordplay in this is very interesting, because these words, "transfigured," and "transformed", also tie into the word *metamorphosis*. Metamorphosis is that process where a dramatic shift takes place, transitioning from one stage to another, e.g., when a caterpillar morphs into a butterfly. I mean, you could be looking at a caterpillar slowly moving on the ground, and suddenly, it's a butterfly! That's the glorious transformation of Jesus at the Transfiguration. He was human-like in one moment, and in the very next moment, He's God-like.

It is in this context that the Daughters of Jerusalem respond by saying to the Bride, "Wow . . . you mean business! You are really awestruck by this one. You are fascinated with Him. Your heart is filled with marvel . . . with wonder. What do you know that we don't know?"

The Scripture gives us a clue about what the Bride knows:

---

[61] See Luke 24.

He is "chief among ten thousand". He is the One who stands out among the crowds. He is the One who is the center of attention just like a large banner preceding a marching military unit in formation. He is eminently superior among all people. The words, "ten thousand" are not to be taken as literal; it means, "incomparable greatness." He is "chief among ten thousand", the "standard bearer", which is a metaphor that means, "He is the greatest of all."

The Bride declares, **"Jesus has no rival . . . no equal. No one compares to Him. He surpasses them all."**

Ten Attributes of the Bridegroom

With this, the Bride continues to describe her beautiful Beloved:

> *His head is like the finest gold; His locks are wavy, and black as a raven. His eyes are like doves by the rivers of waters, washed with milk, and fitly set. His cheeks are like a bed of spices, banks of scented herbs. His lips are lilies, dripping liquid myrrh. His hands are rods of gold set with beryl. His body is carved ivory inlaid with sapphires. His legs are pillars of marble set on bases of fine gold. His countenance is like Lebanon, excellent as the cedars. His mouth is most sweet. Yes, he is altogether lovely. This is my beloved, and this is my friend, O daughters of Jerusalem! (5:11-16)*

> *The way he leads me is divine. His leadership—so pure and dignified as he wears his crown of gold. Upon this crown are letters of black written on a background of glory. He sees everything with pure understanding. How beautiful his insights—without distortion. His eyes rest upon the fullness of the river of revelation, flowing so clean and pure. Looking at his gentle face I see such fullness of emotion. Like a lovely garden where fragrant spices grow—what a man! No*

one speaks words so anointed as this one—words that both pierce and heal, words like lilies dripping with myrrh. See how his hands hold unlimited power! But he never uses it in anger, for he is always holy, displaying his glory.

His innermost place is a work of art—so beautiful and bright. How magnificent and noble is this one—covered in majesty! He's steadfast in all he does. His ways are the way of righteousness, based on truth and holiness. None can rival him, but all will be amazed by him. Most sweet are his kisses, even his whispers of love. He is delightful in every way and perfect from every viewpoint. If you ask me why I love him so, O brides-to-be, it's because there is none like him to me. Everything about him fills me with holy desire! And now he is my beloved—my friend forever (vs 11-16, TPT).

What a stunning description of her Beloved Bridegroom. Let's examine how the Bride develops these ten attributes of her Beloved.

1. **His head:** His sovereign leadership over all
2. **His locks:** His dedication to God and the Church
3. **His eyes:** His infinite knowledge, wisdom, understanding, discernment
4. **His cheeks:** His diverse emotional makeup
5. **His lips:** His Word
6. **His hands:** His divine activity
7. **His body:** His tender compassion
8. **His legs:** His authoritative stride executing His purposes
9. **His countenance:** The impartation of His majesty and splendor to His people
10. **His mouth:** Intimacy with Him

With the review of His glorious attributes, the Bride's summary and fitting conclusion is:

- **He is altogether lovely** . . . His comprehensive incomparable beauty.
- **He is my Beloved and my Friend** . . . He is my His heart's passion.

Becoming Christ-like

The Father has positioned you **in** Christ, and the Holy Spirit is teaching you how to become Christ-like. You are in the process of sanctification, learning how to walk with your Beloved in the abundance of His grace, mercy, and goodness so that every single mistake is covered by His blood. Every day, you are learning to have a much bigger understanding of His mercy than you do of your own weaknesses.

As His Bride, you are the Bridegroom's inheritance. Understanding your high value to God puts everything in proper perspective. Consider this: God loves you as if you were the only person in the world; it's that personal. He doesn't see you as one of hundreds of millions of people. He sees you as one person, and He's forever committed to *you*. God also has a picture of you in His mind—that Christ-like person—and He's going to push you and push you until you become the extraordinary person that He sees you are in Christ. And when *you* see that person—when you wake up to that image of you that He has in His heart—you will begin to fully embrace your destiny and pursue it with the same passion.

You see, God is always focused on your potential. He's got designs on you . . . yes, He's got great big plans for your future. Because He has forever settled the issue of your past, He lives with you in the present and has already secured your future. Hear Him say to you today: "Let's just walk really close together, okay? We'll get better acquainted moment by moment along the way." Do that. Keep walking intimately with Jesus— face-to-face, day in, day out—because remember, the closer you walk *with Him* and *in Him*, the faster you walk *out* of those things you don't want in your life and *into* the territory He has prepared especially for you.

As we look upon the countenance of the face of Jesus in our most intimate exchanges, He communicates and affirms His love to us again and again, and that transforms us inside and out. We can't help but fall in love all over again. He then imparts the majestic nature of His beauty—that Christ-likeness—so that we are overwhelmed with all He is for us. Everything else pales in comparison as we behold His beauty.

This is how to be strong in God and do great things for Him. It's all about beholding His glorious majesty and living in Him. If you get wounded, get healed right away; that annoys the enemy immensely. So many of us get stuck mentally and emotionally in a previous bad relational experience. You can get healed—body, soul, and spirit—very quickly by simply forgiving that person who offended you. None of these other things will hinder you any longer, nor will they sideline you. You'll be able to move quickly forward and be healed on the way as you walk in Him.

As we live in the present with God, we are walking right into the destiny He planned for us from before the foundation of the earth, enjoying His Presence moment by moment along the way. This in itself is the Father's ultimate aim—that you walk with Him and be formed into the image of His Son. There's no striving in this . . . only responding to the abundance of grace and mercy extended to us with a surrendered heart that says, "Yes!"

The Nature of the Bridegroom

Let's take a look at the characteristics of the nature of the Bridegroom that are so attractive to the Bride. It is His beautiful nature that causes her to lay down her own life and surrender completely to Him.

Cheeks and Lips

His cheeks are like a bed of spices, banks of scented herbs. His lips are lilies, dripping liquid myrrh (5:13).

Looking at his gentle face I see such fullness of emotion. Like a lovely garden where fragrant spices grow—what a man! No one speaks words

so anointed as this one—words that both pierce
and heal, words like lilies dripping with myrrh (v
13, TPT).

The "lips" of the Bridegroom are truthful and anointed with grace. His lips speak words that are always life giving and encouraging.

As we said earlier, "cheeks" refer to emotions. Jesus is full of emotions, and He loves to release the full range of His emotions into your heart and through your life. It's so critical for us in our growth to open our emotions to the emotions of Jesus. The cheeks are the windows to the emotions and reflect the countenance of the face that make up His healthy and perfect emotions.

We serve an emotional God. There are many people, however, who think the only emotion God experiences is joy when they are saved, and anger and wrath for any infraction against His law. It's as if He is saying, "I love you . . . and now I'm going to kill you!" How absurd! God's emotions are passionately alive, always well-intentioned toward you, and life-giving. The emotional makeup of Jesus is filled with passion, delight, and longing for you. He loves you with all of His divine emotions, and He would love for you to open your emotions to the emotions He has *for* you. When you do that, look out! You will experience unexpected delights reserved only for His beloved!

In Matthew 22, Jesus quotes Deuteronomy 6:4:

You shall love the Lord your God with all your
heart, with all your soul and with all your mind.
This is the first and great commandment. And the
second is like it: 'You shall love your neighbor as
yourself.' On these two commandments hang all
the Law and the Prophets (vs 37-40).

Sometimes, this world we inhabit makes everything so complex. But there was a moment in Jesus' ministry when He reduced everything down to a radical simplicity: "Love Me . . . love you . . . love others." In other words, He was saying, "Be shocking lovers of God, lovers of yourself, and love other people. That means, love people even if it is totally inconvenient;

love others who are not loving you back; love others who are scary; love others who don't remind you of you; and finally, love yourself. That should keep you pretty busy until I get back!"

Jesus calls us to love Him with everything within us because that's how He loves—with all His heart! He loves you with all His emotions! Have you ever thought about that? The One who created emotions loves you with all His emotions. Be overwhelmed with His love and you will find yourself being captivated by His love, and your response *will* be emotional. That's when you see different expressions of emotions as His love is emotionally connecting with yours. If you are hungry for more of Him, He will touch you. If you are thirsty, He will touch you, and when He does, you will respond. It may be with words, it may be song. It may be in tears, it may be with joyful laughter. It may just be sighing. It may be laying your head in His lap and pouring out all your passionate affections upon Him. That is loving God with your emotions.

Hands

> *His hands are rods of gold set with beryl. His body is carved ivory inlaid with sapphires (5:14).*

> *See how his hands hold unlimited power! But he never uses it in anger, for he is always holy, displaying his glory. His innermost place is a work of art—so beautiful and bright. How magnificent and noble is this one—covered in majesty! (v 14, TPT)*

While it is true that God has unlimited power, He never uses His hands of power in anger against us. Rather, His power is tempered in wisdom, and He always displays it with His goodness and kindness.

Legs

> *His legs are pillars of marble set on bases of fine gold. His countenance is like Lebanon, excellent as the cedars (v 15).*

Legs speak so clearly of God's strength and endurance. He does not waiver when things get tough. In times of testing, He is a pillar—our source of strength.

Mouth

His mouth is most sweet, Yes, he is altogether lovely. This is my beloved, and this is my friend, O daughters of Jerusalem! (v 16)

Most sweet are His kisses, even his whispers of love. He is delightful in every way and perfect from every viewpoint. If you ask me why I love him so, O brides-to-be, it's because there is none like him to me. Everything about him fills me with holy desire! And now he is my beloved—my friend forever (v 16, TPT).

The exchange of intimacy with Jesus releases such sweetness to our soul. His mouth speaks of the power of His words, which is always delivered in such a sweet tone, it is more like a delicious dessert. There is no one who speaks with the tenderness and kindness as Jesus, even when He is putting His finger on something in your life that needs handling. He will always speak specifically and directly to areas that need correction, and He is always at war against anything that hinders—

- our intimate relationship with Him
- our Christ-like maturity in Him
- fulfilling our divine destiny and partnership with Him

However, He only speaks the truth preceded by grace and always wrapped in love. Intimacy with Jesus includes the whispers of His love to our heart. This really is the sweetest, most incredible fulfillment our hearts could ever experience. He is always seeking to enlarge our capacity to mature in this intimate relationship with Him.

At the beginning of the Song, His mouth is defined as the communication of the deepest things that He has on His heart. The Bride is almost at the end of her journey into spiritual maturity, and now she says, "Intimacy with You is the sweetest thing in the human experience." Coming to this conclusion will always cause us to securely protect this intimate relationship and block anything and everything that would seek to its desecration. This place of our intimacy becomes a stronghold of divine love that nothing else can penetrate.

"He is altogether lovely"

The Bride ends this list of attributes to the Daughters of Jerusalem with a great crescendo and summary of her discovery.

> Yes, he is altogether lovely. This is my beloved, and this is my friend, O daughters of Jerusalem! (5:16)

> Most sweet are his kisses, even his whispers of love. He is delightful in every way and perfect from every viewpoint (v 16).

She is saying, "If you ask me why I love Him so, it is because there is none like Him to me. Everything about Him fills me with holy desire! He is my Beloved, my forever Friend!"

The Jesus depicted by the religious world is so different than the one depicted by the Bride. She has given all the attributes of His beauty and now she offers her summary statement: "All told, there is none as beautiful as my Bridegroom." In reality, this is who Jesus really is.

The Bride magnifies Jesus after being asked the question, "What is your Beloved?"

"This is who He is . . . my Beloved. This is the One you asked about and I have described Him in detail for you. You can see now, why I am not offended at Him . . . nor ever will be. This is my Beloved! I love Him."

What a sensational journey of the Bride!

Your Testimony of Jesus: "Who do you say that I am?"

So, the question I ask you is, how would you describe your Beloved—the Lover of your soul? In other words, what is your testimony of God today? In answer to this, we should be able to say: "This is who God is for me today. This is how He works in my life. This is who I know God to be for me."

Remember in the Gospel of Matthew when Jesus asked the disciple, "Who do people say that I am?"[62] They responded by saying, "Well, some say John the Baptist, others Elijah, or Jeremiah, or one of the prophets." Four distorted images.

But then He got really pointed, and asked, "But who do *you* say that I am? Who am I to you?" That may be the most important question you ever answer. What is your personal testimony of God? Who is He to you? Because how you see God, and how you believe He sees you, drives every single event in your life. It determines how you respond or react in crisis-type events, how you respond in human opposition, and in demonic attacks.

"Who do you say that I am?" Who is Jesus to you? What is your **personal** testimony of God—His nature revealed to you?

There are different times in Scripture where God talks about Himself. The first one is found in Exodus 33.

> Then Moses said, "Now show me your glory."
> And the Lord said: "I will cause all my goodness
> to pass in front of you and I will proclaim my
> name, the LORD, in your presence. I will have
> mercy on whom I will have mercy, and I will have
> compassion on whom I will have compassion" (vs
> 18-19, NIV).

From these verses we see that God says three things about His nature:

1) He is good,
2) He is merciful, and
3) He is compassionate.

---

[62] See Matt 16:13.

> *Then the* LORD *came down in the cloud and stood there with him and proclaimed his name, the* LORD. *And he passed in front of Moses, proclaiming, The* LORD, *the* LORD, *the compassionate and gracious God, slow to anger, abounding in love and faithfulness, maintaining love to thousands, and forgiving wickedness, rebellion and sin (34:5-6).*

In these verses we learn more about the nature of God. He tells us that He is compassionate, gracious, slow to anger, abounding in love, and that He forgives sin, iniquity, and transgression. I used to think when I would see that verse about forgiving sin, iniquity, and transgression that God is telling us, "I've already taken care of sin." It's as if He is saying, "I'm repeating this three times because I really want you to get it." And that's what I still believe. But I think there's more. What's so great about these verses is that each one of those words—sin, iniquity, and transgression—hit all areas of **failure**. "Iniquity" means, "that which is crooked, twisted, or perverse." It's used 215 times in the Bible, and it is "a willful devotion to disobey" that springs out of a twisted or perverted thought. The Lord says, "I wash you from iniquity."

"Transgression" is used 80 times in Scripture and it is being rebellious. This is a willful choice to step off the path, or as James says, for the one who knows the right thing to do and doesn't do it, for him it's sin.[63] And God says, "I blot that out."

The word "sin" is used 430 times in Scripture and it means, "the choice to offend." God cleanses us from sin; He has completely dealt with the issue of sin. Years ago, I heard Mike Bickle, the founder of the International House of Prayer in Kansas City, say: "The enemy wants us to think of ourself as a sinner who struggles to love God, when in reality, we are lovers of God who occasionally struggle with sin." You are not a sinner. You are the beloved son/daughter of a heavenly Father whose heart is ravished over you.

God tells Moses about Himself: "Moses, I am so full of

---

[63] See James 4:17.

loving-kindness and truth, I am so full of mercy and grace, I don't know what to do with Myself on some days." That is a message we really have to get into our hearts.

Like I said, your personal testimony of God will drive everything in your life. Your answer to Jesus' question, "Who do you say that I am?" determines how you view yourself, how you view others, how you react or respond in failure, how you react to the enemy's attack, and how you view every single circumstance and event that comes into your life.

Each of these situations presents another opportunity to upgrade your identity of God where you encounter Him beckoning you into a glorious revelation of the resurrected brilliance of Christ. Without a doubt your testimony will be: "My Beloved is altogether lovely . . ."

"The Bridegroom Beckons" Prayer

Hear the Lord say to you:

> Beloved, I am drawing you to this place where
> you fix your eyes solely upon Me, where you
> will trust in Me with all your heart, where you
> will not lean on your own understanding, but
> you will put all your security in your upgraded
> testimony of who I am for you.
>
> I have been longing for this day, when in the
> midst of the trials that come before the blessing,
> you simply refuse to give up on My love.
>
> In this season, I am increasing within you a
> courage to trust Me at new levels, where you
> find yourself relying on your testimony of Me.
> You will hear yourself saying: "I know my God,
> and He is with me, and He is for me!"
>
> I am drawing you, My beloved one, to this place
> where you fix your eyes upon Me and walk in
> this place that I have prepared for you in this
> season.
>
> I am here to sustain you. I am here to bring you
> through—all the way into the place of maturity.
> I am here to lift you up to the next level, where
> you will encounter the nature of My goodness
> and kindness, for I AM for you, and if I AM is for
> you, who can be against you?

Activation #11
The Bridegroom Beckons

1. In 4-6 sentences or phrases, write down your current image of God. Ask yourself:

- Is this a current image I have of God?
- Am I willing to move to the next level for an upgraded image of God?

_____

_____

Sit quietly, relax, and ask the Holy Spirit to give you a vision of God for your next season.

- Are there some character changes and developments coming?
- Am I moving into a new calling in my life, a strengthening, or a deepening of a current call?

_____

_____

How does God see you? How would you answer these following questions?

- Do I really believe that God is pursuing intimacy with me right now because He is passionately in love with me?
- Do I believe that God is **never** disillusioned with me?
- Do I really believe that I could never do anything that would cause God to stop loving me, or be discouraged with me?
- Do I really believe that God never leaves my side . . . ever?
- Do I really believe that God's heart is completely ravished over me, right now, even in this incredible place of weakness I find myself in?

If you answered "no" to any of those questions, it really is time for an upgrade. Go after this with the Holy Spirit. Ask Him to change your mindset on each of these where you answered "no." Record what He shows you.

_____

_____

_____

_____

2. Return to Song of Songs 5:10-16. Write down the attributes of your Bridegroom and consider each one of them as they pertain to you in your life right now. Ask the Holy Spirit for a greater revelation of the characteristics and nature of Jesus and to make them real to your heart.

_____

_____

_____

_____

3. Write out an upgraded testimony according to 5:10-16 answering the question of Jesus: "Who do you say that I am?" This will be the testimony of Jesus you are progressing toward.

_____

_____

_____

_____

_____

_____

Ask the Holy Spirit how you can activate these new things in your life that He is showing you.

_____

_____

_____

_____

_____

_____

_____

_____

_____

_____

_____

_____

_____

_____

_____

_____

_____

_____

TWELVE

Full Bridal Partnership

*But now I have grown and become
a bride, and my love for him has
made me a tower of passion and
contentment for my beloved.*[64]

I n the previous chapter, the Daughters of Jerusalem observed the test imposed upon the Bride, and they asked her a question: "Why do you love your Beloved so much?" From their perspective, they saw how He disappeared from her, watched the leaders of the Church reject her, and observed how she lost the two things she had cried out for: intimacy and ministry. These Daughters do not understand why she is not mad. They ask her another question: "Who is this Beloved one to you, anyway? Why do you love Him so much?" In the last chapter, the Bride responded to those questions by giving one of the greatest descriptions in the entire Bible of Jesus.

But following all of this, the Bride becomes lovesick, and so she begins seeking her Beloved. She's not whining, she's not complaining, she's not depressed or offended; she's just sad and longing to be reconnected to the One she loves. She won't stop her search until she finds Him.

---

[64] Song 8:10, TPT.

Living the Authentic Nature of Jesus

Seeing her situation, the Daughters of Jerusalem inquire:

> *Where has your beloved gone, O fairest among women? Where has your beloved turned aside, that we may seek him with you? (6:1)*

> *O rarest of beauty, where then has your lover gone? We long to see him too. Where may we find him? We will follow you as you seek after him (v 1, TPT).*

The Daughters want to know: "Where can we find Him? We want to follow Him like you do." I love how the Bride and her passion, her love, her authenticity, her humility, her life-testimony, and her sincerity of heart won these Daughters' hearts to a new place of passion for her Beloved as well. We need to really understand that people are watching us in life situations. They want to see us respond differently in adversity, crises, and issues than they do. They have heard all of our words and how a Christian *should* act. But evangelism, especially in this modern era, is not done by simply speaking words; it is best demonstrated by observing our lives. When people see us react to confrontation, to problems, to crises with the fruits of fear, anxiety, anger, resentment, confusion—all fruits of the soulish nature—we lose an opportunity for them to witness the authentic nature of Jesus because we responded the same way they would respond.

But when we respond with the genuine fruit of the Spirit—with love, joy, peace, patience, goodness, kindness, and self-control—that gets their attention. It's just not natural. People want to see a Christian living a supernatural life of peace and joy because they eagerly want to know that there is a greater power outside of themselves with whom they can connect. They want to see that their own fearful, anxious nature can be supernaturally transformed. You and I are the living, breathing example of that to people all around us.

The question of the Daughters changes from, "Who is He?" or "What is He?" to a new question, "**Where** is He?"

"We want to know Him," they announce. "We also want to seek Him. We want what you have. We want that kind of reality in our lives. We really want to know what you know, and we want to have what you have." These Daughters of Jerusalem are no longer content to live at a distance. And this is all because of the living testimony of the Bride.

"My beloved has gone to his garden"

The Bride responds as she suddenly realizes where her Beloved must be.

> *My beloved has gone to his garden, to the beds of spices, to feed his flock in the gardens, and to gather lilies (6:2).*

> *My lover has gone down into his garden of delight, the place where his spices grow, to feast with those pure in heart. I know we shall find him there (v 2, TPT).*

She is saying, "We can always find Jesus hanging out with His people, 'cause He loves to hang out with those who love Him. I know where He has gone . . . I know where His garden is." Then she makes a stunning announcement to the Daughters: "I am His garden."

> *I am my beloved's, and my beloved is mine. He feeds his flock among the lilies (6:3).*

> *He is within me—I am his garden of delight. I have him fully and now he fully has me! (v 3, TPT)*

She tells them, "My Lover has possessed me." The deeper you go into His heart, the more He speaks about our beauty, and the more beautiful you become to Him. Up until now, the Bride has primarily been seeking Him for her own pleasure. But she has progressed into a maturity where her whole life belongs to Him now; her life is for His pleasure alone. This is a very dramatic and revealing statement of the Bride. She says, "I am His and He is mine." This statement has put to rest all the previous statements of ownership, because at last, she is declaring to the whole world: "I am totally His."

Now it's all about Him. Her enjoyment of Jesus is no longer the focus of her life; it is His enjoyment of her.

The Bridegroom's "Delight"

Right in the middle of the Bride's discussion with the Daughters of Jerusalem, the Lord Jesus suddenly breaks His silence and tells her how beautiful she is.

> *O my love, you are as beautiful as Tirzah, lovely as Jerusalem, awesome as an army with banners! (v 4)*

> *More delightful than any delight, you have ravished my heart, stealing away my strength to resist you. Even hosts of angels stand in awe of you (v 4, TPT).*

The Bride walked through this season of testing with a heart full of passionate love for Jesus, and through it all, she remained completely His. There was nothing that could impose itself against her that would cause her to withdraw or lessen her love for Jesus. These tests simply caused her to press in more—to pursue her Bridegroom with deliberate urgency—and her incredible response has even caused the angels to stand in awe of this new person who has emerged.

The result is the response of her Bridegroom to her. In this stunning verse, He is telling His Bride that she has become more delightful than anything He could ever desire, and that she simply ravishes His heart. Wow. To think that our love could cause such a heart response in the Lover of our soul should make us desire Him above everything else! This alone should motivate us to run into His welcoming embrace.

"Turn your eyes away from Me"

The Bride has ravished the heart of Jesus. Think about it: He is completely stunned by you . . . by your beauty. When you come to Him, you delight His heart. Nothing moves Him like you do. Everything you offer to Him is another dazzling glimpse you. He is so overwhelmed that He says:

Turn you eyes away from me, for they have overcome me. Your hair is like a flock of goats going down from Gilead (6:5).

Turn your eyes from me; I can't take it anymore! I can't resist the passion of these eyes that I adore. Overpowered by a glance, my ravished heart— undone. Held captive by your love, I am truly overcome! For your undying devotion to me is the most yielded sacrifice (6:5, TPT).

When He says, "Turn your eyes away from Me," He is using extravagant love language. In essence He is saying, "You are conquering My heart with your love. You are moving Me by your steadfastness. You believe Me even when you feel nothing. You have set your heart upon Me when everything is contrary to what you see. The beauty of your heart has overcome Me."

Then Jesus continues to describe what He sees in you:

The shining of your spirit shows how you have taken my truth to become balanced and complete!

Your beautiful blushing cheeks reveal how real your passion is for me, even hidden behind your veil of humility. I could have chosen any from among the vast multitude of the royal ones who follow me (vs 6-8, TPT).

But one is my beloved dove—unrivaled in your beauty, without equal, beyond compare, the perfect one, the only one for me. Others see your beauty and sing for joy. Brides and queens chant your praise: "How blessed is she!" Look at you now—arising as the dayspring of the dawn, fair as the shining moon.

Bright and brilliant as the sun in all its strength. Astonishing to behold as a majestic army waving banners of victory (vs 9-10, TPT).

Yes, Jesus is talking about *you*. I would love to be in your head right now, listening to the war you are having with yourself. We find it is so difficult to believe that God loves us this much, especially in our weaknesses and failures. But hear Him speak directly to your heart: "You are the one, above all others, for whom I've longed. I have created you for the love you pour out upon Me. I love you so much, my Bride." No one rivals the affections He has for you. Jesus is telling His Bride—that's you!—the same exact thing: "Of all the attendants in My court, you are the only one I desire, and the one I would die for."

Now I decree, I will ascend and arise. I will take hold of you with my power, possessing every part of my fruitful bride. Your love I will drink as wine, and your words will be mine. For your kisses of love are exhilarating, more than any delight I've known before. Your kisses of love awaken even the lips of sleeping ones.

Her Lover owns her heart. He is all she cares about now.

Now I know that I am filled with my beloved and all his desires are fulfilled in me (7:8-10, TPT).

Before this, fears and anxieties controlled her; her weaknesses and failures were an obsession. But, no longer. She has received His forgiveness and taken His love to heart. Now all of her life has been given solely to Him.

That should really excite your heart. You belong wholly to the Lord Jesus, and all of His desires are for you. He longs to release His fiery passion into your heart, because His love for you is so intense. He has looked for one upon whom He can pour out this unrelenting love, and He has chosen you.

Come away, my lover. Come with me to the far away fields. We will run away together to the forgotten places and show them redeeming love (7:11, TPT).

Here the Bridegroom is finally fulfilling the heart cry of the Shulamite from chapter one of the Song when she asked Him to draw her so they could run together in ministry. She is so full of His passionate love, and she is now turning it all around. She is saying, "I want to take You with me wherever I go . . . Wherever You send me, we will run together."

I recall my first mission trip to Nicaragua. I did not feel the call from the Lord to go there, but I was asked to go along with a friend. I invited the Lord to make me a blessing and to come with me with His love, His power, and anointing. He clearly told me that I would have power, breakthroughs, and authority every place I chose to extend His love. For me personally, it was such a life-transforming trip as I observed the results of telling Jesus, "I want to take you with Me wherever I go." It was Jesus and me running together in intimacy and friendship ministering His love and healing to many.

The Response of the Bride

After hearing that, the Bride responds to Him:

> *If only I could show everyone this passionate desire I have for you. If only I could express it fully, no matter who was watching me, without shame or embarrassment (8:1, TPT).*

The Bride again is being so open and vulnerable. She has such a desire to overcome her fear of displaying her passion for her Beloved. She longs to be free, to extravagantly release her affection publicly for the one who has her heart. But she knows that in her culture, displays of affection are a violation—except between blood relatives, such as a brother and sister.

The Furious Fire of the Bridegroom

The overwhelmed Bridegroom Jesus responds to His Bride:

> *Who is this one? Look at her now! She arises from her desert, clinging to her Beloved. When I awakened you under the apple tree, as you were feasting on me, I awakened your innermost being with the travail of birth as you longed for more of me.*

> *Fasten me upon your heart as a seal of fire forevermore. This living, consuming flame will seal you as my prisoner of love. My passion is stronger than the chains of death and the grave,*

287

all consuming as the very flashes of fire from the burning heart of God.

Place this fierce, unrelenting fire over your entire being.

Rivers of pain and persecution will never extinguish this flame. Even floods will be unable to quench this raging fire that burns within you. Everything will be consumed. It will stop at nothing as you yield everything to this furious fire until it won't even seem to you like a sacrifice anymore (8:5-7, TPT).

This fierce love will stop at nothing as you yield everything to His furious fire. Everything in its way will be consumed. Surrendering to His passion won't even seem like a sacrifice anymore. His love is delightfully satisfying to which nothing else compares.

The Lord says, "Fasten me upon your heart." The NKJV says, "Set me . . . upon your heart." He is saying, "Call upon Me to release the seal of fire upon your heart. Call out to Me . . . ask Me . . . invite Me to come." Jesus is calling us to press into Him for a greater increase of the eternal seal, because it is progressive. It grows in terms of the manifestation of God's presence that influences our heart and emotions more and more as we press in for more of Him.

The King's Seal

The journey of this Bride began with a longing for kisses and ends with the fiery seal of divine love, capturing and captivating her at the deepest levels. This seal is His seal of ownership, and a seal of His protection and passion. We receive the seal in its down-payment form[65] the day we are born again—the seal of the Holy Spirit.

Now He gives His promise to His Bride: The waters of sin, the waters of pressure, pain and disappointment, they cannot

---

[65] See Eph 1:13.

quench it. They cannot put it out, nor can it be drowned by the floods of persecution.

The king's seal was a wax seal. The king would place his documents in a container, and then he would put an encasement of wax around it. The king would then put his signet ring right into the hot wax to guarantee the contents inside the container. When a person received a sealed document in ancient times, it was always sealed with the king's signet ring. Affixing the signature seal of the king meant: "All the armies of my kingdom will back up what is in this sealed container."

However, the King's seal referred to in this verse is not one of wax. The Bridegroom is saying to us, "This is not a temporary seal. My seal is affixed with the most ferocious of fires. And the entire power of My Kingdom will back up the promises of what that seal represents." All the power of God will back it up! The enemy may try to raise opposition against it in an attempt to put that flame out by raining down the "water" of temptations, adversity, and troubles. In the natural, water always puts out fire. But this vehement fire of Heaven's decree is anything but natural. It is a supernatural fire—an extraordinary fire that can *never* be put out. Instead this fierce fire will put out all other "water"—the water of sin and temptation. It does not matter what kind of sin it is, or addiction, pain, perversion, or the depths of hell itself. This lower realm "waters" of darkness can never put out the dazzling fierce fires of Heaven's heights. If you will yield to the brilliance of this fire, it will overcome the power of every kind of immorality, the power of every addiction, and the power of bitterness.

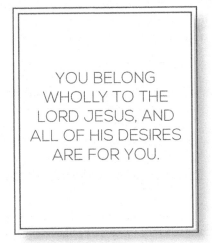

YOU BELONG WHOLLY TO THE LORD JESUS, AND ALL OF HIS DESIRES ARE FOR YOU.

In the end, the zealous fires of God's passionate heart will

incinerate all that opposes His love. **All**. His passion for you will be the only thing left burning.

As we have seen throughout the Song in the journey of the Bride, the way everything begins and is sustained is through intimacy with her Bridegroom Jesus. The seal is placed upon our heart also through our intimacy with Him. This life with Him is all about living in His heart, pursuing intimacy, and walking daily in deep communion and friendship with our Beloved, Jesus.

The Holy Spirit is inviting you to place His seal over your heart, and as you do, it will brand you forever, transforming you from the inside out. You belong wholly to Him. His seal upon your heart brings a guarantee of Heaven's eternal decree of passion and protection. It is His fiery love that will cause you to be radically reconstructed from the inside out.

The Bride makes her final declaration:

> But now I have grown and become a bride, and my love for him has made me a tower of passion and contentment for my beloved. I am now a firm wall of protection for others, guarding them from harm. This is how he sees me—I am the one who brings him bliss, finding favor in his eyes (8:10, TPT).

This is a description of the revelation about whom she has become from the perspective of her Beloved Bridegroom.

I would like to end with the amazing last verse of the Song.

> Arise, my darling! Come quickly, my beloved. Come and be the graceful gazelle with me. Come be like a dancing deer with me. We will dance in the high place in the sky, yes, on the mountains of fragrant spice. Forever we shall be united as one! (v 14, TPT)

The Bride responded to the romancing of the Holy Spirit at the beginning of her journey, and she ends it by living in the deepest chambers in the heart of her Beloved. He draws her, she responds, and they run together.

The dream in her Beloved's heart has become her greatest heart's desires fulfilled.

The Neverending Journey

The Song of all Songs is an active and living book. There is rarely a day goes by that I don't find myself somewhere on this journey and impacted in some tangible way. It may be a particular section, or one of its truths that the Holy Spirit makes real to my heart. We are all in an ongoing journey of maturing our intimate friendship with our Bridegroom.

My prayer is that you will have daily encounters with the Lover of your soul, and with it, a deeper revelation of who Jesus is for you today. I pray for you, dear reader, because you are here at the exact time of history the Lord has called you to live in—for "such a time as this."[66] And because of that, determine to live more fervently in His love and glorious Presence every day of your life.

As you respond to His romancing and drawing you into His heart of affections, I sense in my spirit that He is saying this to you personally:

> As you come to the secret place of My Presence,
> I will **envelope** you in My love and passion and
> send you forth, because I am about to explode
> My love in a measure that the world has never
> seen. And I have chosen You to be in intimate
> partnership with Me. Let us now run together.

May you encounter the passion of your Bridegroom today!

---

[66] See Est 4:14.

"Full Bridal Partnership" Prayer

Hear the words of the Lord over you:

My Beloved, I am on this journey with you. It is a journey of seeing your heart captured and captivated by Me, the way My heart is captured and captivated by you.

I am drawing you nearer and nearer to Me, My love, so I can fill you with new levels of hope, new levels of trust, increasing levels of faith, and of course, fresh stunning encounters with My radical love for you.

I love this place where you are truly trusting that I am good. You no longer walk by what you see, but you choose to trust that I am moving in all things and I am turning everything around for good.

You need to know, beloved, that I have chosen you, and I am faithful, and I am completing every word that I have ever spoken over you. I have sealed you! I am here to sustain you. I am here to bring you through. I am here to lift you up to the next level. I intend to take you to the highest place of My love.

ACTIVATION #12
Full Bridal Partnership

The Bride of the journey began with her longing for kisses and ends with the fiery seal of divine love enveloping her heart.

> *Fasten me upon your heart as a seal of fire forevermore. This living, consuming flame will seal you as my prisoner of love. My passion is stronger than the chains of death and the grave, all consuming as the very flashes of fire from the burning heart of God. Place this fierce, unrelenting fire over your entire being (8:6, TPT).*

This seal is for protection, preservation and passion, and His seal of ownership. She belongs solely to the King. How do we place Jesus as a fiery seal of love over our hearts? It is simply by giving Him our heart; it is by communing with Him, loving Him, and letting Him love us. I would encourage you to pursue Jesus with an even greater level of anticipation. My prayer is that you will sense the anointing of the Holy Spirit drawing you into a deeper intimacy with Jesus. You only need to respond and He will lead you forward.

Activation

Find a quiet place where you can worship God freely. Put on an extended set of worship music and begin to adore Him. Pray that the Lord will open your eyes to see a fresh revelation of who He really, really is. As you ask Him for that, record in your journal what you see and hear, because the Holy Spirit is going to give you a vision of God that really impacts you. You are going to see an aspect of God, and who He is for you that will set you up for years to come.

As you pray about your relationship with Jesus, the Holy Spirit is going to carry you into His private chambers. Expect Him to do this regularly, and respond to Him. As He does, this will be a pivotal point in your spiritual journey—leading you into a deeper place of intimate relationship and fellowship. It is my prayer that these encounters with your Bridegroom will be ongoing, taking you to deeper levels of His passion for you.

Write down:

- The new revelation of Jesus.
- The new ideas for increasing your intimacy.
- The new passion you have for worship.
- The fresh yearning in your heart for discovering more about Jesus.
- The new passion for serving the Lord has put into your heart.

_____

_____

_____

_____

_____

_____

_____

_____

_____

_____

_____

_____

_____

_____

_____

About the Author

Gary Hopkins has served as pastor and teacher for over 40 years. He and his wife, Karissa, presently serve on the core leadership team and are Family Life Pastors at The Mission in Vacaville, California. Gary's authentic and humorous style of speaking and teaching has a unique anointing that opens the way for new encounters with God and spiritual refreshing. He is a lover of the Word, and has an ingenious ability to make it come alive. Gary teaches and trains in the prophetic, personal renewal, practical living, and intimacy.

Gary and Karissa have three married children and three grandchildren.

Resources

Other Resources by Gary Hopkins

- "Captivated by Radical Love" (a 12-part series on flashdrive)
- "The Purpose and Process of Delayed Promises" (an 8-part series on flashdrive)

Audio CD Teachings

- "Divine Favor" (4-part)
- "Happy to Live Unoffended" (2-part)
- "Living Strong in Difficult Times"
- "When Kingdom Beatitudes Invade Your Life"
- "Positioning for Encounters"
- "Finding Your Purpose in Crisis"
- "Follow-through is the Key to Breakthrough"
- "Famous for Love"
- "Discovering Your Truest Identity"
- "Upgrade in Your Identity"
- "Aligning with the Outpouring"
- "The Stunning Power of Supernatural Courage"
- "Psalm 84"

These audio teachings are available for sale at The Mission Bookstore.

www.store.imissionchurch.com

Made in the USA
Monee, IL
17 October 2020

45435129R00164